ALAN ALLPORT was born in Whiston, England, and grew up in East Yorkshire. He moved to the United States in 1994 and earned a doctorate in History from the University of Pennsylvania. An expert on the Second World War, he is currently a lecturer at Princeton University.

# DEMOBBED
## Coming Home After the Second World War

## ALAN ALLPORT

YALE UNIVERSITY PRESS | NEW HAVEN AND LONDON

First printed in paperback 2010

The quotation from 'Casualty – Mental Ward' in Chapter 7 is taken from *Soldiering On: Poems of Military Life* by Vernon Scannell (Robson Books, 1989). Reproduced by permission of Anova Books Company Ltd.
    Arthur Gilbert's testimony in Chapter 2 is taken from WW2 People's War, an online archive of wartime memories contributed by members of the public and gathered by the BBC. The archive can be found at bbc.co.uk/ww2peopleswar.

For information about this and other Yale University Press publications, please contact:

U.S. Office: sales.press@yale.edu    www.yalebooks.com
Europe Office: sales @yaleup.co.uk    www.yaleup.co.uk

Set in ACaslon by IDSUK (DataConnection)
Printed in Great Britain by Hobbs the Printers Ltd, Totton, Hampshire

Library of Congress Cataloging-in-Publication Data

Allport, Alan, 1970–
    Demobbed: coming home after the Second World War/Alan Allport
        p. cm.
    Includes bibliographical references and index
    ISBN 978–0–300–14043–9 (alk. Paper)
1. World War, 1939–1945–Veterans–Great Britain. 2. Great Britain–Armed Forces–
Demoblization–History–20th century. 3.World War, 1939–1945–Veterans–Great Britain–
Social conditions. 4. Great Britain–Social conditions–1945–5. War and society–Great
Britain. I Title.
DA588.A563 2009
305.9'0697094109044–dc22

A catalogue record for this book is available from the British Library.

ISBN 978–0–300–16886–0 (pbk)

10  9  8  7  6  5  4  3  2  1

To the memory of Tony and Grace, and their daughter Sylvia

# Contents

# List of Illustrations

# Acknowledgements

*Demobbed* began as a doctoral dissertation completed in the history department at the University of Pennsylvania, Philadelphia, in the summer of 2007. My first thanks must therefore go to my adviser, Thomas C. Childers, whose inquiries into the experiences of American ex-servicemen (now published by Houghton Mifflin Harcourt as *Soldier From the War Returning*) provided inspiration for my topic. My dissertation committee members, Lynn Lees, Jonathan Steinberg, and Seth Koven, were also indispensable sources of assistance and wisdom. Special thanks go to Lynn and her husband Andrew for allowing my family to stay in their lovely West Philadelphia home during the final year of my Ph.D.

During the two research trips, which I spent in London in 2005 and 2008, I was ably assisted by staff members at the Imperial War Museum's Departments of Documents, Printed Books, and Sound Records; the British Film Institute; the Public Record Office in Kew; and the British Library and British Library Newspaper Archive. Peter Quirk gave up his futon for eight weeks and was a sociable and understanding host. I must also thank Tom and Moira Deveson for their exceptional friendship and hospitality. After I left London, D'Maris Coffman was kind enough to take the time and trouble to copy several PRO documents that I had missed, some of which turned out to be very important to the final work. For practical reasons much of my research had to be conducted in Philadelphia, and I was able to accomplish this in large part thanks to the University of Pennsylvania's amazing Interlibrary Loan Department.

Draft chapters from the original dissertation were read by attendees at two meetings of the annual Mid-Atlantic Conference on British Studies, by members of the Delaware Valley British Studies Group, and by fellows of the 2007 Mellon Summer Seminar in British History at Columbia University, led by Susan Pedersen. My thanks to all of them for their helpful comments. Also, my thanks to my colleagues in the Writing Program at Princeton University.

The editorial team at Yale University Press in London have been a fabulous support throughout the last two years, especially Heather McCallum and Rachael Lonsdale, who helped me to navigate the tricky path from dissertation to book. I should also like to thank Fred Leventhal and Juliet Gardiner, who read early versions of the manuscript and pointed out many errors and ambiguities in the original drafts. Needless to say, the responsibility for any mistakes in the final version is entirely my own.

At the beginning of my research I had the opportunity to speak to several ex-servicemen, and the wives and children of ex-servicemen, either through correspondence or in person. Their thoughts and memories helped to bring this project into life. I would like to thank all of them, with particular thanks to Jim Harper, Barbara Webb, Janet Jacobs, Donald Stables, Fred Walton, and Willie Kitwood.

Lastly, I would like to thank my family. My sisters Carolyn and Susan have supported me both practically and emotionally for many years. My wife Barbara has been a tower of strength in sometimes challenging times during the eight years we have spent our lives together, and I thank her from the bottom of my heart for her consideration, her generosity, and her unconditional love. Thomas, our son, is about as old as this project, and he more than anyone else has had to put up with the inconveniences of its creation, which he has done with (mostly) good grace. Our daughter Katharine sensibly sat out the original dissertation, but has been a wonderful, if noisy, presence in the house during the final completion of *Demobbed*. Thank you; I love you all.

# Prologue

*Smile and joke, young sailor Jack*
*For it's the same old story*
*There'll be no jokes when you come back*
*And bloody little glory.*[1]

The letter, found amongst Cyril Patmore's belongings by the Metropolitan Police, was undated, but was sent around July 1945. By then Patmore's wife Kathleen must have already told her husband, who'd been abroad on active service for three years, that she was expecting the baby of an Italian prisoner of war. 'By now I'm wondering if you are caring to get any letter from me,' she wrote, 'but I feel I must keep on writing until I see you again or you tell me not to.' The letter didn't make it clear whether she yet knew that Cyril had been granted compassionate leave to return from India to their home in Harlesden, northwest London. What it did state, devastatingly, was Kathleen's wish for reconciliation, if not for her own sake then for that of their four children. 'One thing I know is that you loved me otherwise you wouldn't have been so hurt,' she continued:

You ask me why I didn't tell you before, well shame, remorse, frightened call it what you like, but each time I attempted to write to you about it I just hadn't the nerve, and it got worse as time went on until its nearly drove me crazy . . . I have *always* remembered meeting you was the happiest time of my life you stood by me when the rest of them let me down . . . please think my love there is your kiddies to come to even if you don't want me although God knows I couldn't go on without you . . .

Why oh why darling did I have to let you down, me who loves you more than life itself, you who did everything for me, how my heart aches always, bitter tears that will wash away my guilt. I didn't mean to do it sweetheart please believe me, and don't start a divorce I just couldn't stand that. I feel too ashamed for you to see me in this condition yet how I wish I could see you to talk to you it wouldn't matter what you done to me afterwards. Now my *darling* you'll always be that to me.

There was no reconciliation. On 4 August, Private Cyril Patmore of the Royal Scots Fusiliers stabbed his heavily pregnant wife to death in their house on Greenhill Road. 'I live for my children and my wife,' he told the police later. 'I hope the children will be well looked after. They've had a rough time since I've been away.'[2]

Patmore got off lightly. At the Old Bailey the following month he escaped what would have been a mandatory death sentence for murder and was committed to five years' penal servitude on a lesser manslaughter charge instead. Mr. Justice Charles, presiding, was not happy with the jury's decision: he was worried that what he called 'the law of the jungle' was creeping into the English justice system. Just a week before, the trial of another soldier who had stabbed his unfaithful wife to death had also ended in a reduced manslaughter conviction.[3]

*The News of the World* was full of such stories that summer. Talk of the old 'unwritten law' that allowed a cuckolded husband to kill his spouse, a Victorian assumption that had been rejected as 'un-English' for the past fifty years, was creeping back.[4] 'It would seem from some recent murder trials,' wrote an appalled newspaper reader, 'that the unfaithful wife of a serviceman is an outlaw, with no benefit of law whatsoever. She may be murdered with impunity.'[5] Men acclimatised to violence on behalf of the state were, it seemed, finding it hard to restrain the instincts that had been released by war – and a bloodthirsty section of the public was egging them on.

A wave of such 'war problems' beset British society in the months immediately following victory over Germany and Japan in the summer of 1945. The war had dislocated ordinary life in ways that had been unimaginable six years previously. Millions of families had been abruptly broken up, with men, women and children scattered across Britain and the world. The conventions of home and work had been disrupted, often profoundly. New relationships, attitudes and forms of behaviour had evolved, some welcome, many not. Peace offered the prospect of a return to 'normality': the reunion of loved ones, the re-establishment of older ways of doing things, the settling of accounts – and scores.

Of all the changes that the end of the war would bring, the greatest was the return of the men. On V-E Day, over five million Britons were in the uniform of His Majesty's Armed and Auxiliary Forces. Nine out of ten of them were male, the vast majority wartime conscripts or volunteers serving for the duration only.[6] Most had been in the army, navy or air force since at least 1941. Millions were abroad, a vast expatriate community of exiles scattered haphazardly from Norway to the Kenyan highlands to the fringes of Antarctica. Over a quarter of a million of them had been continuously overseas for more than five years.[7] Even the lucky minority who had spent the entire war on 'home' service had usually been billeted or bivouacked far from everyone and everything familiar. By the midpoint of the war, almost half of all British civilians had been separated from someone dear to them by military service.[8]

These husbands, fathers, sons and brothers had been rudely uprooted from their families, friends and workmates by the national emergency. Now, their task done, they would be demobilised – 'demobbed' – and returned home. It is no wonder that servicemen were eager, even desperate, for this to happen as soon as possible:

they formed a greying fraternity. Almost half of them were aged 30 or over by 1945. The war years had been long; there were apprenticeships and careers to resume, relationships to consecrate and children to nurture. The single biggest wartime topic of inquiry amongst letter writers to *Union Jack*, the newspaper of the Eighth Army, had been: 'When are we going to get home?'[9] Wartime servicemen were generally emphatic that they were short-term citizen-soldiers rather than regulars – not 'faceless khaki pieces of a great game of Ludo', as the novelist Anthony Burgess put it, but 'civilians in temporary fancy dress' whose time was now served.[10]

Reabsorbing over a quarter of the working male population back into civilian life was a daunting proposition. The weight of responsibility was enormous. In a December 1943 poll, demobilisation was voted the most urgent postwar challenge facing the nation.[11] It would require 'the greatest social and industrial operation' in British history,[12] a critical first step in building the future.[13] But as Reg Ellery warned, it was foolhardy to presume that one could simply:

> take men indiscriminately from office, factory, farm or school . . . train them in the methods of modern warfare, toughen them and wean them from family and domestic affairs, send them off to fight, and then expect them to fall back into their old jobs again as if they had just returned from a fortnight's holiday.[14]

In the final months of the war, the prospects of demobilisation still seemed 'incalculable and ominous'.[15] After all, many men would be returning as virtual strangers after their long postings to the Middle East, Africa and Asia. What did they expect to find when they got back, and perhaps more to the point, would they be satisfied with what they found when they got there?

The precedents were hardly encouraging. Just over twenty-five years earlier Britain had demobilised another victorious generation of citizen-soldiers, only to see the dreams of the postwar settlement sputter out in anger and despair. The trouble had begun just weeks after the November 1918 Armistice, when a tardy and transparently unjust discharge process had tested the patience of the British Army to destruction and sent tens of thousands of soldiers into what Winston Churchill later called 'a convulsion of indiscipline'.[16]

Hastily released from the Forces en masse, these men had flocked home to their prewar jobs, exacerbating what was already a dangerously overheated postwar boom. In September 1920 the boom bust: trade slumped, orders were cancelled, and ex-servicemen were laid off as briskly as they had been rehired. By November, 300,000 of them were on the dole. The labour market never properly recovered for another twenty years and the penniless veteran begging on the pavement became one of the characteristic motifs of interwar Britain.[17] Many unemployed ex-soldiers rued their decision to come home at all:

*Now the bleeding war is over,*
*Oh how happy was I there;*
*Now old Fritz and I have parted,*
*Life's one everlasting care.*
*No more* estaminets *to sing in,*
*No ma'moiselles to make me gay;*
*Civvy life's a bleeding failure.*
*I was happy yesterday.*[18]

Many men and women remembered this period only too well and feared a recurrence of its broken promises and desperate unemployment, war heroes reduced to selling matches or singing in the streets. It had been a time of irreparable disappointment, mistrust and hardship, a betrayal of the highest hopes.[19] The lingering bitterness of ex-servicemen – the conviction that they had been swindled and betrayed by the politicians, the civilians, the 'men of booming phrases' as C.E. Montague called them – contributed to the sour and irresolute mood of the 1920s and 1930s.[20]

Likewise, many soldiers of the Second World War expected much the same when their job was done. 'When this is bloody over it'll be the same as it was after the last lot,' Anthony Burgess, then an Education Corps sergeant, was told by his soldier pupils: 'The buggers what stayed home will have the jobs and us poor sods go begging.'[21] There were also more personal fears besides the dole. During the war Britain had experienced a friendly invasion of several million Allied troops, predominantly Americans – and rumours of the sexual adventures of the GIs with the wives, sweethearts and daughters of Britain's absent men had spread widely abroad. There would be angry, perhaps violent, recriminations when the British troops returned. 'All the men are thinking about is coming ashore with a Sten gun and moving through the countryside shooting all the Poles and Czechs and the Americans who've been sleeping with their wives and girls,' one colonel warned in early 1945.[22]

There was real fear that mass unrest would result if demobilisation was not handled well. The *Daily Mirror*'s correspondent with the British Army in Germany suggested that a 'League of Angry Men', furious at what they had heard about the behaviour of the civilian establishment at home, was preparing to return from abroad:

> A great change has come over the fighting man . . . at first he was just depressed. Then that depression, as he saw his hopes being betrayed, gave way to a furious anger . . . I came home with the feeling that the serviceman needs his own resistance movement if he is to get justice.[23]

The *Mirror* suggested that this fury would be channelled into political support for the Labour Party, which was then preparing for the first postwar general election. But others worried that soldierly anger would be too volatile for parliamentary democracy, and that ex-servicemen would take literally the call for organised resistance in the form of political extremism: 'They've had a bellyful of being ordered about, and are not going to put up with it when the fighting is finished.'[24]

'Cannot you see what may happen?' predicted *The People* at the beginning of 1945, 'browned-off-warriors – lauded to the skies in war, unprovided for in peace, disillusioned, cynical, angry – marching again at home this time, say on London?'[25] A legion of angry veterans armed and trained in violence was not something to be contemplated lightly. Disillusioned and resentful, ex-servicemen would, it was feared, be easy prey for extremists bearing false promises.[26] No wonder that Ernest Bevin, Churchill's wartime Minister of Labour and the architect of the British reconstruction programme, warned his colleagues that if too many tempers snapped, there would be chaos.[27]

Yet the demobilisation experience in 1945 and all the powerful hopes and fears that it generated has curiously vanished from our collective memory. Few would dispute the claim that Britain has had a national obsession with the Second World War for the last sixty years.[28] Yet the endlessly replayed Greatest Hits of Our Finest Hour omit as much as they revisit – and not just in the sense that the British exaggerate the importance of their role in the victory. Whole episodes of the nation's war story, even important military events, have disappeared from the interpretation of the past we have settled on.

So, we recall D-Day on 6 June 1944, but cannot remember much about the painfully slow Allied advance through Italy that began a year earlier, nor for that matter the final bloody conquest of Germany in the spring of 1945. We are fixated on the Battle of Britain in the summer and autumn of 1940 but have a much hazier awareness – perhaps because of its greater moral ambivalence – of the strategic bombing campaign that followed it. Yet Bomber Command's destruction of Germany's cities absorbed as much as a third of all Britain's wartime resources.

The public memory of 1945 in Britain is dominated by images of gaiety, congratulatory and uncomplicated: the carnival crowds gathered in Trafalgar Square to celebrate V-E Day; the street parties; the victory speeches of Churchill and King George VI. As 'war' becomes 'peace' in this national replaying of the past, so the scene shifts to another moment of myth: the election of Clement Attlee's Labour government and the forging of the postwar welfare state.

It is true that not all the tough legacies of the war are erased in this transition. It is well known that rationing continued into the early years of Queen Elizabeth II's reign, and that the Blitz left Britain with a chronic housing shortage for many years. But the personal experience of the late 1940s is mostly forgotten, and the demobilisation story is regarded as hardly a story at all. It is taken for granted that with the announcement of victory British servicemen returned home without fuss or delay, and that they exchanged their military for their civilian identities as effortlessly as they slipped on the famous demob suits which they were issued with on their discharge.[29]

This is to dismiss what was for millions of people an experience both intense and often sharply double-edged – a national moment rich in joy and relief, certainly, sanguine and self-confident for many, but also one full of doubts, frustrations, sadnesses and private defeats. To be sure, the lurid predictions of postwar anarchy did not come true. Despite tragic individual cases like the Patmores', Britain's gutters did not run red with the blood of unfaithful wives or shop stewards. Ernest Bevin's reconstruction programme was well-intentioned, on the whole humanely (if not always adeptly) administered, in certain respects generous.

But demobilisation was full of human consequence nonetheless, far from trouble-free, and for some ultimately disenchanting. 'How clear it is that many a homecoming will be unhappy and ugly and fearful,' James Hodson was already predicting three months before Germany's surrender on 7 May 1945. 'Many folk must dread the end of the war and the trials it will bring.'[30] The military demobilisation process was not at all quick or uncontroversial. Six months after Japan's surrender on 14 August, British servicemen who had expected a speedy repatriation at the outbreak of peace were still marking time in forgotten camps on the obscure fringes of their empire – a life more 'spiritually devastating' than the war itself, as one British captain in Germany put it.[31] The mechanism of discharge began cautiously and slowly – far too slowly for millions of men in uniform who felt that their contract with the British state had expired with the defeat of Adolf Hitler and General Hideki Tojo.

Frustration bred dissent. Soon a ripple of discontent was sweeping through the British armed forces, worryingly reminiscent of the soldier strikes of 1919. The protests and unofficial strike actions of the second half of 1945 were not a form of khaki *Jacquerie*, but they were alarming nonetheless. By the beginning of 1946 even the War Office was talking about the 'exceptional strain' that the troops' morale was under – strong language from its normally unruffled mandarins.[32]

Even after release from the armed forces the serviceman's troubles were far from over. The military machine had provided a framework for everyday life, a closed and stable world with its rituals and habits and predictable routines. However dreary, dangerous and degrading it had often been, over six years life in the armed forces had acquired a mollifying permanence. Now the demobbed soldier was abruptly being taken away from this world and thrust back into the uncertainties of civilian existence. The writer Nicholas Mosley, then a young platoon commander in the London Irish Regiment, who on V-E Day had been tearing around the devastated roads of Ferrara, Italy, in a looted Mercedes, was not alone in feeling adrift as the wartime apparatus of his life was dismantled. 'For so long the war had provided a structure, a means of getting on with things in spite of doubts and fears.'[33] When the war was over, remembered another soldier, 'I came to the surface like a blinded pit pony'.[34]

The newspapers sometimes made homecoming look easy. In April 1945 *Picture Post* profiled the arrival back in Druid Street, Bermondsey, of Sergeant Jim Ford of the Rifle Brigade after four and a half years in the Middle East. Sergeant Ford was *Picture Post*'s exemplary case study in 'how to welcome a soldier home', a living guide to the ideal demob experience. *Picture Post* provided its readers with a montage of best reception practices – the putting out of the flags, the embrace at the railway station, the family sing-song around the piano, the slippers by the fireside – the full procession of return, in fact, from initial slaps on the back and free pints down at the local to the reassertion of quiet, cosy domesticity. Here, it suggested, was a template for a trouble-free reunion.[35]

But even the relatively unflappable Sergeant Ford admitted to difficulties. On his arrival home he was shocked by the physical desolation of blitzed south London. He could not quite get his head around the idea of women railway porters, unknown in Britain at his embarkation in the summer of 1940. The 6-week-old pup he had left behind had become an adult dog. A prepubescent niece had become a striking young woman. And Betty, the newlywed bride he had left behind during the Battle of Britain, was now his wife of many years, a former factory worker and WAAF and civil servant in the Ministry of Works – a woman of maturity and accomplishment he knew little about. It was all, he confessed, a little bewildering, and he was curt and distant for the first few hours of his return.

Still, Jim and Betty had it easy in many respects. They had no children, and so, unlike other couples, they did not have to negotiate the sudden and volatile arrival into the household of a barely remembered parent. Perhaps most importantly, they had a home of their own. The physical destruction of Britain's housing stock by aerial bombardment had left millions of people, particularly young couples, either living in squalid temporary 'digs' or reliant on the good will of in-laws and relatives, which could strain nerves and restrict the chances of some badly needed privacy.

For other couples less fortunate than the Fords, the reunited home was fraught with domestic tension. Wives were unhappy that their husbands were moody, distant and short-tempered: husbands would spend their evenings with male friends down the pub, treating their homes as lodging houses, and leaving their wives as lonely as they were during the bitter years of separation. 'This neglect and loneliness,' the *Daily Herald* warned, 'is causing such suffering to women that ease and affection may never flourish again.'[36] Demobbed men expecting to ease back into uncomplicated patriarchy grumbled that their wives had lost interest in *them*. 'Now I've come home things seem to have gone wrong,' protested one. 'She can't seem to adjust her life to mine again.'[37] For some, prolonged separation had destroyed the possibility of a happy reunion. 'My husband has returned home after three years in a Japanese prison camp,' wrote one anguished wife in the spring of 1946: 'I thought we should be able to carry on where we left off – but I now find myself repelled by him . . . I somehow cannot return the affection he still feels for me.'[38] The result was a more than tenfold rise in the number of divorce petitions: at its greatest moment of reunion the family seemed to be on the point of collapse.

Outside the household, civilians didn't quite know what to think of soldiers, and vice versa. The relationship between the two wartime communities was more ambivalent than people tend to remember today. Yes, everyone agreed, servicemen had done their duty and suffered for it, but the British homeland had gone through six years of grueling total war in its own right. Civilians were physically and mentally exhausted, and not in the best or most generous of spirits. Some veterans suspected, not without reason, that Britons out of uniform were less than sympathetic towards their difficulties following demobilisation.

Old prejudices about the 'brutal and licentious soldiery' lingered in British culture. The army was seen as a corrupting institution that turned honest young men into crooks, Calibans, libertines and idlers. It may be true that in 1945 ordinary people longed for a return to the certainties of the past, but it wasn't at all clear that the return of the serviceman was going to facilitate this.[39] On the contrary, contaminated as he was by a debased institution like the army, the demobbed Briton was more of a complication than a solution to the country's social problems. Popular *noir* thrillers conjured up an image of a brutalised land haunted by men unable or unwilling to forget the perverted mental legacy of war. No wonder ex-servicemen were treated with as much caution and suspicion as gratitude.

Soon the moral jeremiads were flying fast from the other side. Ex-prisoner of war George Millar detected 'slimy things amid the glory' of London: once the exuberance of homecoming had worn off, he claimed, 'the awe that puts pink lenses before the eyes of the returned soldier when he sees the worldly hub of the thing for which he has fought fell from me. And I saw a stinking stain of shoddiness, cheapness, graspingness and meanness.'[40] Demobbed ex-servicemen grumbled that everyone seemed ill-mannered, boorish, impatient; some of the demobbed felt thoroughly ashamed of their countrymen.[41] The homeland was turning out to be a bitter let-down.

'Within a year of V-E Day,' writes David Kynaston in his magisterial recent history of the period, 'there had set in . . . a widespread sense of disenchantment' across Britain.[42] The irony was that a society which had held together so well for six years of total war seemed to be coming apart in peace. It didn't, of course; but this mood of vague dissatisfaction – which would be a point of departure for a much more protracted sense of national decline throughout the next half-century – began in part with the disappointments of demobilisation. Homecoming seemed to open up, for just a brief moment, limitless, life-altering possibilities. That drabber reality soon closed in again may not have been unexpected, but it was no less disappointing.

Britain has changed a great deal since 1945, but it has lost little of its enthusiasm for sending young men in uniform into harm's way. Tens of thousands of servicemen are stationed abroad, many in the hostile theatre of Afghanistan. At the end of their service these men will return to a country immeasurably wealthier than it was at the end of the Second World War, but not necessarily any better prepared to receive them, or more interested. Perhaps, then, this is the time to reflect on a 'successful' story of homecoming that turns out, on closer examination, to have included plenty of individual tales of distress and disenchantment, injustice and regret.

# CHAPTER ONE

# Now This Bloody War is Over

*This war is ending in a dirty smear.*[1]

It was the dehydrated potatoes that started it. The crew had been promised real, honest-to-goodness spuds for lunch. They had peeled them lovingly the night before. But someone had blundered in the galley. Now they were being served up a runny goop looking, one of them complained, 'like rice pudding'. The men weren't happy one bit. Then there was the corned beef. They didn't like the look of that either. They were always having corned beef. Wasn't it time to do something? Take a stand?

The morning of 6 October 1945 had started off normally enough for the officers and men of HMS *Northway*, which was one of the Royal Navy's seven wartime 'Dock Landing Ships', a ponderous 7,700-ton portable harbour that stored and disgorged landing craft and amphibious vehicles. She had seen action on D-Day and had done valuable work shuttling thousands of men and machines back and forth across the English Channel to support the Anglo-American expeditionary force. In early 1945 she had been sent east to join the vast invasion flotilla assembling for the final assault on Japan – an assault that, as it turned out, the atomic bombings of Hiroshima and Nagasaki on 6 and 9 August would make unnecessary. Now *Northway* sat in Singapore harbour picking up stores, one of thousands of redundant Allied ships scattered around the world waiting to be paid off, sold, or broken up, her crew wondering when they were finally going home.

The trouble started at a quarter past twelve. The petty officer of the watch piped the men due on duty to fall in at the double. Only one of them appeared on deck. The rest, he reported, weren't going to move until they'd had a proper dinner. The PO tried twice more. No response. Then the coxswain of the ship's motor launch refused to go to his station: he'd 'downed tools with the rest of the lads,' he said. *Northway*'s officers spent the next half an hour trying to badger and harangue the crew to obey their orders, producing what the Admiralty's later inquiry called 'considerable shouting and noise', but no result.

The captain appeared and ordered the starboard watch to the quarterdeck. No one stirred. He called the first man on the muster, able seaman Plumb, and personally ordered him to fall in. 'I'm standing by the lads,' said Plumb. Other names were called. 'Nobody fucking well move,' someone muttered in the crowd. No one did. The seriousness of this action could not be exaggerated. Under the Naval Discipline Act a crew's decision to defy the lawful authority of its officers was an act of mutiny, an offence punishable, if a court martial saw fit, by many years of penal service, even hanging. What had started as a grumble over dinner was becoming a matter of life and death.

The impasse went on until quarter to two, when the boatswain made a personal appeal to the men to abandon the protest now before things got out of hand. And yes, he promised they would get their dinner. With that the spell was suddenly broken; the men went back to their duties without incident.[2] *Northway* was no HMS *Bounty*, her captain no cackling, keelhauling Captain Bligh. But in some ways that was what worried the Admiralty Board of Inquiry the most. *Those* kind of mutinies it could at least understand.

A month before *Northway*'s potato rebellion, a similar disturbance had broken out on the destroyer HMS *Javelin* as she lay off the Mediterranean island of Rhodes. The mutiny on *Javelin* had been even more serious: eight petty officers had joined in the protest and were eventually cashiered from the service, along with nineteen seamen. It was an ugly moment for the Royal Navy. But at least the cause was clear enough: *Javelin*'s captain, Lieutenant-Commander James Marjoribanks, was an unpopular martinet. 'He threw the book at us,' recalled one of *Javelin*'s sailors: 'petty regulations governing outward appearances he enforced with neurotic punctiliousness, nagging constantly over trivialities like some compulsively shrewish virago'.[3] 'HMS *Javelin* was an unhappy ship' the crew's defence counsel insisted at their court martial:

> the ship was a clean ship – clean outside – but in the men, [there was] a slow process of deterioration, mentally, a kind of seething discontent for the way in which they were treated; and perhaps what is worse, a feeling of helplessness that there was no-one to whom they could turn.[4]

The Admiralty evidently agreed, removing Marjoribanks from command as soon as the inquiry was over.

But none of this was true of HMS *Northway*. Her commander was no tyrant. Morale was not particularly bad. Even the food, the crew admitted in court, was no worse than on most ships. To the Admiralty it was a mystery why a vessel full of experienced and reasonably contented sailors had suddenly risked prison or worse over a pan of dehydrated potatoes. It was 'an outbreak of mass hysteria', the inquiry board had to conclude: '[men] became caught up in the mentality . . . steadily working themselves up into a heated and mutinous frame of mind over a minor and almost nonexistent grievance'.

The Admiralty decided to tread lightly this time, sentencing Plumb and another seaman to two years in detention, and twenty-seven other members of the crew to short spells in the naval stockade. But if the British military authorities hoped that by this magnanimous attitude the *Northway* incident would be a solitary act of madness brought on by the tropical heat, a freak one-off, they were soon to get a nasty shock.

It is fairly well known that at the end of the First World War the British Army had erupted in protest at its slow demobilisation. Acts of insubordination had broken out in hundreds of camps across Britain. Over ten thousand soldiers on leave in Folkestone in January 1919 had refused to embark on troopships that were supposed to return them to France. A convoy of lorries filled with striking soldiers, sporting chalked messages such as 'we're fed up' and 'no more sausage and rabbits', had descended on the War Office in Whitehall. Whiffs of revolutionary ferment had begun spreading westwards from Russia; a patrol vessel at Milford Haven lowered the White Ensign and raised the Red Flag. Detachments of the Army Service Corps had briefly taken over the town of Calais in a strike against long working hours and slow release from armed service, and Field Marshal Douglas Haig had only been dissuaded with difficulty from shooting the ringleaders.[5]

What is less well known is that during the six months that followed the end of the Second World War, a similar swell of discontent was to flow through His Majesty's armed forces across the world. Soldiers would break out of camps and refuse to board troopships. In India and the Middle East, airmen would down tools in protest at squalid conditions and draconian discipline. Over 260 paratroopers in Malaya would be court-martialled en masse for disobeying orders. In Aldershot, traditional home of the British Army, 300 inmates would set fire to the town's famous 86-year-old military prison – the 'Glasshouse', named after its elaborate lanterned roof – and reduce an icon of Crown authority to a burnt-out shell.

During the Second World War British serviceman had been, on the whole, much better behaved than their predecessors. There had been fewer court-martial cases than in the previous conflict, even though the punishments available to military courts during the First World War had been much more savage. So it says something about the depth of unhappiness and frustration in the ranks of the British Army, Royal Navy and RAF in the months following the surrender of Nazi Germany and Imperial Japan that even stolid, undemonstrative, wryly resigned men like the crew of HMS *Northway* were being driven to the brink of mutiny. 'Thousands of us are becoming embittered and demoralized,' complained an RAF airman to the *Daily Herald*; other servicemen spoke of 'disgust and rebellion' and how 'bitter, frustrated, and completely disillusioned' they felt.[6] Something had gone very badly wrong.

## When They Sound the Last All-Clear

It had all been very different on V-E Day, Tuesday, 8 May 1945. Corporal H.A. Wilson, a high-grade cipher clerk from Northampton attached to the headquarters of Twenty-Third Armoured Brigade, had recorded in his diary the celebrations in Loutraki, a coastal town a few miles northeast of Corinth, Greece. 'Every Tommy was either drunk or cheerfully heading that way,' he wrote:

> The beach party had lost none of its determination to keep knocking off the bottles, but its roaring song had slackened to a drunken drawl. Soldiers of all ranks were staggering round, singing dolefully or shouting to the stars . . . the bonfire flames had subsided but the vocal din was as strong as ever. The little Scottish pianist was literally blind drunk; his eyes were tight shut but his groping fingers worked on like independent mechanisms. Elsewhere by the light of the beach lights I could see soldiers sailing in little boats . . .[7]

As the news of Germany's surrender was broadcast to the troops on the BBC General Forces Programme across Europe and the Mediterranean, so their celebrations had begun. Unsurprisingly, many British servicemen spent the first day of peace paralytically drunk. Perhaps the best parties were to be found in the broad swathe of newly liberated territory from Denmark to the Po valley in Italy, where cellars full of champagne, brandy, gin and schnapps once greedily hoarded by the *Wehrmacht* were now broken open by their conquerors for what was intended to be the booze-up of the century.

In Klagenfurt in Austria, medical officer Guy Blackburn reported 'a measure of euphoria, almost in disbelief' amongst his fellow troops that was complemented by crate upon crate of requisitioned beer.[8] On the outskirts of Hamburg, the men of Lieutenant Sydney Beck's artillery battery, stupefied by rum punch, built and set alight a huge bonfire and tried to throw the unit's piano on it.[9] Casualties were inevitable. Private Harold Harrington of the Sherwood Foresters fell down some wooden stairs while drunk, cut open the bridge of his nose, and had a huge field dressing plastered over the whole of his face by an equally intoxicated sergeant. Next morning when he woke up he thought he had gone blind.[10]

The people of Britain, in and out of uniform, had much to celebrate that Tuesday night. Six years of deprivation and sacrifice had been vindicated in the destruction of the hated Nazi regime. 'I am not ashamed to say that I cheered lustily when I heard last night that Hitler was dead,' recorded Sydney Beck in his war diary a few days earlier. 'I shouted so loudly that the echo rang back from the dark trees through the stillness as clear as my own voice.'[11] That howl of relief was replicated across the world. 'Advance, Britannia! Long live the cause of freedom! God save the King!' Churchill exclaimed in his victory broadcast. Millions of Britons responded with unembarrassed pride and satisfaction.

But not everyone found themselves as deliriously happy at the news of victory as they had expected they would be. However welcome the defeat of the Third Reich was, for some British servicemen the end of the war was accompanied by doubt, confusion and suspicion. Fighting had already sputtered out untidily in many places. In Italy the *Wehrmacht* had surrendered days before. The men of the Eighth Army, who had suffered through years of bitter close-quarter fighting in atrocious conditions, found themselves hundreds of miles away from the military climax in Germany, and especially Berlin, marginal extras in a drama that had now passed them by.

'For us the war just fizzled out – and that was that,' wrote signaler H.W.F. Charles at the end of his three and a half year journey from

Egypt to the Alps. The end of the war 'was real in the sense that it was information received and understood,' he added, 'but it didn't make the slightest difference to our lives and nobody seemed particularly excited.'[12] Artillery officer Christopher Seton-Watson made the best of the surrender celebrations, setting off a huge petrol-drenched bonfire with a flare pistol. But as a highly decorated soldier who had fought all the way from Dunkirk to Bologna, he admitted in his diary to an 'acute feeling of disappointment and frustration' that he had had to 'finish the war in a backwater and miss all the thrill of the final pursuit and triumph'.[13]

The war in northwestern Europe was supposed to have ended on 4 May, when delegates from the de facto Nazi capital in Flensburg surrendered all forces in the theatre to Field Marshal Bernard Montgomery. But many *Wehrmacht* troops were still fighting ferociously up to the last minute. The Germans defending the eastern bank of the River Elbe near Cuxhaven continued to shell British positions throughout the surrender negotiations, and even when surrender was formally announced the following day they refused to let Royal Engineer sappers repair any bridges because they argued that technically there was only a truce. 'Why, oh why, won't they give in and realize it is so hopeless to resist any further?' wrote Sydney Beck in exasperation.[14]

For troops at the 'sharp end' of combat, the final days had been amongst the most psychologically gruelling of the whole war. Physical tiredness had been combined with the fear of being killed or crippled at the brink of victory. During April, soldiers in Germany had been furious at hints in the London press that the campaign was as good as over, and that armoured columns were 'racing along the roads with no opposition' – a suggestion that people at home were no longer taking the war seriously.[15] In reality, organised resistance might have been melting away, but until the moment of surrender every verge and copse in Westphalia could still contain a fanatical teenager with a *Panzerfaust* anti-tank rocket determined to take a few Tommies with him.

It is not surprising that for men in the thick of battle, the end of the war – the end of being shot at by strangers on a day-to-day basis, the end of expecting each morning to be one's last – was not easy to come to terms with. 'There should have been a great sense of relief – we should have all gathered round and raised our mugs and said "here's to the Poor Bloody Infantry",' thought Corporal Eric Lord, an NCO with the Coldstream Guards in north Germany:

> There was no grand celebration at all . . . I sat down on the grassy stretch of the aerodrome at Cuxhaven and tried to collect my thoughts and all I could think of was *well, that's the end of that*. We don't have to dig slit trenches and hear the awful sound of the *Nebelwerfer*, the multi-barrelled mortar. No more shells screeching over.[16]

Paratrooper Christopher Cross wrote to his parents shortly after hearing the news of the German surrender:

> As such dates go, this, I suppose, will be an important one. For us, it's not any different from yesterday or the day before . . . well anyway, this bit of the war is over. I suppose I should feel elated, but I feel tired and disgusted, and I can't get the smell of Germans out of my mouth no matter how hard I clean my teeth. Disgust, contempt and a little pity mix ill. What now, I wonder?[17]

For the hundreds of thousands of British servicemen stationed in the Pacific and South East Asia, V-E Day meant little at all. On 9 May 1945, as Europe's celebrants were sleeping off their victory hangovers, kamikaze suicide planes smashed into the decks of the Royal Navy carriers HMS *Formidable* and *Victorious* as they conducted ground-support operations off the Okinawa Islands. Fortunately the damage was not too severe. But five days earlier another kamikaze had started a fire in one of *Formidable*'s hanger bays that had killed eight of her crew. There was plenty of killing and dying still going on.

In Burma, General 'Uncle Bill' Slim's Fourteenth Army, the largest British Commonwealth field force of the war, was continuing its southeastward progress after taking Rangoon on 3 May. The novelist George MacDonald Fraser, then a lance corporal in a Border Regiment battalion in the spearhead of the advance, remembered V-E Day vividly. 'An officer – he must have been a new arrival, and a right clown – ran out in front of the company and shouted, with enthusiasm: *Men! The war in Europe is over!*' Fraser continued:

> There was a long silence, while we digested this, and looked through the heat haze to the village where Jap might be waiting, and I'm not sure the officer wasn't waving his hat and shouting hip, hip, hooray. The silence continued, and then someone laughed, and it ran down the line in a great extended torrent of mirth, punctuated by cries of *Git the boogers oot 'ere!* and *Ev ye told Tojo, like?* and *Hey, son, is it awreet if we a' gan yam?*[18]

If anything cooled the enthusiasm of British servicemen in Europe and the Middle East on V-E Day, it was the thought of a unit such as Fraser's Cumbrian battalion sweating it out in faraway Burma. For everyone knew that the liberation of Britain's South East Asian colonies would only be a preliminary to the apocalyptic finale of the Pacific War: the invasion of the Japanese home islands themselves. And now that hostilities in Europe were ended, thousands upon thousands of British troops would presumably soon be heading eastwards to join the gathering Allied armada.

Enthusiasm for this bloody and protracted crusade was slight. Few Britons had ever felt much emotional investment in the distant war against Japan. A posting to the Far East had long been the nightmare at the back of many men's minds. Captain A.M. Bell MacDonald returned from a tour of duty in Italy in the spring of 1944 only to find that his unit was being redeployed to India. 'It's the thing I dreaded most of all,' he wrote in his diary:

> I never thought for a moment that they were going to do it on us . . . Burma now seems a certainty. Some poor devils have to fight

in that hateful little country against those hateful little Japs, but I did pray it wouldn't need to be me. . . . Oh God, help us all and please get me back quick![19]

Corporal H.A. Wilson in Loutraki, Greece, weighed up the prospect of a Far East transfer with a quietly mutinous intransigence that was shared by many of his comrades: 'Burma's one little square I'm not being pushed into. I've no intention of getting my tonsils slit by a squint-eyed Jap. I've strength enough for one war but not two . . . I've come to the end of my tether; I've had enough.' Sergeant George Teal, a Coldstream Guards tank commander in Germany, felt much the same way. 'Montgomery told us that were now off to Japan and we all muttered *testicles!* under our breath. We didn't want to be off nowhere.'[20]

There was no way to know for sure who would be needed in the Pacific. Wartime British servicemen, whether they were volunteers or conscripts, had 'hostilities only', or some variation on that theme, scribbled into their paybooks: they had agreed to serve until the king's enemies were defeated. Japan had not even been at war with Britain when most of them joined the Forces. But there was no legal obligation to release them just because Germany was now no longer a threat. Indeed, the government had never defined what 'hostilities' meant. Did it include occupation service? What about the little wars already simmering on the fringes of empire? How long would the Second World War go on for, anyway?

Army balladeers, vying with one another in the depth of their pessimism, spun gloomy predictions about their military service stretching years into the future. The anonymous author of 'The Gallant Ninth' foresaw that by 1950 soldiers in the Middle East would have gone native, wearing caftans and speaking Arabic; others predicted that 'we're going to get demobbed – in Nineteen Fifty-Three', and that:

*All the ships have buggered off to sea, fellows*
*Fret awhile, sweat awhile, you'll soon forget*
*Civvy street, slippered feet,*

*All those things you ever dreamed of . . .*
*You can all box on to 1963, fellows.*[21]

Indeed, according to a War Office report on the mood of the troops in Germany, soldiers were worried that they would be expected to serve for another five, six, or seven years – perhaps for the whole occupation stretching decades ahead.[22] 'The future is a hundred times more uncertain than it ever was,' wrote Christopher Seton-Watson in Bologna on the day the war ended. 'No one has a ghost of an idea as to what happens next. So the only thing to do is to be patient and wait till the very important persons make up their minds.'[23]

## Release and Resettlement

Nonetheless, on V-E Day even the most determined barracks cynic knew that *some* men would be going home soon. It was neither necessary nor possible for Britain to maintain five million men and women in HM Forces just to defeat Japan. In any event, the country's role in the Pacific War was becoming increasingly symbolic, and it was not clear that the Americans even really wanted, let alone needed, British help any longer. So there was little surprise when on 12 May, a week after the German surrender, Ernest Bevin announced in the House of Commons that the first release cohort would be discharged on 18 June – 'D' (for demobilisation) Day.

The essential details of Bevin's demob plan had been announced back in September 1944. It divided servicemen into two categories, or classes. Most men – nine out of ten – were in Class A. For these men, the order in which they would be demobilised was calculated according to two factors: their date of birth, and the month in which their war service began. Two months of service were equivalent in value to one year of age. Each serviceman could calculate his Release Group Number in a simple table published in the official Forces guidebook, *Release and Resettlement*. The older you were and the longer you had served, the lower your Group

Number would be. Groups were to be released in turn, with Group 1 first, then Group 2, and so on.

The exceptional one in ten servicemen were known as the Class B 'key men'. They had been in prewar civilian occupations considered so vital to reconstruction – coal mining, building and civil engineering, teaching, the police service – that it was justifiable on grounds of national interest to discharge them ahead of the rest of their Release Group.

The plan was well received because it emphasised simplicity and transparency. Everyone's place in the Class A order of release was based on two straightforward pieces of information; anyone could easily calculate anyone else's Group Number if they wanted to. Officers and other ranks were to be treated identically. Men stationed abroad would be returned to the United Kingdom to be released at the same time as men on home service. As for Class B, Bevin was emphatic that this was not a soft option or an attractive way of jumping the queue. Anyone released in Class B was expected to work for his reconstruction employer only, and if he left that job he became immediately liable for recall to the Forces. Whereas newly released Class A servicemen would get eight weeks' leave with full pay upon their release, those in Class B would receive only three weeks.[24]

A lack of sensitivity to this issue had helped to precipitate the fiasco of 1919. David Lloyd George's coalition government had devised an elaborate release scheme which favoured men with pre-existing civilian work guarantees (so-called 'slip men', named after the contract chits that they carried from their employers). Whatever economic rationality this system might have had was more than cancelled out by the outrage it committed against common-sense justice. The men pushed to the back of the queue were those who had been out of contact with the civilian job market since 1914 – in other words, the very men who had volunteered for service at the outbreak of war. 'The ordinary soldier,' wrote Churchill in his postwar memoir *The Aftermath*:

Saw his lately joined comrade hurrying home to take his job . . . while he, after years of peril and privations on a soldier's pay, wounded and sent back to the carnage three or sometimes four times, was to be left until all the plums at home had been picked up and every vacancy filled.[25]

By contrast, Bevin's rules were so straightforward they could be written on the back of a beer mat. The scheme seemed to defy dodges and shortcuts, and offered no favourites to insiders. It was just what a tired and cynical and somewhat short-tempered group of men needed in 1945. Mass-Observation's study of demibilisation, *The Journey Home*, had predicted that the only really successful plan would be one:

> which has no loopholes, in which everyone is sure where they stand and know in advance what is going to happen to them; a system which has the main virtues of being clearcut and unambiguous, so that everyone shall know that however they are placed, everyone else with a similar record and qualifications is in the same boat.[26]

The simple principle of 'fair shares for all' had been a compelling way of justifying the food-rationing system during the war, and Bevin's plan made a similar appeal to straightforwardness and even-handedness. The response from the troops was overwhelmingly favourable. An Eighth Army officer reported to *The Times* that his men found it 'practical . . . and a sincere and honest attempt to deal fairly with the problem'. Even 'confirmed grouchers' like Captain A.M. Bell MacDonald was willing to concede that 'the plan sounds very good and most people seem pleased'. 'I'm looking for snags,' said one private to Corporal H.A. Wilson, 'but I can't find none. It's pukka genuine, the real thing at last.'[27]

Servicemen keenly scrutinised *Release and Resettlement*, learning by heart every detail of the plan. The letters pages of the Forces newspapers filled with queries about arcane qualifications and exceptions to the basic scheme. Each man's Release Group Number, committed to memory, became as important a feature of his service identity as his name, rank, or serial number. 'Demob,' as one lieutenant in the Royal Electrical and Mechanical Engineers put it, 'is the only subject of Army conversation. The first thing you ask of any newcomer is his demob number. The job he is given depends on his number, his likelihood of taking interest in it depends on his number.'[28] Bombardier Arthur Harris of the Royal Artillery noted in a letter home from Schleswig-Holstein that 'everybody from the colonel downwards seems to be suffering from demobilisation fever'. Soon he had advanced symptoms too:

> My state of mind can best be described rather vulgarly by the common phrase, 'sweating on the top line' as the days, the hours, the minutes, the seconds slide inexorably on. I am very wary of staircases in the darkness . . .[29]

## We Did Our Part . . . Get Us Out

Monday, 18 June 1945 – Demob Day – arrived and went without a hitch. Several thousand of Britain's oldest and longest-serving men and women emerged into civilian life to a barrage of photographers' flashbulbs. As June became July and then turned to August, the discharge machine went through its well-oiled if undramatic motions. True, there were grumbles at the languid pace. By the end of the first two months, barely 200,000 of the first cohorts at the front of the queue had been released, fewer than one in twenty of all servicemen. The rate was sluggish, barely 3,000 a day. In 1919 the discharge centres had processed ten times as many. That had been a flood; this was barely a trickle.

Churchill's caretaker government, which had come into office when the wartime coalition had broken up at the end of May, could defend its hesitancy by pointing to the ongoing war in the Far East. While the Japanese threat continued to exist, the nation's efforts still had to be carefully planned and directed by the state. 'The national emergency is far from over,' argued *The Times*; and the logic of this, though unwelcome to the troops, had been grudgingly accepted.[30] But all this changed on 6 August, when the United States dropped the first atomic bomb on Hiroshima. Two days later the Soviet Union declared war on Japan. A day after that a second A-Bomb destroyed Nagasaki. On 15 August the Japanese government declared its unconditional surrender to the Allies. The Second World War was suddenly over.

Nobody in Britain was unhappy to see the Pacific War ended. The catastrophic destruction of the warships HMS *Prince of Wales* and *Repulse* in December 1941, the surrender of Hong Kong a few weeks later on Christmas Day, and the humiliating rout of imperial forces in Malaya and Burma the year after, had all been avenged. For hundreds of thousands of servicemen expecting imminent transfer to the Pacific, Japan's surrender meant that a Homeric struggle on the invasion beaches of Japan was now unnecessary. It also meant that surviving Far Eastern prisoners of war (Fepows) held by the Japanese under atrocious conditions, some for more than three and a half years, would at last be reunited with their families. These facts alone made V-J Day something well worth celebrating.

But the end of the war against Japan also made the demand for faster demobilisation all the more compelling. British servicemen had never been enthusiastic about the war in the Far East, but it had helped to justify their retention in the ranks. Hiroshima had altered the moral terms of call-up completely. The troops had agreed to fight fascism, and had been willing to forgo many of their basic rights as citizens to that end. Now the fascists were beaten, however, it was time to go home. 'We entered military service because of the national necessity', insisted one lance-corporal in the Mediterranean theatre:

> We did our part, and now we only ask for the just repayment – our release from a hateful bondage . . . get us out. Let us build. Let us work. We won the war. Give us a chance to win the peace.[31]

So when George Isaacs, the new Minister for Labour and National Service, made his first major announcement about demo-bilisation in the House of Commons on 23 August, the nation in arms awaited expectantly. The news was anticlimactic. Isaacs revealed that an additional 250,000 releases would be made on top of the 750,000 who were already due to be discharged by the end of the year. But that was as far as the peace dividend went. Four out of five men serving on V-E Day would still be in the Forces on 1 January 1946, including some of the longest-serving soldiers of all, men whose Release Groups were still relatively high because of their youth. The 26-year-old 'militia men,' who had been conscripted in the spring of 1939, for instance, were not among the million. They would be spending a seventh Christmas in uniform.

'A shock greater than the news of the atomic bomb hit our mess-deck when we heard on the radio that we have months, and perhaps years, more of this soul-destroying service life,' complained one group of naval ratings.[32] What gave Isaacs' decision a sour twist was that it was accompanied by the news that over a million civilian war workers would be demobilised from industrial conscription in armaments factories. There had been enough resentment within the Forces in May when the Ministry of Labour had decided not to call up any more civilians over the age of 30. The news of faster releases from factories was not calculated to improve the mood of disappointed servicemen. 'We are delighted to see that munition workers are to be released in time to pick the best jobs, while we carry on with fatigues,' snapped a group of RAF aircraftmen to the *Daily Herald*.[33]

It didn't help that a Labour government was now handing out the bad news. On 27 July, the People's Party had formed its first ever majority government after winning a historic landslide victory. Winston Churchill had been removed from Downing Street and his former wartime deputy Clement Attlee had become Prime Minister in his place.

It was an open secret that most servicemen who had voted in July had supported Labour.[34] The Party had explicitly presented itself as the guarantor of the hopes of the ordinary soldier, whose welfare it claimed to hold in 'sacred trust'.[35] The *Daily Mirror*, loudest and lustiest of Attlee's Fleet Street chorus, considered itself the 'paper of the Forces' and had exhorted its readers to 'Vote for Him – Vote the Soldier's Way'.[36] Many servicemen felt that it was their support that had decided the election.

In fact, the significance of the service vote in 1945 was greatly exaggerated. It increased the overall margin of victory but it didn't alter the outcome. There were simply too few voters from the armed forces. Barely half of all eligible service personnel registered to vote, and of those, four out of ten didn't bother to cast a ballot on the day. If every serviceman who voted Labour in the election had abstained, Attlee would probably have won anyway.[37] But that is not what anyone believed in the summer of 1945. Labour, everyone assumed, owed its victory to the Forces. And now the serviceman expected to be rewarded for his support. Demobilisation would be the first test of how well his government was going to honour its debt.

But the Labour administration in which so many hopes were invested had other things to worry about than the demands of its voters. When the government had drawn up its reconstruction plans back in 1944, it had made the reasonable assumption that the war against Japan would continue for at least another twelve to eighteen months after Germany's defeat. From a strictly practical point of view, there was something to be said for such a two-stage ending to the war. It would ensure the continuation of vital American Lend-Lease aid and justify the extension of state controls on production and manpower. Japan's stubborn refusal to surrender might perversely turn out to be a lucky break for a Britain struggling to readjust to the harsh accounting realities of peace. 'Bring me victory', cried John Bull; but – he added, *sotto voce* – 'not *just* yet'.

The atomic bombs smashed all of Labour's assumptions to smithereens. 'There is no prospect now,' *The Times* lamented a few days after the Japanese surrender, 'of a prolonged and steady "tapering off" . . . the end has burst suddenly . . . reconversion has become an emergency operation.'[38] On 20 August, President Harry Truman abruptly cut off all further financial assistance to Britain. The country's reconstruction efforts had been predicated on a continuing supply of vital dollar-aid; now John Maynard Keynes had to be dispatched to Washington to barter with US Treasury Department officials for an extension of American largesse. The $3.75 billion loan which he eventually negotiated proved completely inadequate; only Marshall Plan assistance, a severe devaluation of the pound in 1949, and years of pinched consumerism at home would eventually resolve Britain's 'dollar-gap' of hard currency.

There was, then, a strong case for faster demobilisation on economic grounds. Defence expenditure in the final year of the war had reached £100 million a week, now an impossible amount to sustain. As Keynes had pointed out in a memorandum to the new Cabinet, the British had got into the unfortunate habit of maintaining large and expensive establishments all over the world to police vast areas eastwards from Tunis to Burma and northwards from East Africa to Germany. He warned that this extravagant military overstretch was contributing to an imminent 'financial Dunkirk'.[39]

If the UK were to rebuild its export markets aggressively, men in uniform were needed back in the factories churning out machine tools and textiles. Civilian industry was critically short of manpower. Employees long past retirement age who had stayed on during the war were now leaving the workforce. Not enough school leavers were taking their place. Soldiers were required back on the shop floor.

But Britain had inherited daunting global responsibilities that it couldn't simply ignore. In liberated Europe the immediate problems of peace were as complex as those of war. British troops in northwest Germany were trying to restore some kind of order in the midst of chaos: repairing roads and bridges, telephone lines, water supplies and electrical power cables; clearing minefields, defusing unexploded bombs; reopening ports, canals and waterways blocked by sunken vessels and anti-invasion obstacles. Above all, they were confronted with a horde of lost human flotsam: millions of refugees, former prisoners of war, freed slave labourers and concentration camp survivors, known in bureaucratic parlance as 'displaced persons', or DPs. Many were passive and bewildered; some, including escaped Russian prisoners, 'half-civilized Mongols and Tartars' in the army's view, were running amok raping and murdering any German civilians they could get their hands on.[40] All had to be rounded up, disarmed, fed and sheltered until someone could decide what to do with them.

Moreover, Britain was still a great world power – or, at least, Attlee's government was committed to the collective fiction that it was still a great world power. Labour might have espoused a formal policy of anti-imperialism, but His Majesty's new administration was just as insistent about the need to defend the British Empire and aggressively contain communism as the previous government had been. And the empire was unsettled. Security forces in the Palestine mandate were targets as the conflict between Jewish colonists and Palestinian Arabs simmered to the boil once again. In India resistance to the retreating Raj was coupled with growing sectarian violence. Peace might have been declared across the world, but emergencies such as these were still self-evidently going on.

Nor were Britain's imperial responsibilities confined to its own turf. The French and Dutch colonies in the Far East, which had still been under Japanese control on V-J Day, needed occupying and policing, despite the fact that many local nationalists, radicalised by the defeat of their former masters in 1942, were in no mood to welcome the Europeans back. French Indochina and the Dutch East Indies had declared independence immediately after Japan's surrender, and the new government in London was determined to stamp out this native impertinence on behalf of its allies. By October, in one of Britannia's forgotten proxy wars of decolonisation, tens of thousands of British troops supported by tanks, aircraft and naval gunfire would be fighting a ferocious street-by-street battle with revolutionary irregulars in the Indonesian city of Surabaya.

Meanwhile, across Europe, former allies were busy haggling over the spoils of victory. In Venezia Giulia, at the northern head of the Adriatic, British and Yugoslav troops were engaged in a tense standoff over the status of the Italian port of Trieste, which had been occupied by Marshal Tito's communist partisans. In Greece, British units were monitoring an uneasy ceasefire between monarchist and communist forces. And eleven million soldiers of the Red Army remained on the frontiers of Joseph Stalin's vastly expanded empire, his intentions for them as yet unknown.

The service ministries in London insisted that these security commitments required the retention of large numbers of men.

They estimated that in mid-1946 Britain would still need an army, navy and air force of two and a quarter million. So it is not surprising that the Labour government, pulled in both directions, at first acted cautiously on demobilisation. But its servicemen were not particularly sympathetic. The empire meant little to many of them, and the idea that they should play colonial enforcers in the service of the French or the Dutch was not at all appealing. As for Europe, shouldn't it look after itself? And anyway hadn't the atomic bomb made the traditional mass army obsolete? Churchill, the Victorian sabre rattler, had wanted to play toy soldiers; Labour was supposed to be the Soldier's Party, which meant the Demob Party. 'We are not enemies of the government, which we helped put in power,' warned a RN signalman in the *Daily Mirror*, 'but we soon will be if they don't treat us as human beings with wishes and longings, and not just as many service numbers.'[41]

By the autumn of 1945 the Minister of Labour found himself the target of every newspaper in Britain. Isaacs, a much less prepossessing figure than Bevin, lacked his predecessor's natural authority and charisma. His insistence that 'we are not going to be stampeded . . . we shall avoid hysterical demands for releases which are plainly impossible' came across as shrill and unconvincing.[42] Dissatisfaction multiplied. When Mass-Observation asked a sample of soldiers how demob was progressing, the answers were virtually unanimous: 'It can really be answered in two words,' wrote a major in the British Army of the Rhine. 'IT STINKS! That is as mild as I can bring myself to be.'[43]

By the end of the year, demobilisation was being described by one of the Labour Party's own MPs as 'the Achilles heel' of the Attlee government.[44] Even the *New Statesman*, journal of the intellectual Left, found Labour's appeals for patience unconvincing:

When Mr. Attlee pleads vaguely our 'commitments and obligations' in Europe and the Far East as reasons why 'over-optimistic' forecasts of accelerated demobilization may not be fulfilled, listeners to his broadcasts feel that policy is still being sold to them in a poke . . . an end must be put to the waste represented by unemployed soldiers.[45]

## What a Thing it is to Be in a Peacetime Army!

'Do you suffer from overworked elbows – the new occupational disease which is caused by leaning the elbows on hard surfaces, such as canteen counters and fences, while waiting to be demobilized?'[46] This question, asked by the *Daily Mail* in September 1945, would have struck a chord with hundreds of thousands of servicemen hanging around depots and base camps across Britain at that moment with literally nothing to do. For these men, the autumn and winter of 1945 was a period largely defined by boredom, muddle, waste and inactivity.

The victory hangovers had worn off a long time ago. The day-to-day routines that servicemen had endured for five or more years – the spud peeling, the saluting, the everything-in-triplicate – remained unaltered by peace. 'My life is precisely the same now as it was before in wartime,' complained one soldier to Mass-Observation in September 1945. War or no war, soldiers still had to put up with the small but vexing inconveniences of being part of the military machine – the lack of privacy and freedom, the separation from friends and family, the uncertainty about the future.[47]

What *was* new was the absence of any sense of purpose to this captivity. These were men who were trapped only by the elegant simplicity of the Bevin demobilisation plan. As previously noted, demob was based on the principle that all servicemen with the same age and service criteria should be released at the same time, regardless of where they were stationed. This meant that men in the United Kingdom who were surplus to military requirements could not be demobbed until their comrades in the same Release Group had been repatriated from abroad. Men whose Group Numbers were low could not even be sent abroad on overseas duty. This was logical and even humane, but it meant that during the remainder of their service they were often effectively useless. Some of them spent weeks being passed around from depot to depot like unwanted parcels.

'What a thing it is to be in a peacetime army!' lamented gunner John White, as he sketched out in his diary a typical four days in his barracks in October 1945:

Fine sunny day. No parades. Detailed for guard tonight . . .

Played table tennis for a while this evening. Had a hair cut in the afternoon . . .

Cookhouse fatigue today. Played table tennis again . . .

No parades this afternoon. Wrote a letter and played a few games of table tennis.[48]

H.W.F. Charles wrote to his mother from his depot camp in Thirsk, North Yorkshire, which he had been dumped in after returning from Austria: 'It's completely unintelligible . . . I don't even feel annoyed. It all seems so hopelessly irrational that it has become amusing.'[49] Two days later he was sent to a tank regiment in Bury St. Edmunds. They didn't want him either.

If peacetime Britain had been awash in unemployed ex-servicemen at that moment, then those left in the Forces might have been a good deal less insistent about their right to release. Indeed, in the more uncertain mood of 1944, when the spectre of the interwar dole queue was much stronger, feelings about rapid demobilisation had been ambivalent. 'Many feel that *anything* would be better than to allow servicemen to return without some guarantee of work,' suggested Mass-Observation's *The Journey Home*.[50] Better, perhaps, to take things slowly than risk another wasted generation.

But by the autumn of 1945 it was becoming clear that there was not going to be a postwar speculative bubble, and that Britain's biggest economic difficulty was going to be a shortage of manpower, not a surplus. In September, the Oxford political economist Sir Hubert Henderson complained to *The Times* that up to five and a half million servicemen and civilians were being lost to industry by being uselessly detained in the Forces or in war factories.[51] Employers began complaining about their difficulties restarting civilian production in the absence of their workforces.[52]

Men at a loose end were supposed to have been diverted by the Educational and Vocational Training (EVT) programme, which had been introduced to much ballyhoo in mid-1944. The idea of giving servicemen a taste of civilian work experience while they were biding their time in uniform was laudable, but in practice it was hard to put into effect. Some senior officers, who disliked the EVT's faint traces of intellectuality, made it clear from the start that they would have nothing to do with it. By 1946 the War Office was forced to admit that EVT 'had fallen far short of what had been hoped'.[53] The head of the Royal Navy's EVT centre at Chatham complained to the *Contemporary Review* that the scheme had faced 'massive disregard' by the Forces, and that it had been dogged by administrative chaos:

> I recall, for instance, starting a large mathematics class . . . at the third meeting, its size was no less, but the personnel entirely different. I have visited a language classroom, and found everyone absent – picking sugar beet. I have fought, not always with success, to secure talented seamen for EVT who would otherwise have been mowing grass or cleaning lavatories. My entire staff of teachers has spent idle afternoons while their students were being paid.[54]

So they sat. And they waited. 'Here is a glimpse of life today for a medical practitioner in the RAF,' recounted one service doctor to the *News Chronicle*:

*Scene*: An RAF Station.

*Dramatis Personae*: 750 of nation's fittest young people. Two medical practitioners.

9–9.30am: Sick parade which averages five cases. 9.30–10am: signing mail.

10am onwards: anything to pass the time . . .[55]

## Service East of Suez

'It's a scandal . . . if we can be compelled to do three years' service, mostly abroad, on top of the four years war service, solely because of the incompetence and over-staffing of the RAF, I would like to know just what the last war was all about.'[56] Flying Officer Charles Crichton, the author of these words, was no one's idea of a natural malcontent. He had had, as the phrase went, a 'Good War'. After joining the RAF as a sergeant in early 1941, Crichton had spent over two years training to be a Spitfire pilot, first in the southeast of England and then for ten months in Canada as part of the British Commonwealth Air Training Plan. He arrived in Italy in March 1944 attached to 682 Squadron, a photo-reconnaissance unit that flew a special version of the Spitfire loaded with extra fuel tanks and armed with vertically mounted cameras rather than cannons. Crichton spent thirteen exhilarating months flying high-altitude scouting missions over the battlefields of Italy and southern France, dodging flak and Luftwaffe interceptors. He loved being in the air. His job was every overgrown schoolboy's dream.

But by September 1945, he and his squadron were being shuttled desultorily around the Near East – first to Palestine, then Egypt, then Palestine again, then Iraq, posted to a succession of ugly, forgotten tented shanties in the desert scrub. 'As far as the eye can see there is nothing but a jumble of huts, hangers, telephone wires and rusting barbed wire,' he wrote to his parents from one strip of hard gravel somewhere in Mesopotamia. 'The mess is bad, the food below average, and the camp cinema shows films that I can remember seeing at school.'

There was little going on. The days of damn-the-consequences flying were over. Most of the squadron's Spitfires and Mosquitoes were grounded to keep maintenance and fuel costs down. 'I am doing very nearly nothing,' Crichton complained: 'In fact things are worse than that; they are inventing work to keep us from being too idle.' And he had no idea when he was going to be able to go home. Despite four years of active service, his place in the demobilisation queue seemed depressingly low: according to the vague guesstimates given out by the Air Ministry, 1948 looked to be his earliest possible release date.

Just to make life even more uncomfortable, prewar RAF stuffiness was reasserting itself, the slackness and easy camaraderie of wartime life giving way to spit-and-polish and snobbery. 'I am beginning to get a fair idea of the peacetime RAF,' Crichton wrote. 'The regular officers maintained a discreet silence about wartime volunteers during the fighting. But now that we are no longer essential quite a different attitude is apparent. They are trying hard to return to '39 standards.' These complaints – of squalid conditions, the lack of any meaningful work to do, pointless drills and fatigues to fill in the time, and conspiracies by self-serving brass-hats – would reverberate wherever British servicemen were stationed around the world during the first twelve months of demob. But they had a special significance in the benighted military posts east of Suez.

Conditions at bases in Britain were not always good either. At one Royal Navy depot in Glasgow, there were said to be two hand-basins and one shower for every hundred of the unlucky ratings who passed through its verminous workhouse walls.[57] Nor were men in Germany always spared what one soldier called the 'dreariness and sickening sordidness of life' on garrison duty.[58] But servicemen in the UK were usually able to receive one week's leave every three months, which meant at least intermittent contact with their loved ones. And men posted to western Europe also had reasonable opportunities to get home; in fact, the allegedly luxurious conditions for some of the more fortunate occupiers of Germany and Italy were to cause a minor scandal back in Austerity Britain.[59]

It was the men posted to the Near East and beyond – North Africa, the Persian Gulf, India and the tropics – who had the most thankless and demoralising demob experiences of all. Cut off almost completely from family friends and community during their service, their expatriation a cruel exile from everything they had known as civilians, they felt themselves especially damned and unwanted – 'a legion of lost men who are doomed to rot,' as one soldier in Burma put it.[60] Bitterness was not concealed. 'We languish hopelessly in the British Belsen, as we lovingly term it,' wrote Sergeant Bill Points from the Middle East in the summer of 1945: 'this hellspot in the desert, sand-swept, oven-heated, blistering, waterless, green-starved, soul-killing stretch of nothingness . . .'[61]

The troops' strength of feeling has been passed down to us in an insightful report prepared for the War Office by Lieutenant-Colonel John Sparrow, just the sort of unlikely warrior thrown up by the exigencies of wartime. Sparrow was a barrister, a classical scholar, an acerbic commentator for the literary press and the cultivator of a ferocious temper that would make him a feared but highly respected postwar Warden of All Souls, Oxford. But he was also someone with an innate gift for talking to, and perhaps more importantly listening to, ordinary people, and under the reforming influence of the army's adjutant-general, Sir Ronald Forbes Adam, he had found a perfect niche for his talents as the War Office's expert on troop morale. Since January 1942 he had been producing regular summaries for the Army Council on the 'mood of the forces', compiled from a range of sources that included field commanders' reports, postal censorship statistics and queries from servicemen addressed to the BBC broadcaster Professor John Hilton.[62] On 28 June 1945 he arrived in India for what was to be a four-month tour of the subcontinent and South East Asia Command (SEAC).

What Sparrow found was not encouraging. India Command and SEAC suffered from every deficiency in basic army welfare, with a chronic shortage of radios, gramophones, newspapers, books, films and decent live entertainment. A 'barrier of mistrust and even hostility' had formed between soldiers and senior officers in the East: 'The troops,' Sparrow reported, 'have succeeded in persuading themselves that "they" could perfectly well improve the conditions and shorten the period of service overseas if they wished, and that it is lack of interest and selfishness that prevents them from doing so.' Churchill (who never visited the Far East during the war) was reportedly booed whenever he appeared on a newsreel screen.[63]

A Royal Army Medical Corps report on conditions in Burma at the same time came to similar conclusions. 'The Army, in the mind of the [ordinary British soldier],' it lamented, 'is all feet, no head, and vaguely malignant, like one of the more incoherent tropical insects magnified ten million times.' Senior commanders, it suggested, were undermining good relations between the ranks because of an excessive insistence on what the report called the specious and showy – or as rank-and-file soldiers put it more bluntly, bullshit.[64] The army's 'present air of all-pervading witlessness' was making military service in the east 'a Rip Van Winkle's nightmare'.[65] Wartime Burma had always been notorious as the worst of all postings. Logistics were so stretched, the rudiments of welfare so difficult to obtain, that even cigarettes had to be airdropped to the troops in waterproof packages; beer amounted to three bottles a man per month, sweets and chocolate were practically unavailable.[66] Dysentery, malaria and sepsis cut down soldiers in their prime.

But conditions offshore could be equally bad. Tropical tours on dilapidated vessels of First World War vintage, unsuited to hot conditions, were infamous. One stoker described life on a battleship to the MP Hannen Swaffer:

> We live on a mess flat roughly thirty five feet by seventeen feet. Eighty men live, eat and sleep in this confined space with no portholes. Daylight has never penetrated down where we live since the ship was built . . . the only ventilation is through ten small blowers which usually give you a stiff neck instead of a breath of fresh air. I wish the Health Minister could be present when we are called out in the morning. Racking coughs and the stench of sweating bodies is enough to make the healthiest of us ill . . . to make matters worse, we are constantly working on the officers' living quarters and their luxurious bathrooms.[67]

By 1945 repatriation had become an *idée fixe* amongst men who had served in the tropics for any appreciable length of time. 'It is nothing less than an obsession,' wrote John Sparrow to the

War Office: 'how complete may be judged from the instantaneous reply of a private soldier to my casual enquiry [of] how long he had been overseas: *Three years, two months and nine days sir*. This was typical.'[68]

Indeed, many overseas servicemen would have happily foregone immediate demobilisation if only they could have been posted back to Britain. But the army's theatre rotation system, known as PYTHON, had by the end of 1945 become almost as controversial as demob. PYTHON had been introduced a year earlier, and it was supposed to guarantee that all soldiers would be rotated back to the UK after a set period of overseas service. This was originally set at six years, and by the early summer of 1945 it had been reduced to four years for men in Europe and the Middle East, and three years and eight months for those in the Far East. With the defeat of Germany, however, impatience grew for further cuts.

At the beginning of June, Churchill's secretary of state for war, Sir James Grigg, made a well-publicised announcement that PYTHON for troops in India and SEAC would be reduced to three years and four months. This meant that many thousands of men who had been hurriedly shipped to India in the spring of 1942 to forestall a possible Japanese invasion would soon become eligible for rotation. A few weeks later, however, Grigg was forced to clarify that his earlier promise had been a target to work towards rather than a firm pledge. His announcement provoked a howl of anger from men whose hopes had been temporarily raised.[69] 'After today's news,' wrote one soldier to the Forces' paper *SEAC*, 'most of us out here are feeling like waving a few red flags . . . the lads are hopping mad about the whole "set-up", and the general opinion is that we've been victimized.'[70]

The authorities were facing genuine logistical problems. Transportation was critically short. RAF Transport Command was stretched to the limit air-trooping men back from the Far East and the Mediterranean – during 1945 its aircraft flew 284 million miles – and its fleet of Dakota cargo aircraft were worn out after years of excessive wartime use.[71] Accidents started mounting up. Fifty ex-Fepows just liberated from prison camps in Siam and

Indochina were killed in plane crashes along the mountainous Bangkok-to-Rangoon air route alone.[72] In November 1945 over 160 service personnel died in Transport Command crashes. More stringent safety precautions were introduced but this cut down on flying time, slowing down the repatriation process even more.[73]

Surface ships were in equally short supply. Britain had lost over eleven million gross tons of shipping through enemy action during the war. The government did itself no publicity favours by lending the two giant liners RMS *Queen Elizabeth* and RMS *Queen Mary* to the Americans for the repatriation of GIs in Europe. It was not an unreasonable decision: the superliners could be used far more efficiently on transatlantic runs, for they were too big to travel through the Suez Canal, and the Americans had returned the favour by loaning equivalent shipping space.[74] But the point was lost on resentful British servicemen, who saw only pampered GIs going home while they stayed put. 'An ugly mood is setting in,' thought one ranker in the Far East. 'If things are not hurried up there will be a considerable amount of trouble.'[75]

## Strike

Discontent was already simmering amongst the thousands of airmen in the Far East when Leading Aircraftman L.A. Gillam arrived at RAF Seletar in Singapore in January 1946, one of Transport Command's vast and sprawling tropical maintenance bases. Overcrowded, without proper canteens or welfare facilities, Seletar was in 'a shocking state', Gillam later recalled. With the base seemingly cut off from the outside world, information about demobilisation was unavailable or confusing; airmen received their mail weeks late. Hundreds of men were camped in tents filled with water. 'Things had been better during the war.'[76]

The miseries of malaria and dysentery were accentuated by prickly heat, caused by the constant sweltering humidity. Yet with the onset of peace many air force commanders continued to insist on regular kit inspections and parades, military 'bull' consisting of drills, march pasts, fatigues, including turnouts in 'best blues' – the heavy woollen tunics and trousers designed for European temperatures. 'There has been a great tightening up of so-called discipline overseas,' complained one airman in December 1945. 'This includes frequent parades, inspections, and all the other petty irritations in which the authorities apparently delight in piling on to the unfortunate . . .':

> On my own station, in the heat of a Middle East summer, men would be compelled to mount guard in the sun with sleeves rolled down and fastened, collars buttoned up and ties worn, long slacks, and full webbing for four two-hour stretches in twenty four, at the end of which duty they had two hours' stand-off in which to breakfast &c., before resuming work in the hangars . . . it is small wonder that the men are disgruntled when they realize that as a result of winning the war they are a lot worse off.[77]

Moreover, demob seemed to be malfunctioning at these bases. Buried within *Release and Resettlement* was a warning that 'It will be necessary in some Services to deal separately with the several branches and trades and probably with ranks (or ratings) in those branches.'[78] It was always going to be difficult to release men based purely on age and time served. Not all servicemen were of equal importance to the running of ships, units and air stations. Officers were more important than other ranks, technicians more important than the unskilled. Many clerical staff would be needed to handle the vast amounts of paperwork created by demobilisation. Men with higher rank and more experience tended by definition to be older and to have been in the Forces longer, and therefore had low Release Group numbers. Their absence would be felt most keenly.

Of all the services, the RAF was struggling hardest with the logic of the Bevin plan. It relied more than the army or navy on tradesmen. And because RAF Transport Command's aircraft were expected to repatriate millions of overseas personnel, many squadrons were now being kept busier than they had been during the war. So the Air Ministry had decided to interpret the age-plus-service principle very flexibly. Its demobilisation notices were broken down trade by trade. For November and December 1945, for example, it anticipated releasing the following:

Aircrew – Groups 23–24.

Ground trades – accounting clerks, Groups 14–16; cooks, Groups 18–19; equipment assistants, Groups 19–21; clerks, Groups 21–22; chiropodists, dispensers, laboratory assistants, masseurs, nursing orderlies, operating rooms assistants, radiographers, sanitary assistants, nurses, dental mechanics – Groups 20–22 . . . *et cetera*.[79]

Technically, the Bevin plan allowed this kind of selective discharge. But from the ordinary airman's point of view, it was a flagrant disavowal of everything he believed he had been promised. A cook with exactly the same age-and-service criteria as a masseur expected to be released on the same day. If the RAF valued his skills more than those of the masseur then that was the RAF's problem, not his. Bevin had stressed that every person in Class A would be treated according to the same formula. Servicemen had understood this to mean that all members of the same Release Group would be demobilised at the same time *without exception*. This misunderstanding was to prove incendiary.

The first act of what were to become known to history as the RAF 'demob strikes' took place at RAF Jodhpur in northwestern India. Airmen from two maintenance units refused to assemble on the parade ground for a morning inspection, going to their normal places of work instead. They appointed a twelve-man delegation to meet with the commanding officer and present a petition of their grievances: bad food, pedantic discipline and slow demobilisation. Then the airmen of RAF Drigh Road near Karachi ignored an order to parade in best blues. At nearby RAF Mauripur, airmen refused to work for four days. Word of the protests spread to airfields in Ceylon, where airmen also downed tools. Men at Cawnpore, the largest air force base in India, came out in sympathy. Four thousand men at Selatar joined in. By the end of January 1946, around 50,000 airmen from Egypt to Malaya had joined in the protest. It was one of the largest acts of collective indiscipline in British military history.[80] Sir Keith Park, the former Battle of Britain commander who had been appointed Allied Air Commander in South East Asia, reported with alarm to the Air Ministry. 'Would emphasize serious consequences of strikes on Indian population and particularly on our prestige out here,' he telegraphed: 'I consider the situation serious and may get out of control.'[81]

The authorities in India were already jittery in early 1946; the mood in the subcontinent on the brink of independence was volatile enough – like 'sitting on top of a boiling kettle', as one of the protestors put it.[82] Airmen of the Indian Air Force were also refusing to obey orders, and 20,000 Royal Indian Naval ratings were soon to follow. The naval mutiny turned ugly; a RIN sloop was bombarded by shore artillery, killing six crewmen. Under the circumstances, it is to the credit of many RAF station commanders that they did not overreact. Waiting for demobilisation themselves, many of them may have quietly sympathised with the querulous conscripts in their charge. The airmen themselves, many of whom were trade unionists in civilian life, interpreted the withdrawal of their labour as a strike – a peaceful and legitimate act of remonstration in the industrial tradition. But the concept of a strike did not exist in the RAF; there was only a sharp line distinguishing lawful obedience from mutiny.

The Air Ministry was therefore not in a very forgiving mood. Convinced that communist infiltrators were rabble rousing, the Special Investigation Branch of the RAF Service Police began systematically touring bases, identifying and punishing suspected ringleaders. One, Aircraftman Norris Cymbalist from RAF Seletar, was sentenced to an astonishingly severe ten years' penal servitude until a vocal public campaign back in Britain led by the barrister and MP Denis Pritt was able to secure his release in November 1947.[83]

Though the RAF strikes were to become the best-known acts of indiscipline during the demob period, they were far from being the only ones. They had, in fact, been preceded by a series of refusals by troops to board vessels that they insisted were filthy and unsafe. Complaints about the poor conditions on troopships were

44

becoming common by the end of the war, evidence of a growing truculence within the ranks. For example, an officer who had just completed a journey from Liverpool to East Africa on a requisitioned passenger liner in December 1945, was moved to protest to the *Manchester Guardian* about the conditions he saw on board. In a cargo space 96 feet (29m.) by 60 feet (18m.) by 7 feet (2m.), 250 men were packed along with their full kits. This mass of humanity had to live, eat and sleep within these tiny confines in permanent artificial light. 'At night,' wrote the irate officer, 'those who were sick in the furthest corners of the room had to crawl underneath scores of hammocks before they could reach the lavatories, which were on the deck above.'[84] 'The scene below resembled one of those photographs of Belsen,' recalled H.A. Wilson of a troopship returning from Italy: 'naked or semi-naked bodies lying close together on the floor or on or under mess tables while others swung restlessly in hammocks above'.[85]

The disciplinary problems on the troopship *Otranto* (HMS *Belsen*, as she became known in the press) on her voyage to Sydney in the autumn of 1945 illustrated how difficult it was going to be to corral 'hostilities only' soldiers no longer impressed by military discipline. The source of the trouble on *Otranto*, according to an Admiralty inquiry, was a group of Australian ex-prisoners of war who refused to remain supine in the face of King's Regulations:

> Defiance of all rules was quite evident . . . they objected to anything in the nature of orders and any type of discipline . . . instructions issued to them were often treated as though they were given by their German captors.[86]

In November 1945, 300 Australian and New Zealand officers and NCOs awaiting repatriation walked off the liner *Orion* at Southampton after they found out that she would be sailing with three times as many passengers as she had been designed for.[87] Two days before Christmas, another 1,000 men refused to board *Orion* in Liverpool following a 'lusty demonstration' at the quayside.[88] Similar trouble broke out on the overpacked Dutch steamer *Johann de Witt*, which was ferrying soldiers back from leave to Italy.[89] One of the more colourful of these protests took place in Liverpool a week before Christmas the following year, when 200 soldiers bound for Singapore on the *Empress of Scotland* rushed down the ship's side on scramble nets, fought their way past military policemen, and marched off to their transit camp in Huyton shouting 'we want justice'. When they were finally rounded up on to another ship, they booed the dockside band and threw tin cans at the MPs.[90]

In November 1946 several thousand soldiers at the giant ordnance depot at Tel El Kebir, between Cairo and the Suez Canal, refused to work for five days in a protest at their delayed demobilisation. Afterwards the War Office's instinct was to make an example of the protesters, just as the Air Ministry had tried to do with its strikers some months previously, though in the end it was no more successful in making the charges stick. Dozens of soldiers were arrested and taken for questioning to the detention cells of an abandoned German prisoner-of-war camp at Tahag. For twenty-three out of twenty-four hours the men were held in pitch-dark cement box cells, some 5 feet (1.5m.) by 8 feet (2.4m.) and crawling with lice and vermin. This went on for several weeks. Ten men were eventually charged with conspiracy to cause a mutiny, and six were convicted. Their sentences, however, were quashed on appeal.[91]

It was much the same story in August 1946 when the army decided to court-martial en masse 263 men of the 13th Parachute Battalion, who three months earlier had refused orders to attend company parade in protest at the filthy conditions at their barracks at Muar, near Kuala Lumpur.[92] All bar three of the defendants were found guilty and sentenced to between three and five years' penal servitude. Back in Britain thousands of signatures protesting the decision were collected by sympathetic MPs. Then, in October, the War Office suddenly announced that due to irregularities at the trial all the sentences were being quashed. It was an embarrassing moment for the army, particularly as it had spent some weeks emphasising the scandalous nature of the mutiny and the salutary effect that a stern punishment would have on discipline in the armed forces.

'This,' said *The Times*, in a summing-up that could well apply to all the demob protests, 'brings to a disquieting end a case that has been profoundly unsatisfactory from the beginning.' It was lamentable, the newspaper thought, that soldiers should have so far forgotten their duty as to resort to mutiny. But it was just as lamentable that the men had been ordered to occupy a camp in the condition of Muar in the first place.[93]

## A Parting Lesson

By the time that the Muar paratroopers were released in late 1946, however, the threat of a more widespread revolt within the ranks of the British armed forces had receded, for the simple reason that so many of the war's citizen-servicemen had finally gone home. After the dawdling pace of the early months of demobilisation, improved transport conditions and the willingness of the service chiefs to release more men (possibly encouraged by the discontent stirring in their ranks) had helped to speed things up. In the first half of 1946, the four largest of all the Release Groups were discharged, demobilising almost two million servicemen.[94]

So perhaps it could be said that demobilisation after the Second World War was a success. Ernest Bevin's biographer, Alan Bullock, had few doubts on that score: 'the scheme,' he wrote, 'worked so well that it was continued without modification . . . [there was] hardly a hitch'.[95] And it's undeniable that the release programme in 1945 did not descend into the kind of chaos that had overwhelmed the military authorities after the First World War, when the original plan had to be abruptly abandoned halfway through and a new demobilisation scheme with a much faster overall rate of release was improvised by Winston Churchill, the then secretary of state for war.[96]

This is not to say that the final months of demob in 1946 were without controversy. Many servicemen in the higher Release Groups, particularly younger men who had completed several years of wartime duty but whose lack of years penalised them in the age-and-service calculation, remained in uniform and were as frustrated as ever. 'I joined the RAF in September 1942, at eighteen-and-a-half, but as my release group is 49, my date of release has not even been announced,' complained one to the *Daily Herald* in August 1946: 'Thousands of us are becoming embittered and demoralized, living a life many of us detest, kept away from our homes and wives, some of us still overseas, and all prevented from beginning our postwar careers.'[97] Nonetheless, by the end of 1946, four in five men who had been serving on V-E Day had been discharged. Bevin's Release Group scheme would trickle on until March 1949, but by that time the great majority of non-regulars serving in HM Forces were teenage National Servicemen who remained in uniform for a fixed term of duty. By the beginning of 1947, wartime demob was effectively over.

In the eighteen months that followed the start of demob in June 1945, millions of men and several hundred thousand women were returned to civilian life. After some hesitation and false starts, the machinery of release worked. The sporadic acts of protest within the ranks were an embarrassment to the authorities, but outright insubordination remained the exception; most servicemen expended their frustrations in barrack-room bull sessions and letters to the editor, not mutiny. But just because the process didn't end in abject disarray does not mean that it left those who went through it unmarked. The Labour government had been unprepared for the strength of popular feeling provoked at the end of the war with Japan when it failed adequately to improve the rate of release, and it scrambled for some time to regain popular confidence, not always very artfully.

Perhaps most ominously, there was an unwillingness to share basic information with the general public throughout the demob process, which augured ill for the state's commitment to open government. Labour in 1945 remained altogether wedded to wartime habits of secrecy that were far less justifiable in a peacetime democracy. Even *The Times*, which was generally sympathetic towards Labour's demobilisation policy, by September 1945 was complaining that discrepancies had not been explained:

And any disappointment of the expectations which have been aroused will breed discontent and unrest, however fair the proposed order of release, unless the Government takes the public completely into their confidence . . . public collaboration with the Government must be sought increasingly by information and persuasion rather than by decrees and compulsion.[98]

Labour complained that conservative papers such as the *Daily Express* were inflaming the situation by spreading irresponsible rumours about demobilisation. There was some truth to this. 'What excuse can I give to my wife for not being home on leave,' bewailed a sergeant of the Royal Engineers in July 1945, 'when, according to what she has read in the papers, I should have been home weeks ago?'[99] The following month *Union Jack* wrote an open letter of censure to Fleet Street about the 'garbled half-truths or faulty conjectures' that were causing acute mental distress within service families. 'Wives accept [press] forecasts as the truth. They write to men abroad saying: *I believe you don't want to come home.*'[100]

But rumours were only flowing because of the dearth of any official information in the first place. The gentlemen in Whitehall were not, it seemed, about to start sharing secrets with the hoi polloi.

Servicemen in 1945 wanted the 'fair deal' they had earned from a government they had (in their estimation) put in place. Instead, what many of them felt they received were equivocation, denials and indifference – in other words, the kind of runaround they had always experienced in the Forces. It was a first bitter little taste of disenchantment with postwar life that would be replicated many times again in Civvy Street over the months and years to follow. 'What kind of England are we exiles coming back to?' wondered Sergeant Bill Points during the month in which Japan surrendered, August 1945.[101] For some of his comrades, the demob process had already shown the way. 'Never has a victory been so shamelessly betrayed,' wrote driver W.A. Charlotte in June: 'we know it is not a victory for us – we are condemned and not wanted in England.'[102]

An exaggeration? To be sure. Still, it was not the best of starts for a New Jerusalem.

# CHAPTER TWO

## So, You're Back Then

*I've lost the best six years of my wife.*[1]

The Firth of Clyde, a warm summer evening in June 1945. Corporal H.A. Wilson returns home from Greece after four years overseas. 'The ship slowly edged its way round Gourock and came within view of the mainland,' he wrote in his diary:

I gazed in silent wonder at the fresh greenness, the hedged fields, the velvet hills, and although my heart was as dry as dust I felt something stir within it. Yet I could only gaze and gaze as if I had never seen the country before. And all the others lined up at the rails and gazed too; but not a cap went up into the air and not a cheer rang out across the water. The only sounds were the gentle purring of the ship and the lapping of little waves against its sides. The tongue cannot speak much when the heart is drinking.

After what seemed like a long time one or two found their voices.

*Well, here it is at last!*
*Blimey, look at the boozer!*
*Hey, look at the red double-decker buses!*

*This is England, all right!*
*It's not, you fool. It's Scotland!*
And so on.[2]

Other returning servicemen's first glimpses of Blighty were less lyrical. Royal Marine Cecil Wareham, who had spent the last two years of the war in the Far East, arrived at Tilbury Docks under mackerel skies and drizzle after a 12,000-mile voyage from Australia. 'The large dockside cranes were well rusted,' he recalled: 'the buildings looked drab, windows broken, the dockside workers silent and expressionless . . . neither customs officials or dockside staff were helpful and had a couldn't-care-less attitude towards us.'[3] 'The sky, the sea, the buildings, the half-dozen disinterested onlookers – all [were] so greyly apathetic and coldly unwelcoming,' thought one lieutenant who had been captured at the fall of Singapore back in February 1942; as his ship eased into Southampton harbour it seemed he and his comrades 'were being sneaked in by the back door lest anyone should notice . . .':

The overriding impression is of an exercise going through the motions so that the appropriate forms can be completed and signed without much of a guilt complex. All very impersonal. *Next please. So – you've had malaria sixteen times, dysentery five times, dengue fever twice, beri beri, tropical ulcers, etc. etc. Thank you. Next please.*[4]

Thanks to the languorous pace of demobilisation, repatriated servicemen didn't trickle home until months and even years after V-E Day. In Queen Victoria's day, British soldiers had returned from foreign wars together with the rest of their units; at the end of the 1899–1902 South African War, Lord Roberts' volunteers had marched in triumph through the streets of London, Manchester and Glasgow, standards flying and spectators applauding.

And in 1945, when the novelty was still fresh, early arrivals *were* fêted. The first ships to return carrying liberated prisoners from Singapore and Rangoon received a rapturous welcome. When the vessel carrying Sergeant W. Innes-Kerr and other repatriates from the Far East eased into Liverpool docks, it seemed as though the entire city had turned out at the wharves to greet them: the lord mayor, municipal MPs and military top brass were among the dignitaries on the quayside as brass bands pounded out celebratory marches. 'It took a good couple of hours of bull and blare before we disembarked,' remembered Innes-Kerr: 'the streets were jammed with cheering crowds; everyone was crying.'[5]

But given that most of the servicemen of Churchill's war shuffled slowly and anonymously home one by one, it didn't take long for homecoming to become passé. When the *Duchess of Richmond* sailed up the rain-drenched Mersey river bringing home men of the Fourteenth Army in November 1945, the mood was very different than it had been a few months earlier. 'Half a dozen bandsmen with ground-sheets over their heads dashed out onto the quayside, played a few bars of *God Save the King*, and dashed off again,' one junior officer, Arthur Gilbert, recalled; a barking voice on the tannoy system then announced that the ship was to be searched, and anyone found in possession of contraband goods court-martialled.[6] Demobbed ex-servicemen had become two a penny. One ex-serviceman from Perth discovered by accident that his local church had held a party to welcome home demobilised parishioners three weeks before he had got back. Everyone had been too embarrassed to tell him.[7]

### Scared of Your Wife, Soldier?

Still, it must have been personal hopes and fears rather than the size of the crowd that dominated the minds of most returning servicemen as they disembarked from their troopships and trains on the final leg of the journey home. Half of the discharged men were married.[8] That means there were more than four and a half million husbands and wives waiting for one another in 1945, often after years of separation.

Fantasies of reunion, often highly elaborate, had been spun in servicemen's minds during the long months awaiting their demobilisation. 'We all speculate on when and how we will arrive at our own homes', wrote David Scott Daniell in December 1945, as his own demob approached. 'To be met at a station or not to be met? To walk in unannounced, the element of limited surprise, or to announce the time of arrival?'[9] These imagined scenarios were all part of what Anthony Burgess called the extensive mythology of marital homecoming in 1945.

George Millar, who escaped from an Italian prisoner-of-war camp to make his way back to England via Spain and Gibraltar, reconstructed two of his fantasy homecomings, 'stock dreams [that] had so persisted that to him they amounted to reality', in his 1946 memoir *Horned Pigeon*:

> In the first he arrived in a sunny morning at that platform in Victoria Station where all the boat trains used to arrive. . . . Anne stood at the end of the platform, peering at the crowds in that peculiarly expressive, myopic way, the body slightly tensed upwards, the eyes a little screwed up (she would not want to wear her glasses when she knew that he was going to see her there for the first time in three years). Sometimes he was glad to present a prison companion or two to her. Sometimes they were alone, an island in the crowd . . .

> In the second dream he arrived unexpectedly and he had to ask the porter how to find her flat. He rang an unknown doorbell, waited, rang again. Then he heard her hesitating, slightly heavy step within. She opened the door, her eyes puckered with their effort to see who stood there on the dark landing . . . he stood there waiting – and then anything might happen, depending on his mood while he dreamed.[10]

Mostly, Burgess suspected that what the lonely soldier really yearned for was the cosy vision of his wife 'waiting in a bright kitchen apron, a hot cup of tea in her hand'.[11]

But there was fear beneath the fantasy. The *Daily Mirror* received so many inquiries from worried servicemen approaching their demobilisation that it ran an article – '*Scared of your wife, soldier?*' –

trying to assuage their fears.[12] 'I haven't seen much of the wife and kids,' wrote one man who had been absent from home for five years, 'and now I find I'm plain frightened to go back to them. I still love them . . . but I feel if they expect me to show my feelings I'll run away because I have no energy left.'[13] Happiness at impending reunion sometimes had to be faked. George Moreton, a former prisoner of war, recalled that he and a group of his fellow ex-captives formed a 'hysterical happy party' on their way home, affecting a *joie de vivre* they did not really feel.[14] Hugh Dewhurst, a returnee from the Far East, celebrated for hours with his friends in a local pub knocking back pint after pint, knotted up with unspoken anxiety.[15]

Wives were, of course, anxious about the moment of their husbands' homecoming too. In the spring of 1945 the correspondence columns of newspapers and magazines filled up with questions about the best way to greet imminently returning men. There was a tone of censure to the advice. *Woman* scolded that years of solitary 'slackness' had left too many of its readers 'bleary, bedraggled, [and] festooned with curlers' – and that the wise wife would do well to take a crash-course in grooming before the big day.[16] 'Brush and smooth your hair, cleanse and polish your nail tips, and keep your skin pink and white and peach-soft . . . [be] prettier than before, better company than before, more desirable than ever.'[17]

It is hardly surprising that many otherwise rational and competent women admitted to being in a fright over their husbands' looming return. 'Having been tied to the house and the children through the war, I have let my looks and figure and my "charm" go,' fretted one wife to the *Daily Mail*'s advice columnist Ann Temple. 'My movements are as clumsy as my conversation is limited. Now I am in a panic because my husband will be home in three weeks.'[18] '[Mother] was nervous, almost apprehensive, at the prospect of seeing [father] again after so many years,' recalled one returning soldier's daughter: 'As from the day she received his letter she messed about in the mirror every morning with the few precious cosmetics she had left and then changed her hairstyle.'[19]

Short stories in women's magazines of the period are a useful barometer of the public mood. Throughout 1945 and 1946 the anxious serviceman's wife or sweetheart became a stock figure in the lunchtime fiction of magazines such as *Woman*, *Good Housekeeping* and *Woman's Own*. For example, *As Ricky's homecoming approaches, Rebecca's heart is haunted by fear. Will this man she married prove a stranger? Will he want her as his wife?*, or, *I'm a different person, thought Derris, in panic. Will John like me now?*[20]

Servicing the national anxiety, the pop psychology handbook became a new phenomenon in publishing. During the 1940s there was an extraordinary growth in the range of advice available to British couples, from the Marriage Guidance Council – soon bankrolled by a government worried about the skyrocketting divorce figures – to tabloid agony aunts such as the *Daily Mail*'s Ann Temple.[21] Books such as *Living Together Again*, *Soldier to Civilian* and *Sex Problems of the Returning Soldier* (less lurid than it sounded) catered to the apprehension of women at home. Some of these publications were bestsellers: Dr. Eustace Chesser's *Love Without Fear* had sold 720,000 copies by 1951.[22] Groundbreaking works like Marie Stopes' *Married Love*, first published in 1918, had pioneered the franker discussion of personal relationships a generation earlier. But it took the Second World War and its attendant social problems to give the self-help guide a wholly respectable place on the nation's bookshelves. Demobilisation fears accelerated the British embrace of therapy culture.

## What's the Matter With Me?

When Eighth Army driver Maurice Merritt arrived home after six years abroad, no one was at home. Even the cat 'couldn't wait to get outside for a wee,' he recalled years later:

> There was a short note on the kitchen table: 'Make a cup of cocoa if you like – *bloody cocoa, after all that time in the desert* – and there's a tin of pilchards in the larder if you feel peckish. Joan.' Pilchards! Ask any man who has been in the army what he thinks of pilchards and see what reply you get . . .

It was the first time in six years that I had entered an unoccupied room . . . here I was, in one of the greatest cities in the world, yet lonelier than in the middle of the desert, feeling more cut off from civilisation or contact with other people than when in the desolate regions of North Africa . . . somehow, something seemed to be missing.[23]

It was not always easy to predict an exact hour of homecoming in a land with a creaking transport network and limited private ownership of the telephone. Men about to be discharged had to report to collecting and dispersal centres across the United Kingdom, often many miles from their homes, where they attended to the legalities of their demobilisation and were issued with civilian documents, rations and clothing. All of this took time and it was difficult to know when the paperwork would be done. As a result, many newly coined civilians showed up on the family doorstep with little or no warning.

This did not necessarily guarantee disaster. The reunion of liberated prisoner of war Harold Knowles with his parents was all the more touching for its surprise:

My mother was just outside eating an apple . . . at first she did not see me, but eventually looked up at me, looked away again and then carried on peeling, slicing and eating the apple, but there was no other reaction. . . . Then it seemed to come to her suddenly that she had seen someone standing near her. She stopped eating, looked up at me, stared for a few seconds, and then said 'Harold'. I went to her, kissed her and cuddled her, and then she burst into tears. 'Dad,' she called, 'Harold's here.' My father came out of the house to me, shook hands, put his arm around me, and said 'Hullo Harold. It's grand to have you home.' We then went into the bungalow for some tea.[24]

Sometimes the moment of reunion lived up to the fantasy in every way. 'There was no disappointment or disillusion or anti-climax,' Captain A.M. Bell MacDonald wrote with relief to a friend shortly after his return home from India in the spring of

1945: 'It was sheer heaven. Frances is lovely and hasn't changed an atom.'[25] Novelist Ralph Finn's description of a homecoming he saw in December 1945 was a romantic one, to be sure, but no doubt it reflected the experience of many reunited sweethearts:

> The light in the porch, the happiness and delight shining from the welcoming faces, the bent head of the man from Burma, the still London indigo dust outside. . . . A perfect portrait of light and shade. The darkness of the streets and the light of the porchway. The gloom of four years abroad and the radiance of an unexpected and permanent return.[26]

Inevitably, however, other homecoming moments were anticlimactic. Loading the event with so much emotional significance was often a guarantee of disappointment. 'I suppose I should have expected Mother's greeting to be without visible emotion as we had been brought up like this,' thought Royal Marine Cecil Wareham, 'but when she said "*So, you're back then*" after three years' absence I was somewhat deflated.'[27] The wife of ex-POW Bill Franklin, Marjorie, did not initially recognise him when they were reunited in Southampton:

> ' "*You have changed!*" was her comment, with a brief embrace. I was embarrassed, and could not reply. . . . I realized that after four years, with no communication, we were total strangers. It was difficult to convey to my buddies just how awful an experience it was. Mine was not a case of falling into each other's arms.[28]

Soon after the start of demobilisation, the advice columns of British newspapers and magazines were being filled with the stories of men and women whose reunions were going awry. 'My wife and I met the night before I sailed to Africa', began a typical story in a November 1945 issue of *John Bull*:

> For three years we kept on writing to each other and finally decided to marry on my return home. When I eventually came back I found

to my dismay that I had a totally false idea of the girl . . . our marriage is a total failure.[29]

'Four years ago, while serving in the WAAF, I met an airman', began another:

After we married he went overseas. We were very much in love – faithful, always building castles for the future. Now he has come home, and after a few months I find myself hating him. He is ill-mannered in company, bad-tempered, shows off. He loves me, but I can't bear him. What's the matter with me?[30]

There were discreet hints in the press of sexual incompatibilities. One returned husband complained that his wife could no longer 'express her love for me at all'.[31]

The finality of demobilisation often arrived with an uncomfortable thud. Brief wartime meetings could be misleading, for the 'steaming, heart-warming glow' of the frantically snatched leave was a very different matter from the 'tepid bath' of permanent reunion.[32] Sweethearts and spouses were on their best behaviour during a leave, with all the irritating distractions of domesticity momentarily disregarded. Doubts and annoyances could be set aside for forty-eight hours. This 'honeymoon on the instalment system', as one wife called it, provided a series of bracing interludes during the drab loneliness of wartime. But for newly married couples it was a poor preparation for life with a long-term partner. Demobilisation meant facing up to rather more mundane realities.[33]

The truth was that many husbands and wives in 1945 barely knew one other. At the outbreak of war there had been a rush to the altar as men were conscripted into the Forces. The nuptiality rate in 1940 was the highest in British history.[34] After a rushed honeymoon the new husbands often disappeared on faraway postings and had little contact with their wives for the remainder of the war. Partners who had been married for years were still virtual newlyweds at the end of it. Millions of wartime sweethearts now had to learn to live with one another for the first time, and under far from ideal conditions.

Maintaining even a long-term relationship during the war's enforced separation had been a trial. Mail was the only means of communication. Recognising its importance to morale, the Forces had gone to great lengths to secure a regular and speedy service despite an enormous volume of traffic. In 1944 alone, four and three quarter million letters, packets and parcels were sent from Britain to troops abroad by the Royal Engineers Home Postal Service. By heroic efforts, the delivery time of letters to the Far East had been reduced from up to four weeks to just eleven days.[35] But servicemen often made poor correspondents. 'No letter from you for a whole week', one wife wrote to a rifleman in the Mediterranean. 'When Ruth went off to school this morning she cheerily remarked: *"Don't worry mum, I expect he's dead."* '[36] Army chaplain N.R.M. Hawthorn lamented the pathetic truth that so many soldiers had been utterly incapable of keeping up regular communication with their wives.[37] Even the most assiduous letter-writers must have found it difficult to work literary legerdemain week after week, month after month. Most servicemen did not have a secondary education; by one estimate, one in five of them was functionally illiterate.[38]

Magazines offered wives advice on good letter-writing practices, usually recommending bland pick-me-ups over more difficult topics. 'Little domestic worries . . . should never be mentioned,' cautioned Alice Millard in *Good Housekeeping*: 'Letters should be full of jolly family incidents, fun, music and congenial work.'[39] Men often dared not express their true feelings either, for fear of upsetting their loved ones. 'I say that I am cheerful,' Royal Artilleryman Alan Harris said of his letters home from Italy, 'when in fact I am nearly always miserable to the point of despondency – to the point of committing suicide . . .':

I say that I am fit and well, when in fact my bowels are wrenched with diarrhoea, when my stomach is retching and my head aches . . .

I say that I am eating fine and the food is excellent, when in fact not a morsel has passed my lips for twenty-four hours . . .

I suppose I could describe dripping bayonets, gashed mutilated bodies, the blood gushing from open wounds, the pathetic top boot standing alone, the limb inside smashed off at the knee . . . all very fine, brave and heroic. But not very comforting.[40]

There was surely much common sense to this. But a relationship lived out through page after page of inoffensive chit-chat must, in the long term, have acquired a somewhat unreal quality. 'Letters were a thin thread,' noted psychologists Eliot Slater and Moya Woodside in their study of wartime service marriages, 'a sense of loss of touch was universal.'[41] No wonder that some husbands and wives had little idea what to expect when they met their partners again. However, separation also occasionally improved marriages. Some wives, reported Slater and Woodside, had been able to assess their returning husbands more objectively with fresh eyes, and liked what they saw.[42] A *Woman* reader said that she no longer harboured doubts about her husband after five years of fidelity under the toughest of circumstances.[43]

Improvement in a marriage after separation due to wartime activities was the optimistic premise of Alexander Korda's cinematic reflection on demob, *Perfect Strangers* (1945), starring Robert Donat and Deborah Kerr as a drippy couple invigorated by the war. Robert and Catherine Wilson are dull, timid, sickly, sexually limpid, professionally unambitious and quietly seething with resentment towards one another. In 1939 Robert is conscripted into the Royal Navy, while Catherine enlists in the WRNS to take her mind off things. After a bumpy start, navy life slowly builds each of them up physically and mentally – so much so that after three years of separation they dread the prospect of returning home. Dazed by the transformation that each sees in the other, their initial reunion is hostile: Catherine, now a glamorous, lipsticked brunette, brusquely informs her husband that she has no plans to become 'a weak child-wife' again. Of course, after a cathartic row common sense prevails and the pair head into the postwar future together.[44]

But *Perfect Strangers* supposed that husbands and wives would change mutually and compatibly – an assumption not always borne out in real life. Some homebodies became outgoing during the war; some extroverts morphed into stay-at-homes. 'Before the war we went out a lot together dancing,' complained one returned soldier: 'We were also keen on weekend cycling and walks together. I'm so happy just to be home again that I don't seem to want more. Yet I feel my wife does.'[45] Returned prisoner of war Philip Meninsky and his wife had married young, and after four and a half years of separation had come to inhabit 'two totally different worlds . . . I had grown up to become a very much [more] serious person than I had been when I left . . . she wanted to go to parties, she wanted to play bridge, she liked company – she had no interest in the work I wanted to do.'[46]

Other men and women who had once rubbed along fine could no longer understand one another. A woman whose fiancé returned after two years in a prisoner-of-war camp found him 'rather given to showing off, full of exaggerated mannerisms, gestures and grimaces, and overflowing with empty talk which got nowhere . . . I was bitterly disillusioned,' she admitted.[47] A husband who had become a superb bridge player during his military service embarked on violent post-mortems when his still averagely skilled wife played a bad hand.[48] One wife walked around rehearsing highbrow conversation pieces while doing the dusting, for fear that she no longer matched her husband's scholarly horizons; another worried that her husband had 'gone mental' when he started philosophising about life in his letters.[49]

After years of life in tents and barracks, many servicemen had lost their social graces. A common complaint was that previously reserved and neat men now swore with glee and dressed sloppily.[50] Dick Fiddament, a veteran of the Burma campaign, horrified his relatives by slurping his tea in great gulps and throwing any leftovers on the fire in army style.[51] Men had forgotten how to use knives and forks.[52] Some could no longer sleep on a normal bed. Soldiers of the Fourteenth Army still looked for scorpions in their shoes and examined the bread on the breakfast table for weevils.[53]

Some couples were, in short, a complete mystery to one another. 'Natural excitement carried us over the first few hours,' wrote the disillusioned wife of one demobbed man. 'Then the edge of boredom insinuated itself between us. We, who should have had so much, had nothing to talk about.'[54]

## The Thrill Has Gone and I Don't Seem to Care

One recently released ex-serviceman was overheard carping on a bus by a *Daily Herald* journalist:

> The curse of England is that all the wives have got so dull. . . . Oh, they've been wonderful of course, and have had a hard time, but what do they talk about? Queues, rations, babies, coupons, their poor feet – one long dirge, and all the same, as though the gramophone record had got stuck. So I go off with the boys most evenings.[55]

One of agony aunt Evelyn Home's correspondents in *Woman* had found that his wife, formerly 'a real home-bird', had entered full-time employment in his absence and 'seems to enjoy it too much for my peace of mind'. Though the family earnings had doubled as a result of her job, he stubbornly refused to touch a penny of it.[56] Resentment masquerading as chivalry coloured other men's attitudes towards women's prosperity. The fiancé of a well-paid war worker stubbornly refused to borrow from her the £300 he needed to enrol in a vocational course because it would be demeaning.[57] Men returning from the Forces were very conscious of the changes *they* had gone through. But they did not always appreciate, still less like, the alterations that their wives had experienced while they'd been away, especially if these changes had meant a new and more interesting life outside the home, or increased financial independence.

For most women left behind, the war years had brought mostly hardship: hard work, little spare time, less money and no material or psychological support from absent husbands. Until the last year of the war, the wife of a private soldier with two children only received thirty-eight shillings a week in state allowance and compulsory allotment from her husband's pay, while on average factory labourers were earning over twice as much – pushing up the national cost of living fast.[58] As a result, then, by mid-1943 more than four out of five wives without children in the home were in full-time war work. Women who had dependants under the age of 14 were exempt from compulsory direction into war industry, but they often had to work as well just to make ends meet.[59]

The normal routines of housekeeping were horribly complicated by the war. By 1945 civilian consumption of household goods had fallen by over four-fifths.[60] Most basic foods were price-controlled, but other consumer goods were fantastically inflated in cost or simply unobtainable. Kitchenware, linens and furniture were particularly irreplaceable. Hours of 'leisure' time during the working week were eaten up by queuing at the shops for rations, often without success. This burden was particularly discomforting for middle-class housewives, who before 1939 had been able to rely on hired help to handle the more tedious chores around the home; the truculent domestic 'daily', well aware of the shift in power between her and her employer, was a stock comic character by the end of the war.[61] For a housewife to hold down a physically demanding and monotonous job while trying to look after a family, keep a house clean and endure the Sisyphean trials of wartime shopping, must have been exhausting.

By V-J Day the dreary indignities of wartime – the 'drabness, drudgery, shoddiness, discontent, and red tape,' as the *Daily Mail* put it[62] – were taking their toll on civilian nerves. What official historian Richard Titmuss would later call the 'arithmetic of stress' was multiplying dangerously.[63] 'War strain' amongst working women over 30 was rapidly rising, according to mental health clinics.[64] Salons were being bombarded by requests for scarce hair dyes by younger women turning prematurely grey.[65]

Victory did not improve things. By August 1946, over half of Gallup's respondents said they were receiving less, and worse, food than they had during the war.[66] 'Peace nerves' now replaced war strain. The intake of neurotic cases at Birmingham's main psychiatric hospital stood one third higher in 1946 than it had done in

1940.[67] The GP Anthony Weymouth recorded in his diary that dozens of women patients were complaining of being:

> mentally and physically exhausted by the cooking, cleaning and queuing. . . . Only the other day, one explained to me that she was able to carry on her life while the war was on only because she believed that it was 'for the duration'. Now . . . she can see no end to her life of hardship and the hope which buoyed her up during the war years has left her.[68]

Wives endured. They created new lives for themselves in the absence of their husbands. In the years since there has been a temptation to romanticise these wartime women, to reimagine them as flagbearers of feminist liberation. That is not the way most British wives saw themselves at the time. There was nothing glamorous or empowering about working double shifts in a dirty aircraft factory, only to return home to two hungry and demanding children. The majority of service wives made no secret of their dislike of war work. Some deliberately got pregnant in order to exempt themselves.[69] By 1945 they had had quite enough of being the household breadwinners and looked forward to handing that responsibility back to their homecoming husbands.

Yet much to their own puzzlement and shame, there were some wives who found themselves unexcited about their husbands' return when the day finally came. 'I was thrilled when I heard he'd be back by the autumn,' admitted one woman who had only spent three months of married life with her husband. 'But now I find the thrill has gone and I don't seem to care. I'm so ashamed, but somehow all the enthusiasm has gone out of me.'[70] 'I thought I should be contented and happy when the war would be over,' wrote one troubled wife to the *Daily Mail* in November 1945:

> Instead I feel worse. Everything seems wrong. . . . I have no patience with the children. I don't enjoy anything, don't laugh at anything – in general life is all wrong. My health is excellent.

My husband – the best of all husbands – is home again. Am I an extraordinary case or is it happening to everyone?[71]

The 'skin of indifference' that had protected forlorn wives during their long isolation could not be shed easily.[72] Coping mechanisms that had been necessary for the continuation of normal life were becoming dysfunctional. 'All I have been doing for four years is just waiting for my husband to come home,' said one. 'I have taken no interest in anything for so long that I now find it impossible to be interested in even the prospect of his return.'[73] 'I'm burnt out,' confessed a *News Chronicle* reader: 'I know I adore him – or rather I did when we were really married; I do not honestly know what I feel now.'[74]

As Margaret Goldsmith warned in her 1946 book *Women and the Future*, many English women had formed habits of independence that would be difficult to break even if they weren't fully conscious of how much their enforced independence had changed them.[75] 'I'm thrilled at the prospect of seeing [my husband] again,' wrote one wife to *Modern Woman*:

but honestly, the idea of settling into the old married rut appals me. I've enjoyed living alone. I like early tea in the morning, in my dressing gown, with a newspaper for company. I hate the thought of dressing straight away, cooking bacon and making conversation . . . I have loved a room to myself and hate the idea of sharing the dressing-table, not being able to read in bed, and having reproachful looks when I sit up leisurely giving my hair and face their nightly beauty care. Trivialities, of course, but I have so much enjoyed my small freedoms. Am I abnormal?[76]

*Yes*, said the press. The nation's agony aunts were fairly unanimous that it was up to women to adjust to the new realities brought about by demobilisation. When *Modern Woman*'s Muriel Forth (writing under the pseudonym of Ray Allister) was asked by a full-time working wife whether she should quit her job on the insistence of her newly returned husband, even though she didn't want to abandon her independence and dreaded the 'dreary monotony of keeping house on inadequate money', Forth maintained that it would be for the best nonetheless: 'when he is so sensitive to change, the sense of defeat just when he needs confidence in himself, may leave a scar'.[77] 'It's her job . . . she took it on,' chided the *Daily Mail*'s Ann Temple when told about a wife who loathed and detested housework after having had an interesting wartime job.[78]

But some women remained forthright. The *Daily Herald*'s Janet Grey reported on a mood of rather resentful aggressiveness amongst wives expecting husbands home: 'It's no good his thinking he's going to find me the same mouse-like creature I was a few years ago.'[79] Husbands were warned by the *Daily Mirror* not to cramp the style of wives in this mood.[80] The repatriate, warned Dr. H. Leonard Browne in a 1945 Guildhall lecture, might find on his return that he was now living in a 'dual monarchy' of a marriage in which he had been demoted to a mere co-ruler along with his wife – whether he liked it or not.[81]

## Meet Your Children

If 6-year-old Jo Mary Stafford had had her way, the war would have gone on forever. Whereas for other British families war meant death and displacement, for the three Stafford girls growing up in the Warwickshire Black Country it brought a peace and security never again to be repeated in their childhoods. Bombs fell on the homes of nearby Birmingham, not sleepy Walsall. As a serviceman's wife receiving a compulsory deduction from her husband's army pay, their mother, although far from wealthy, nonetheless had a reliable and independent source of income for the first and only time in her life. 'We prospered,' Jo wrote years later in her memoir of childhood: 'If we didn't grow fat we certainly grew healthy . . . we were a united family, vibrant and warm, cosy and content in the home our mother ran.'[82]

But the war had to end. Jo's father, up until then a shadowy figure whose intermittent appearances on leave had not seriously disturbed the family's tranquillity, was demobbed. He had prospered in the army, with a comfortable sinecure as a sergeant in the catering section of a home-service depot far from the dangers of battle. His ego had swelled during years of barking parade-ground orders at luckless Tommies. Now surplus to military requirements, he had been stripped of his perks and his authority. He felt powerless, emasculated. The only people he could still order around were his unfortunate wife and children, and they would have to do. 'He chose to run our "barracks" on Army lines,' Jo recalled:

> *From now on*, he told us as he lined us up for inspection, shoulders back, tummies in, feet straight, heads up, *this unit will cease to be run in the old slip-shod way* . . . when he had finished addressing the squaddies he bade us fall out, and as I slunk away I noticed, with dreadful apprehension, the stout leather Army belt lying innocently across the table before him.[83]

What followed were years of systematic physical and mental abuse. Jo's mother, previously a confident, happy and able woman, was reduced to a 'helpless zombie devoid of willpower'.[84] It wasn't until fifteen years later as a teenager, when a hysterical Jo threw a cup of scalding hot tea over her father and fled his house never to return, that she was free of her tormentor. The power of military rank had warped the man, who could never adjust to its loss. 'He didn't know any better; perhaps he never had a chance,' she mused generously after his death years later. 'Forgiving, unfortunately, is not forgetting.'[85]

The Staffords' catastrophe was thankfully the exception. But the end of the war was traumatic enough even for children with better fathers. Many of these children had only just returned home themselves. Within a few days of the outbreak of war in September 1939, up to three and a quarter million of them had been evacuated from Britain's cities to be provided with shelter in rural areas from the apocalyptic bombing that was expected at any moment. Others followed in successive waves of dispersal. Although by the last year of the war most of these evacuees had been sent back or drifted back to their homes, some stayed for a surprisingly long time: as late as August 1945, it was believed that 76,000 children had still not returned from their wartime billets.[86]

Some evacuees enjoyed material privileges and psychological liberation during their wartime exodus. The less fortunate were victims of loneliness, neglect and abuse. Schooling for many thousands of children came more or less to a halt, an educational interregnum which shocked the nation when years later the boys were called up as 18-year-old conscripts and often found to be effectively illiterate.[87] For children such as these, home in 1945 was an exotic, perhaps forgotten, place. Their postwar demobilisation was just as disorientating as their fathers'.[88]

Who was father, anyway? For children too young to have conscious memories of him before his departure, the concept of 'Daddy' had by 1945 often reached the levels of the purest abstraction. 'Perhaps Dad was like Father Christmas,' wondered one child: 'You knew he existed, but you never saw him.'[89] Logically, many children seem to have come to identify their father literally as a photograph on the mantelpiece.[90] David Scott Daniell's son went one further and announced that any passing soldier was his daddy, which must have made for some uncomfortable moments for his mother.[91] Three-year-old Margaret MacLeod had come to believe that her father would arrive on the doorstep in an aeroplane, while a Cambridge girl assumed that daddy had no legs because his picture only showed him from the waist upwards.[92]

This confusion only made his eventual moment of homecoming all the more awkward. 'I was playing in the garden with a group of friends,' recalled one daughter who had not seen her father for five years:

> It was a few minutes before father distinguished myself and my sister from the group . . . although we knew his arrival was imminent there had been so many returning servicemen, both members of the family and friends, calling on us during the past few days that we were confused. I hid behind mother and asked: *Mummy, who is that man?*[93]

John Brum spent four years away from Britain fighting in Burma with the Royal Norfolk Infantry. 'Every soldier imagines he's going to get off the train, run down the platform and put his arms around his wife,' he recalled years later, 'but none of that happened. My wife was hiding behind a pillar. When we got in the taxi she said to my son, *that's your Daddy*. He said to me: *You're not my Daddy, my Daddy's on the wall*. It was a picture he couldn't associate with me. It broke my heart.'[94] To Oliver Bland, who had been repatriated, 'my daughter was a complete stranger – she didn't know who I was'.[95]

Even children who had been able to see their fathers occasionally during the war were in for a rude awakening. Just as the honeymoon atmosphere of leave did not prepare husbands and wives well for the more pedestrian grind of married life, so a father's brief holidays had an air of fantasy that was bound to lead to disappointment later on. 'It was easy enough then; no problems, no real rows or conflicts,' warned Leslie Brewer in a 1946 advice column. 'For that all-too-short three or four weeks you were the fabulous man mother had talked about for years, the splendid fellow who was coming all the way from India, who'd take us all out to the pictures or out for a spree.' But, as Brewer pointed out, demobilisation would come to have less jolly connotations:

> The brief encounter with you came to be associated with, naturally, presents and treats and being allowed to stay up later and all the havoc your short visit worked in the usual, rather dull, domestic routine . . . for dad it was easy; very pleasant to be a sugar-daddy for a few weeks and then take refuge in the quiet of a tent or billet . . . but this time you're home for good . . . you've now to stay on and see the big tin of sweets become empty and the donkey from Cairo broken. You've to share with your wife the task (and unpopularity) of enforcing all the small but important 'musts'. In short, you've to take your rightful place in your family as a partner with your wife.[96]

Children who had remained in the home during their fathers' absence had got used to monopolising their mothers' attention. It was natural that they would begrudge this strange interloper's claims on her time. Those who had recently returned from evacuation and who were eager to re-establish their own relationships with their mothers resented the competition even more. Once praised as 'a glorious ally, the fount of all good things, the man who upsets bedtime and the most willing of all playmates', Brewer warned that the demobbed dad would soon turn out to be 'a bit of a flop . . . all the build-up, all the excitement of your homecoming may just end up in an anti-climax of a shy or even hostile *hello* or a refusal to come down'.[97]

Night-time was a particular problem. Many youngsters had slept in their parents' bed during the war. This was partly because of the lack of a comfortable alternative: blankets and linens were scarce, and with coal scrupulously rationed the warmth provided by huddling together really counted in winter. But it also provided emotional consolation to lonely mothers and children. It was not easy to explain to a young bedmate that his or her presence was no longer wanted.

A reader of *Housewife* worried that her daughter of two and a half had begun waking up and screaming in the middle of the night since her father had returned. 'When I have gone to her [she] asks for a drink, then chocolate, and anything else she can think of to keep me by her side. I have tried to explain to her that she cannot have me all by herself now and must learn to love Daddy as well.'[98] 'I had always shared a bed with my mother,' Julie Burville recalled of life before her father's demobilisation, but when he arrived unexpectedly one night she was unceremoniously bundled out forever. 'He seemed utterly foreign, no part of me or her . . . and what followed was worse: I didn't sleep with Mummy any more.'[99] Five-year-old Wendy Reeves came to a blunter conclusion: 'I did not like this tall, weird, cold man.'[100]

Working-class fathers had always been distant and vaguely hostile figures within the family.[101] A sort of domestic cold war between dad and the rest of the family was considered a normal state of affairs in many British households in the 1930s. Coordinated acts of 'resistance' by mother and the children against this unwelcome, beery brute were celebrated in popular song:

When father came home at night and drunk we used to rob
And after the course of a week or two we saved up seven bob.[102]

Knowledge or enthusiasm about fatherhood retained a taint of effeminacy. 'I knew nothing about babies,' recalled Francis Lucas after his return from the war. 'I was embarrassed with babies . . . I felt embarrassed when we walked out and my wife pushed the pram. It was only with great reluctance that I would be persuaded to push the pram myself.'[103] Some mothers were keen to maintain this stigma. Fathers sometimes complained that they were deliberately excluded from the affections of their offspring by wives emphatic about maintaining a monopoly of influence in the nursery. In some cases fathers had to develop relationships with their children in secret.[104]

But the idea of fatherhood was slowly changing. Notions of a more active and participatory role for the male parent had begun filtering down from the middle classes during the interwar years. It was all the more hurtful and bewildering, then, when demobilised men received a cold reception from the boys and girls they had missed so much. Stung, many fathers concluded that their wives had been too lax with discipline during their absence. The belief that Britain's youngsters, particularly its boys, were becoming delinquent without the proper corrective influence of their fathers had become widespread during the war. Some of the complaints about the slow pace of demobilisation were framed around this crisis in the home. As early as 1943, MP J.A. Cecil Wright had been urging the early release of parents, arguing that Britain was unwittingly cultivating 'a generation of uncontrollable children' because of the absence of the stern hand of the father within the home.[105] Many mothers agreed, some pleading for the compassionate return of their soldier-husbands as boisterous older boys grew up unchecked.[106] 'They're getting too big for a woman to manage,' worried Norah Burke: 'every misdemeanour or bad habit you have to deal with by yourself; every decision you have to make alone'.[107]

This fear continued to inform much of the debate about juvenile crime that followed in the late 1940s and 1950s. Delinquency amongst boys and girls was assumed to be rampant and increasing. 'Daily we read of children of tender years who are beyond the control of their parents,' suggested the *Daily Mirror*; 'of children who are becoming little thieves and looters . . . of children who are tragically neglected or cruelly treated.'[108]

The number of juveniles found guilty of criminal offences in England and Wales did rise by a third during the war.[109] The official historian of the wartime social services, Richard Titmuss, suspected however that the panic had more to do with less tolerant standards of conduct demanded by tired and testy adults than a real change in behaviour. 'The aspirations and prejudices of the moment' were, he argued, 'reflected in the birching of more little boys.'[110] The sociologist Geoffrey Gorer agreed that mid-century British parents were unhealthily preoccupied with what he called the 'pleasures of severity'.[111]

There was masculine cachet to strict discipline. Working-class men who were felt to have 'lost control' of their children lost face in public.[112] It must have been particularly vexing for the demobbed – accustomed as they were to the harsh and mechanical obedience of the Forces, and insecure about their status in the home – to discover children who appeared to be wilfully hostile and defiant. But, as Jo Mary Stafford's family discovered, attempts to introduce military standards in the household could be disastrous. The mother of a 2-year-old boy whose husband had returned from active service had to spend four months persuading him that stentorian orders and peremptory field punishments would not have the effect he hoped. 'I realize,' she wrote afterwards, 'that much harm has been done by this treatment.'[113] Otherwise doting fathers, warned *Housewife*'s Ann Cuthbert, 'accustomed to a position of authority in a service where there is no answering back, may not realize that parade-ground methods are entirely unsuited to four-year-old intelligence and requirements.'[114]

Alice Truman's sailor husband had been captured by the Germans in May 1940 when his submarine HMS *Seal* was bombed to the surface off the Danish coast. He did not see his family for five and a half years. When he returned home at the end of the war, Alice had to explain to her children who their daddy was. 'He was very short tempered,' she remembered:

> Being in the Navy he expected immediate obedience. . . . The little boy who was by then six years old didn't come when his father told him to and he ignored it. My husband slapped him on his leg. This little boy with a red face looked at this great big man and said *Why don't you go back to where you came from? We managed very well without you.* Many times I thought I could break my heart both for my husband, because he'd missed so much, and for my children, who had to adapt to a man telling them what they could and couldn't do.[115]

But some fathers resented the bogeyman image that their wives might have luridly conjured up during their absence. 'May I protest,' wrote one to *Woman*'s advice page, 'against the unfair practice of so many mothers of insuring their children's good behaviour with the threat of: *I'll tell daddy when he comes home?* We fathers crave our children's love and also their respect, but not if the latter only implies fear induced by the mothers . . . why make an ogre of Daddy by threatening the child with some future retribution?'[116]

'Things have gone terribly wrong,' lamented a returned serviceman who hadn't seen his 4-year-old son for three years. 'He can't stand me – screams when I come near him . . . my wife's always telling him: *You can't do this now daddy's back.* Or: *Daddy will smack you if you're naughty.* Or: *Everything's different now – daddy's here.* When she says things like this he begins to cry and runs away from me.'[117] 'I am allowed no say nor interest in my daughter,' complained a veteran of the Burmese campaign: 'she is very spoilt, but if I correct her my wife says, *Don't mind this cruel man, come to Mum!*'[118]

Fathers discharged from the Forces in 1945 and 1946 had a shock coming to them if they expected seamlessly to reassume the role of paterfamilias. Demobilised men, often barely remembered as parents, had to be reintroduced to the household. Their offspring were not always impressed with the new arrival. Some openly demanded that he leave. Others, cowed by their home-coming father's violence or alienated by his coldness, never rebuilt their relationship with him. Their 'real' fathers, the men they had prayed for and wondered about for so many lonely years, never returned from the war.

## My Home Is a Misery

'The returning soldier expects a home – meals at his own table without queuing, an armchair by the fire, a lie-in on a Sunday morning. He will want to have a home of his very own, where he has privacy and is not overcrowded.'[119] This, according to William Shebbeare, a Labour Party activist who wrote extensively on the wartime army under the alias 'Captain X', was a bedrock requirement that would measure the success of demobilisation.

During the interwar years Britain had increasingly become a home-centred society, a country in which the family dwelling was the emotional bedrock of the citizen and the seat of all comfort, safety and familiarity.[120] In *The Uses of Literacy* (1957) Richard Hoggart would characterise the mid-century working-class home as the critical line of defence against a capriciously authoritarian world: 'where almost everything else is ruled from outside, is chancy, and likely to knock you down when you least expect it,' he wrote, 'the home is yours and real'.[121]

This ideal of domestic intimacy could not have arisen at a worse time, however. The state of Britain's housing at the end of the Second World War was catastrophic. Over 200,000 houses had been totally destroyed or damaged beyond repair by enemy action. A further three and a half million – two houses in seven overall – had received some kind of damage, often leaving the buildings temporarily uninhabitable.[122] Targets of sustained aerial bombard-ment such as London were particularly ravaged. The V1 and V2 pilotless rocket attacks in the final year of the war had not caused great loss of life, but they had wreaked havoc across the capital's already dilapidated housing stock, damaging over a million homes.

Other than London, the cities that had born the brunt of the Blitz in 1940 and 1941 – Liverpool, Coventry, Portsmouth, Hull – still showed their gaping wounds five years later. As for the capital, 'bruised and afflicted' as B. Ifor Evans described it in his 1946 homecoming novel *The Shop on the King's Road*, it was grimy with a war's worth of accumulated dirt.[123] You could see the particles of brick dust in the air. Tarpaulins nailed over vanished windows and shattered roof tiles flapped incessantly. Vivid wild flowers had sprouted up amongst the bombsites. Here and there the cellars of demolished houses had been turned into static water tanks, and in some cases stocked with fish from the Thames by enterprising anglers. Packs of feral dogs, their former owners dead or disappeared, roamed the rubble at night.

Even towns and cities unaffected by bombing had felt the blast of wartime change. The British population had been reshuffled; sixty million changes of address had taken place since September 1939.[124] Industrial workers had poured into the aircraft and munitions factories of the West Midlands and the southeast, billeted in every spare room available. Workers had brought their wives and children and had made new lives for themselves. With jobs in the manufacturing export trades plentiful and wages high, there was little incentive to leave. Some servicemen returned to find that their sleepy prewar towns had doubled in population during their absence.

For austerity Britain, then, chronic homelessness became the norm. By the autumn of 1945 one-third of all Britons, according to a Gallup poll, were looking for somewhere new to live.[125] Anxiety about finding a home was rife amongst servicemen awaiting demobilisation: one Scottish minister suggested that the troops should receive no further bulletins on the matter, because the situation was so hopeless it could only cause further depression in the ranks.[126] Such doom-laden talk was not excessive. At the beginning of 1949 there were over one and a half million households on local-authority housing waiting lists in England and Wales, two-thirds of which were made up of parents with at least one child. Four in ten had been on the list since at least 1946.[127]

Demobilisation sometimes had an unfortunate knock-on effect, with the return of one man ousting another. Many house-owners had rented out their properties in 1939 and 1940 when they had left for an industrial job elsewhere or the Forces; their home-coming meant there was no longer space for tenants. In January 1945, Leading Aircraftman D.W. Williams pleaded without success in Birmingham County Court to stay an eviction from a tiny one-bedroom flat in Sutton Coldfield after the landlady learned that her husband was returning from India. Williams's wife and six children had been renting it ever since they were bombed out of their own home two and a half years earlier. But the town housing authority was unmoved: it already had 900 other urgent applications in the queue.[128]

Local housing committees faced a barrage of requests for accommodation. Prioritising cases from the chaos was awkward. Lucky families were chosen at the committee's own discretion. Many committees used a points system to try and identify the most urgent cases on the list. Though councils were encouraged by central government to award extra points to the demobbed, a man's status as an ex-serviceman was not always a guarantee of high priority. And it was difficult to argue that, say, a returning soldier with a wife and two small children necessarily had any greater claim to a house than a bombed-out family of four who had been living in a squalid temporary shelter. The war's equality of sacrifice undermined the discharged man's entitlement to special treatment.

Opportunistic landlords were known to exploit the desperation of house-seekers, particularly ex-servicemen with gratuity payments from their demobilisation in their pockets. Some unscrupulous proprietors illegally demanded 'key money,' or a cash premium over and above the listed rent, before they would sign a lease. By 1946 a £110-a-year two-room flat in Chelsea needed an advance payment of a staggering £1,500.[129]

Some ex-servicemen took matters into their own hands. The thousands of squatters who took over disused army camps in mid-1946, and the Communist Party's noisy occupation of fashionable

Kensington addresses that winter, are well-known facts. But direct action of this sort had been pioneered a year earlier by the Brighton 'vigilantes', briefly darlings of the popular press, who took over empty properties and moved homeless families of ex-servicemen into them. The vigilantes were led by Harry Cowley, a bowler-hatted chimney sweep known as 'the Guv'nor' who was already a local legend because of his confrontations with Oswald Mosley's blackshirts before the war. His 400-odd vigilantes, mostly ex-servicemen themselves, would smuggle squatters into the houses at night, carting their belongings on barrows. Though the legal owners of these houses often responded with eviction notices, the proceedings were inevitably lengthy.[130]

The vigilante idea briefly spread to London during the summer of 1945 and Cowley addressed large crowds in Hyde Park, promulgating his theory of direct citizens' action.[131] Perhaps alarmed by his populist appeal, the government moved quickly to neutralise Cowley's message by granting local councils greater powers to requisition vacant properties.[132] However, this peremptory action made little immediate difference to the housing problem, as many empty houses were bomb-damaged or beyond repair.[133]

In the absence of any alternative, many young couples had no choice but to share accommodation. This usually meant living with the parents of the husband or wife: in 1947, almost one in ten British households were organised this way.[134] One in five of the families on the 1949 waiting lists were currently living with a set of in-laws.[135] For many, it was a long-term situation. Demobbed RAF mechanic Jack Clabburn lived with his mother-in-law for fourteen years until he was able to get a house of his own.[136]

Cramped conditions bred frustration. 'Every woman knows by instinct that a happy family life is impossible without a home of one's own,' noted Jean Bird in *Modern Woman* of April 1946. The British found themselves in a permanent battle of attrition over access to sculleries and pantries. Young mothers evacuated along with their children had tried, without success, to share sinks and ovens with their begrudging hostesses during the war; now ex-servicemen's brides were squabbling with mothers-in-law.[137] Many

British houses of the time lacked what would now be considered the most basic fittings. One quarter of all working-class residences had no bath, not even a portable tub. Almost half had no hot running water.[138] Indoor toilets had still not replaced wooden outhouses in filthy back alleys. Tempers were frayed as housewives tried to cook and wash in cramped kitchens.

To demobbed men, there was something unpleasantly familiar about this situation. To be in the wartime Forces was to live constantly in the presence of others. Servicemen ate together, worked together, slept together. Continually under observation, their routines inspected and examined, their decisions largely made for them, their lives were not their own. Even their private thoughts, if committed to paper, could be scrutinised by the postal censor. Personal space shrank and disappeared. The simple lost pleasures of solitude and answering to no one assumed commensurate importance.

In June 1945 the *Daily Express* asked a group of servicemen what they would appreciate the most about being back in Civvy Street. These were some of the answers they got:

No shaving in cold water in a dark room with an old blade; or no shaving at all if I don't want to . . .

A chair to sit on for breakfast and the day's paper to read with it . . .

Food off a china plate and tea from a china cup with my own requirements of sugar and milk in it . . .

Somebody else to do the washing up and make my bed . . .

The wearing of a shirt with a collar and tie, and shoes . . .

No more drill or anything else that is good for discipline or morale when an hour's rest with a book would do me a lot more good . . .

No need to call anybody 'sir' unless I feel the required amount of respect . . .

Stand with my feet apart and my hands in my pockets whoever I talk to . . .

Go to bed when I like in a room of my own and put the light out when I wish.[139]

Canadian Bernard McElwaine made up a similar roster of wishes in the *News Chronicle*. What he was looking forward to, he wrote, was 'eating at a table with a knife and fork – and a different plate for each course . . . spending a lot of time in the bath tub . . . the pleasure of reading a paper on the day it's published . . . reading it in a warm, lighted room without four or five people peering over your shoulder'.[140]

The attraction of demob became more and more defined by these promises of isolation and freedom. And the best guarantee of all these things was a house of one's own. 'Home,' wrote one soldier in 1942, 'means leisure, quiet, privacy, courtesy, relative luxury and comfort, forgetfulness of the Army and all idiocy and petty oppression, muddle, hurry and noise and squalor and discomfort, anxiety and worry.'[141] The ideal home necessarily kept outsiders at arm's length. 'Any idea of having to share a home, even to share a gateway or front porch, is repugnant to a great many people,' noted Mass-Observation's 1943 report on postwar housing: there was, it thought, an 'almost monotonous iteration' about the emphasis that ordinary people placed on having a separate house on its own.[142] In a wartime survey of men and women in HM Forces, the overwhelming majority wanted a small garden specifically because of the extra seclusion it would bring.[143]

It was, then, as J.L. Hodson wrote in 1945, a 'war misery in the second degree' that servicemen who had fantasised about William Shebbeare's 'home of their own' so often found themselves living under someone else's roof in Civvy Street.[144] Couples trying to re-establish their relationships under already difficult circumstances had next to no privacy. 'They were never alone,' Barbara Kendall-Davies recalled of her parents after the war: her demobilised father 'resented having to live in my grandmother's house, where she ruled the roost with a firm hand'.[145] 'My home is a misery,' bewailed one demobbed soldier whose wife could not get on with his sisters.[146]

It is little wonder that reunited husbands and wives living in these cramped confines often irritated one another intensely. 'We always seem to be quarrelling over silly little things,' worried the wife of one man returned from three years overseas. 'He is restless at night if I want to read in bed . . . in the evenings, once he has looked at the newspaper, he doesn't settle to anything else and it fidgets me to see him lolling about . . . you see how small these things are, but when you are living in rooms they seem important and get on your nerves all the time'.[147] Trivial rows sometimes became the tipping point of the marriage. One newly returned officer asked his wife to sew some medal ribbons on his jacket. Two minutes later she announced she was leaving him.[148]

Postwar Britain was a land of nerves fraught by the day-to-day cheerlessness of years of austerity and overwork. Recreating a happy home in such stressful circumstances required patience and a willingness to make material and emotional concessions, but patience and willingness were not always there. Unspoken miseries accumulated; sometimes the bottled-up rage and frustration became too much.

But the greatest menace of all to married life – the spectre that the wartime Archbishop of Canterbury, William Temple, had blamed in 1943 for the virtual 'disintegration' of the British family – was not overcrowding, or overwork, or bad parenting, or a lack of understanding.[149] It was sexual jealousy. Two-thirds of the record number of divorce petitions in 1946 and 1947 cited adultery as the cause for the marriage's breakdown.[150] The war had broken up the family unit, scattered men and women far and wide, and introduced the lonely, vulnerable and curious to new temptations. The transience of life on the home front and in the theatres of combat had encouraged experimentation and lowered the thresholds of caution. Britons had acted in haste. Now they would repent at leisure.

# CHAPTER THREE

# My Faithless English Rose

*Dogs, did you think that I should not come back from Troy? You have wasted my substance, have forced my women servants to lie with you, and have wooed my wife while I was still living. You have feared neither God nor man, and now you shall die.*[1]

Jock Cairns was drunk and angry by the time he got back to the house of his in-laws at 10.45 p.m. on 1 March 1945, but as witnesses told the police afterwards, no one thought he was capable of violence. After twelve pints and five double gins, it was a wonder that he could even stand. But barely fifteen minutes later, two people were going to be dead.

After almost a year with the British occupation forces in Italy, Jock, a sergeant in the 697th Artizan Works Company, Royal Engineers, had been looking forward to his leave when he had arrived back in Britain two weeks previously on 16 February 1945. But his wife Emily's homecoming reception for him was reportedly 'off-handish', and after a few days of tension, perhaps exacerbated by the fact that they were lodging with her parents in Feltham Road in Ashford, Middlesex, Jock had taken his two young sons with him to visit their paternal grandmother in Glasgow. This was supposed to give Mrs. Cairns – 'a neurotic type' who had been seeing a doctor for symptoms of nervous exhaustion – a chance for a recuperative holiday alone in Bournemouth. Instead she headed straight for Twickenham, where she met up with Ronald D'Alcorn, an ex-airman recently demobbed from the RAF. Emily had been secretly having an affair with him since the beginning of the year.[2]

The Cairns had not always been unhappy. Jock had had a long war, serving with the British Expeditionary Force in France in 1940 and later with 21 Army Group in Belgium and Germany. The couple had been separated for many months. But according to Emily's mother, Mrs. Cane, they were still 'on affectionate terms' when her son-in-law returned to her home in January 1945. Problems only began after Jock was posted to Italy that March. Emily sent a stream of letters and parcels to him, but received only irregular replies, which so distressed her that eventually she became convinced he was seeing another woman.

She met D'Alcorn in a Twickenham restaurant sometime around January 1946, shortly after his discharge. He wrote her love letters in a soppy, matinee-idol style which played on her distress and loneliness: 'Dearest darling, I know now that there can never be anyone else; my devotion to you is everlasting, and to make you happy is going to be my job for life.' Mrs. Cairns appears to have fallen hopelessly in love with him. 'Oh, I can't help it, I like Ronnie ever so much,' she told her sister Margaret. 'He is very good to me and I feel I can't live without him . . . I hate Jock.'

Emily returned to Ashford a few hours before her husband and the children on the morning of 1 March. The couple's reunion was 'far from affectionate', and they retired for a private thirty-minute talk, after which Jock, acting in a 'perfectly calm and resigned' way (as his in-laws later said), emerged to explain that his wife had revealed her affair and her intention to leave him. She would be taking the children with her. Mr. and Mrs. Cane, who apparently had been kept in the dark about D'Alcorn, told Emily to get out. She left Feltham Road alone and phoned her lover, who was startled by the news: he did not appear to have been taking the relationship nearly as seriously as she was. Nonetheless, he invited her to his home in Twickenham, and after several hours managed to console her with the promise that she and the two boys could move in with him. She left Twickenham about 7.30 p.m., apparently much more cheerful, and returned home to pack.

Meanwhile, Jock had spent the whole day in the pub along with his father-in-law and Emily's brother Richard, a sailor who had just returned on leave. They stumbled home around closing time. It was shortly after they arrived back at the house that Richard first noticed the cocked automatic pistol tucked into Jock's battledress. Alarmed, he took the gun off him. But Richard couldn't work out how to remove the bullet from the chamber and so he discharged a round into a bucket under the kitchen sink, sending his mother – who was distraught enough already from the events of the day – into outright hysterics. Richard then hid the gun in the kitchen pantry and went to bed. It was just after 11 o'clock.

Perhaps Jock was less drunk than he seemed. Perhaps the gunshot revivified him. Either way, a few minutes after Richard had gone upstairs he quietly recovered the pistol and put it back in his army blouse. He then joined Emily and his mother-in-law in the front room and stood before the fireplace. Mrs. Cane, tired and in despair, had her face buried in her hands, and so her account to the police of what happened next was necessarily incomplete. She remembered Jock mumbling something to his wife, to which Emily replied 'no, definitely not'. She then heard two sharp bangs. When she looked up both Jock and Emily were lying next to one another, he collapsed on the floor, she slumped in her chair, both quite dead.

Jock Cairns' murder–suicide was not the first homecoming that had turned deadly. Seven months earlier on a warm August evening, 1945, residents of Shoreditch had seen a shaking, blood-smeared man pacing back and forth beside a police telephone box on the Hackney Road. When a policeman eventually approached him, the man had said simply: 'I have killed my wife. I have stabbed her.' He turned out to be Frederick James Hooker, a former private in the Army Pioneer Corps, who had been demobbed three weeks earlier. Hooker had confronted his wife Lilian about the on-again, off-again affair she had been having with another soldier since

May 1941. He demanded that his wife take him to meet the other man. She refused. Hooker pulled out a pocket knife and stabbed her in the neck several times. 'I have been going crazy for the last three weeks,' he told the police later. 'I kept asking her to be fair to me but she wouldn't. I idolized her and thought the world of her . . . I just longed for the time I could get back to her. . . . I kept thinking about my children,' he added. They had eleven boys and girls.[3]

Then there had been ex-staff sergeant Albert Nettleton, described as a 'devoted and attentive husband', who a few months after his demob had bludgeoned his wife to death with an iron when her persistent adultery drove him into a 'terrible rage'.[4] A crowd of over a thousand turned out to see his arrival at Holyhead police station.[5] And there was Private Frederick Marshall, who returned from four years in Burma to discover his wife Ivy associating with a gunner in the Royal Artillery, and who, after his pleas for reconciliation failed, had strangled her one morning in bed.[6] There was also Edward William Jones, a driver with the Highland Division in liberated Holland and a veteran campaigner of North Africa, Sicily and Italy, who arrived home on leave one day and shot dead his wife's boyfriend with a Sten gun.[7]

In the eighteen months that followed the end of the war in Europe, scarcely a Sunday went by without at least one story in the *News of the World* about a returning serviceman killing or assaulting his errant wife or her lover – or, in a few cases, being pre-emptively killed by them before he could act himself.[8] Demobilisation had given life to, and guaranteed death from, that most un-British of offences, the *crime passionnel*. Despite the media hype, however, the number of tragic stories like these was very small. Violent crimes of any kind were still rare in Britain. The wife-killings of the demobilisation period attracted the attention that they did partly because of their novelty – and their ferocity. These were, after all, not genteel murders like those found in the pages of Agatha Christie novels: polite poisonings in the conservatory. They were brutal, even feral attacks, animated by a primal rage unknown in British crime lore since the days of Jack the Ripper.

So their lurid qualities alone appealed to postwar newspaper readers. But these murders had a special timeliness too. The deaths of women like Emily Cairns had been predicted long before the return of their soldier husbands. Such women, it was said, were paying the price for a nation that had sinned. The wives and sweethearts of Britain had supposedly broken faith with their absent menfolk. They had committed the unforgivable betrayal: adultery. And not just adultery, but adultery with Americans, Canadians, Poles, Italians – in other words, *foreigners*. Now there was to be a terrible reckoning.

Britain in 1945 was a country quietly tormented by sexual suspicion – and not just of women. Men, too, had behaved discreditably during their absence from the family home. With the war over, many broken promises and shameful secrets could no longer be hidden. Demobilisation meant confronting unwelcome truths. The results were rarely as violent as those seen in Feltham Road, but they could bring humiliation, anger and disgrace nonetheless. As the troops marched home, unhappy revelations took place behind many thousands of British front doors.

## Untying the Knot

'Nothing like it has ever been seen in our social history before . . . [it is] a modern matrimonial landslide'.[9] Writing in *John Bull* in June 1946, the Reverend W.E. Purcell was not alone in lamenting what he regarded as the wartime collapse of the British family. Three years earlier the Archbishop of Canterbury had congratulated his fellow countrymen and women on the 'splendid endurance, mutual helpfulness and constancy' they had shown during the long years of struggle. But even he had been alarmed at the 'collapse in respect of honesty and sex morality' that he had seen all around him; all the old conventions of British life were visibly failing.[10] By V-E Day it seemed to such Jeremiahs that the price of victory had been altogether too high. Britons had defeated fascism abroad, but destroyed their own moral fabric in the process.

The *Daily Mail*'s Ann Temple cited the 'depressingly numerous' cases in her postbag of men who had written to their wives and children after an absence of three or four years to say they were not returning.[11] Women had to be counselled on how to explain to their children that their father was not coming home. For some, the heartbreak was too great. Marie Burgess received a letter from her husband, a lieutenant-colonel stationed in Italy, explaining he was leaving her for another woman. 'May God forgive you for the misery I saw on a small boy's face when I told him tonight,' she wrote before trying to gas herself and her 7-year-old son in their Clacton-on-Sea home. She survived. The child died.[12]

Some symptoms of national decadence had developed a notoriety quite out of proportion to their actual frequency. Bigamy, for instance, had become, according to the parliamentarian Lord Elton, 'almost a national institution'.[13] It's true that wartime conditions had created new possibilities for fraudulent marriage. With the population in permanent flux, and stolen and forged identity cards readily available – by 1945 it was estimated that half a million Britons were either using illegal papers or none at all[14] – it was easier than ever to misrepresent oneself. By 1945, prosecutions for bigamy made up one in ten of the cases on the Old Bailey calendar. A printed warning was included for the first time with every civil marriage form.[15]

Some men absent from their legal wives set up second homes with their mistresses, marrying them for respectability's sake. A sergeant major in the Royal Artillery garrisoned in Leicester divided his war between two wives and seven children, living with one family during the week and the other at weekends.[16] One lieutenant worked his way through a trio of wives during the war, and might have added his three additional girlfriends to the roster had the law not finally caught up with him.[17] Some bigamists created entire shadow lives for themselves. Edrick Findon, a 24-year-old private soldier who ended up before Winchester Assizes, not only married twice but also appeared at various times as a lieutenant, a captain and a major, before joining the RAF for good measure.[18]

One in three bigamists was a woman. In March 1945, Leeds Assizes heard the case of Evie Beecroft, who had remarried during the war despite knowing full well that her first husband, who had been captured at Dunkirk, was still alive in a German prisoner-of-war camp. Beecroft had taken her spouse's absence as an opportunity to begin again without fussing too much over the details, and so told her children that their father was dead before marrying an unwitting substitute. Inconveniently, her legal spouse survived to return to Britain at the end of the war, and her flexible understanding of widowhood led to twelve months in prison.[19]

But although the annual number of fraudulent marriage convictions tripled during the war, the total number of cases nationwide remained in the hundreds.[20] Bigamy was small beer. Far more worrying to moral traditionalists were the divorce figures, which really did make for grim reading. In 1935, 4,100 decrees absolute had been granted in England and Wales. By 1945 the figure was up to 15,600. In 1947 it reached the extraordinary total of 60,300.[21]

What had gone wrong with British marriage? Perhaps, as some thought, young people had debased the sacred institution by entering into it recklessly. Perhaps the skyrocketing divorce rate was a reflection of the moral shallowness of a generation lacking a proper Christian education, heedless of the gravity of their commitments. 'The modern "easy come, easy go" view of marriage' was to blame for 'a gradual cheapening and lowering of standards,' wrote W.E. Purcell.[22] The chief medical officer of the Ministry of Health, Sir Arthur McNalty, agreed that because of the war:

Prudential considerations [have been] disregarded . . . after the wedding the bridegroom, if a serviceman, rejoins his unit and the bride goes back to her war work. They may meet at intervals for periods of short leave, or they may not see one another until the end of the war. In the meantime both partners have been exposed to trials and temptations. They have often little thought of planning for their future life together.[23]

In fact, a number of factors were responsible for the postwar divorce spike, some only tangentially related to the war. The 1937

Divorce Reform Act had broken down significant roadblocks to the dissolution of unhappy marriages, in particular by creating new grounds for desertion and cruelty. The divorce rate had already been rising rapidly in the two years before the German invasion of Poland in 1939, and presumably would have carried on increasing, though at a less hectic rate, even if peace had been preserved.

Equally important, the legal-aid schemes introduced into the wartime Forces – the precursors to the general opening up of legal aid to the poor in 1948 – for the first time made divorce economically possible for large numbers of men and women. The result was a flood of applications. Between July 1942 and December 1945, the legal-aid departments in the armed services received 48,000 petitions for divorce, of which by the end of that period only 5,000 had been successfully completed.[24] By V-E Day it was taking up to three and a half years to finalise a case in the armed services, and the barrister and Labour MP Moss Turner-Samuels was complaining that 'the existing machinery for dealing with divorce is creaking woefully'.[25]

So the remarkable divorce figure in 1947 was, to some extent, a statistical anomaly owing to the enormous number of backlogged wartime applications that were now finally being processed. The accumulation was cleared by the introduction of Special Commissioners to hear petitions, and the time needed to declare absolute a decree nisi was cut from six months to six weeks. After that, the number of annual awards granted fell sharply and stayed low for a decade. There were fewer divorces in 1962 than in 1946.[26] The British family stumbled on.

But something *was* different about divorce in 1946 and 1947, the two record petition years. For the first and only time, more husbands than wives initiated the breakup of the marriage; and two-thirds of those husbands cited adultery as the cause of their estrangement from their spouses.[27] It's true that some of these allegations may have been legal contrivances, for the no-fault category didn't yet exist. But such a wave of allegations can't just be dismissed as a statistical blip. For millions of British families the war's consequences were clearly real and deeply distressing. And it wasn't just feckless newlyweds who were struggling. The divorce figures for England and Wales show that for every two recent marriages that failed in the late 1940s, one couple that had been married for much longer – perhaps fifteen to eighteen years – divorced as well. These were husbands and wives who had long passed the seven-year-itch phase; the collapse of their marriages was unprecedented.[28] The stolid middle-aged were struggling to readjust to peace along with everyone else.

## Bloody Yanks

'I had trouble at home . . . I got fed up.' As Fusilier Alan McLeod's personal life had begun to unravel, so had his army career. The 23-year-old husband and father already had a string of wartime convictions for absconding from his unit when he was sent on garrison duty to Germany in October 1945. Frustrated that he could not get the compassionate leave he felt he needed to save his marriage, McLeod fell into bad company. One night, after a bellyful of schnapps, he raided a Hamburg warehouse to steal goods for the black market. The nightwatchman discovered him; McLeod shot him with a machine gun, killing him instantly. 'I felt that if only I could get back I could put things right,' the young fusilier wrote in his unsuccessful plea for clemency following his court martial. The court was not inclined to show mercy. On 18 June 1946, McLeod was executed by firing squad.[29]

Although few cases ended as dramatically as his, McLeod's personal anxieties were certainly not unusual. During the last ten months of the war, the Soldiers, Sailors, Airmen and Families' Association (SSAFA) received over 50,000 requests for help with family problems from soldiers in northwestern Europe alone.[30] By autumn 1945 the War Office was having to arrange 300 interviews a day to handle requests for compassionate leave.[31] 'Anxiety about domestic affairs . . . is rife,' wrote Lieutenant-Colonel Sparrow, the expert on morale, after his visit to the Mediterranean and Middle East.[32] 'Troubles at home are general,' agreed the Air Ministry, 'domestic problems extremely serious'.[33]

Adultery, or the fear of it, was at the root of many of these problems: 'no disease was more infectious than the anxiety and depression arising from this topic,' acknowledged the War Office's official postwar report on morale.[34] A combination of barrack-room gossip and prurient press stories encouraged what psychologists Eliot Slater and Moya Woodside would later call 'an atmosphere of mass suggestion' within the ranks during the war.[35] In his *Sex Problems of the Returning Soldier*, Kenneth Howard described the anxiety that festered when soldiers overinterpreted the scraps of information they received from their wives' correspondence:

> He is constantly on the alert for any sign in letters from home of waning affection or other sentiments. Every possible shade of meaning is read into the most innocent sentences . . . he is apt to be surly and suspicious, to imagine that someone is trying to usurp his place. His awareness of his own sexual desires and temptations and his own possible weakness add to his suspicions . . . any sign in a letter from home that all is not well, or that love is fading, is a source of torturing anxiety and resentment to him . . . remember that nothing makes anxiety more acute and more intolerable than a feeling of helplessness, an inability to 'do something about it'.[36]

Prisoners of war especially dreaded being abandoned by their loved ones. Of all servicemen, they had the most time and inclination to worry: cut off almost completely from contact with home, depressed, lacking confidence, often physically ill, the anxiety of suspicion could be a daily torture.[37] Some at least found gallows humour in the situation. Colonel G.H. Shorland, incarcerated in a Japanese compound, pitied his wife 'churning out cards at twenty-five words a time with no reply . . . shan't be surprised if you run amok one day and say *all dead or dying. Hope you never come back. Keep miserable. Bored. Betty*'.[38]

This fear of being forgotten occasionally, and tragically, turned out to be well founded. During the first months of liberation, a few former prisoners who were assumed to be long dead turned up at home alive only to find out that their 'widows' had married again in their absence. This was most common amongst former captives of the Japanese, who had not always been able to pass along information home through the International Red Cross. 'I'm nearly crazy with worry, and I just don't know what to do,' wrote one distraught reader to *Woman*'s agony aunt Evelyn Home in January 1946:

> I have recently received word that my husband, supposed lost in Singapore, is alive and recuperating in hospital in Australia. This has come as a tremendous shock to me, for I had resigned myself to losing him and had deliberately started a completely new life. After a period of misery I was lucky enough to meet and love my American husband, who is now back in the US making a home for me . . . I am shortly expecting a baby . . . I must be honest and say that I have considered my first husband dead for so long that to me he is not quite real – a ghost and a dream – whereas my American husband has all my heart.[39]

And it was the Americans – the 'bloody Yanks' – who were the root cause of so much of this anxiety. By June 1944 more than one and a half million US servicemen were stationed in the UK. Overall, more than three million would pass through Great Britain at one time or another during the war, along with several hundred thousand Canadians, Frenchmen, Belgians, Dutchmen, Czechs, Norwegians and Poles.[40] From the moment that American troops began to deploy in Europe in large numbers in mid-1942, Britain's servicemen began to nurse what became an increasingly rancorous inferiority complex towards these allegedly oversexed, certainly overpaid interlopers. The sartorial gap between the two Allies was stark. Ordinary British soldiers wore only battledress blouses without collars and ties, more akin to a prison jacket than a smart blazer, whereas enlisted men in the US army were issued with service uniforms for off-duty wear that to foreign eyes made them look like officers. The contrast did not go unnoticed by women, their interest already piqued by Hollywood glamour and the access that American troops had to scarce items such as stockings and chocolate.

The 'colonisation' of Britain by these foreign interlopers became a preoccupation of troops abroad. 'Far across the ocean lies a land so fair and sweet,' suggested the bitter ballad 'Our Country':

Rugged hills and valleys, with their houses small and neat,
Once a land so free and easy, home of England's fighting sons,
Now a home of Poles and Frenchmen, Yanks and some Canadians.[41]

An adaptation of 'Lili Marlene' told a similar story:

I've been away a long time with thoughts of coming home
My heart was full of gladness, and love I'd never known;
But during my absence long and grim
The Yanks had bought, with lime and gin
My good-time English sweetheart,
My faithless English Rose.[42]

There was, warned a welfare officer in the Mediterranean, a widespread feeling amongst the rank-and-file overseas that the young women of Great Britain had 'let the boys down very badly' by throwing themselves at such men.[43] 'Girls I knew and respected have fallen for foreigners,' wrote one disgusted veteran returning to Britain after four years abroad.[44] The Germans played on these sexual insecurities, distributing propaganda leaflets to British troops in Italy suggesting that Americans were habitually sleeping with their wives.

But doing something about your anxieties was not easy. The army, which had traditionally relied on commanding officers to assist their men, was making an attempt to professionalise its counselling responsibilities. Domestic cases were now referred to local army welfare officers (LAWOs), distributed around the United Kingdom, who investigated marital difficulties reported by servicemen and could recommend a course of action that might include compassionate leave, a posting closer to home, or even early release from the army.[45] But many applications acknowledged by the War Office to be legitimate were nonetheless turned down because of manpower shortages.[46] And not surprisingly, women resented the idea of state snoopers checking up on them and asking impertinent questions of their friends and neighbours.[47] Clumsy intervention by a welfare officer could make a domestic problem even worse. Often, then, there was little choice for the servicemen but to wait and worry.

## In a Way, They're Worse than Jerry

Ironically, the image of the GI as a gleeful Lothario may be a myth. According to army chaplain N.R.M. Hawthorn, who investigated 3,000 cases of wartime adultery by servicemen's wives, fewer than one in twenty of the villains turned out to be a foreign soldier. In fact, three-quarters of the adulterers were British civilians; and the typical Tommy was over three times more likely to be cuckolded by one of his own comrades as he was by a GI.[48] Perhaps the Americans were not the Casanovas everyone assumed. This uncertainty illustrates that despite all the infamy attached to wartime sexual adventures, we have virtually no way of knowing how common they actually were. We would need, as a starting point, a British equivalent to the famous Kinsey Reports compiled in the United States in the late 1940s and early 1950s; but no such study exists. Mass-Observation did produce something called the 'Little Kinsey' in 1949, but its scope was much smaller and its methodology open to criticism.[49] Surviving evidence is fragmentary, often anecdotal, and very difficult to interpret. In other words, we can only guess at the truth.

We do know, for example, that the number of reported illegitimate births to married women in Birmingham trebled from 1940 to 1945, and that just over half of these women were wives of servicemen. We know that in Lindsey, north Lincolnshire, and Southsea, Hampshire, half of all illegitimate children were born to married women.[50] But we don't know how representative any of these figures are for Britain as a whole. Nor can we be entirely sure what they mean. Some of these putatively 'married' women were actually divorced or widowed. Others were long separated from their husbands and were in a stable existing relationship with the baby's father.

And what of the illegitimate children who escaped the notice of the statistician? If a married mother did not explicitly state otherwise on her baby's birth certificate, then her husband was assumed in law to be its father, even if this was prima facie implausible. An unknown number of servicemen accepted cuckoos as their own kin; an unknown number were unwittingly duped. Some illegitimate children were presumably aborted or abandoned, while in other cases unofficial adoptions by sisters or other female relatives may have taken place. And of course illegitimacy figures tell us nothing about adulterous women who through attentiveness or luck avoided pregnancy.

The only attempt to study the problem systematically during the war was made by a group of army chaplains led by the Reverend Hawthorn. They surveyed 8,000 married soldiers who had been away from Britain for at least three years, and their calculations showed that between 6–10 per cent of such men 'had reason to know their wives had been unfaithful' during their absence.[51] Hawthorn argued that, since there must have been many adulterous liaisons that were successfully concealed by wives, the real rate of infidelity was much higher: he proposed that after an extended separation one in five service wives committed adultery. But even these figures are speculative, since we don't know what Hawthorn meant by 'reason to know'. Did these wronged soldiers have definite proof of adultery, or were they just guessing? Suspicions were presumably not always well founded.[52]

So maybe the problem was much less serious than the legends suggested. But returning British servicemen were not to know this, and perhaps they wouldn't have cared about such dry nuances anyway. They were angry, and they wanted justice. Perhaps they also wanted an excuse to punish women.

It is noticeable that many official and public comments about women in the 1940s were unapologetically accusative. A War Office morale report blamed 90 per cent of servicemen's marital failures on the actions of what it called 'selfish women'.[53] By 1944, soldiers in the Middle East were:

> assert[ing] in strong terms that they have lost faith in women. . . . They do not pretend to be paragons of virtue themselves, but in comparison to the laxity of the women, men claim as a rule that for their part they have played the game, and they fail to see why women should not have done the same. Disillusion is widely expressed.[54]

By the end of the war there was more than a hint of misogyny in the air. 'I notice,' wrote the *News Chronicle*'s agony uncle John Aubrey in July 1945, 'that the vast majority of the villains of my post-bag are women . . . can it be that a general outbreak of anti-feminism is one of the inevitable consequences of war?'[55] Tropes of treachery appeared. A parson stationed in North Africa condemned the women of England as 'the most efficient fifth column' in the service of the Axis.[56] '*In a way they're worse than Jerry, do more harm to us than guns*', agreed a balladeer of the Eighth Army.[57]

An army psychiatrist, T.F. Main, worried that some returning servicemen would find women legitimate targets for their anger. 'The feeling of being cheated,' he wrote – cheated sexually, economically and emotionally – might 'give rise to angry desire [amongst repatriates] to destroy all womankind as monsters, cocottes, harlots, drunkards, foolish empty-headed hard-boiled gold-diggers.'[58] The British public sometimes seemed to sympathise with this thirst for revenge. Private Reginald Keymer walked free from a cheering Nottingham courtroom in July 1945, despite his admission that he had strangled his adulterous wife in a local maternity hospital. 'The provocation,' said Justice Macnaughten, presiding, 'was such that an ordinary frail man might have done what he did.'[59] When Frederick Booth, who had also strangled his unfaithful spouse in a jealous rage, stood before a Chester court a year later, he was found not guilty after just seven minutes' deliberation.[60]

Sometimes sympathetic juries defied the advice of their own judges. After Kathleen Patmore's killer Cyril escaped the death penalty at his trial in September 1945, Justice Charles made it plain that he disagreed with the finding: if men coming back from abroad were allowed to draw the conclusion that their unfaithful wives were denied the protection of the law and could be killed without consequences, Britain would have surrendered to what he called 'the law of the jungle'.[61] Two months later another jury deliberating over a naval officer who had shot his wife's paramour, found the officer guilty only of unlawful wounding, upon which the incensed Charles berated them: 'The only thing you have not done is to give this man a medal.'[62]

Some commentators were alarmed. Juanita Frances of the Married Women's Association complained about the letters she had received from soldiers defending the right to 'do in' adulterous wives. 'Sentimental juries', as she called them, were undermining the rule of law by encouraging angry men to take their possessiveness and jealousy to its extreme conclusion: 'we feel it is imperative that the public should be made to realize this'.[63]

## The Law of the Jungle

So were these wife-killings of 1945 and 1946 part of what Susan Gubar once called a wartime 'Blitz on women', a brutal, gendered vendetta by the frustrated and angry?[64] Certainly, the attitude towards domestic violence in the 1940s was far more casual than it is today. In working-class neighbourhoods the Victorian assumption that husbands had the right, within certain limits, to beat their wives still lingered on. Black eyes and bruises after a Friday night row were accepted with a shrug. The police were still reluctant to intervene in household disputes. Moreover, if a wife had broken a sexual taboo, it was still felt that she had brought destruction down on herself. Men, the assumption went, could not be expected to remain passive in the face of such extreme provocation. The 'unwritten rule' still held good. The public was reluctant to see wronged husbands hang; any killer of a harlot deserved a measure of mercy.

But there were voices in defence of British women in 1945. The press certainly entertained topical stories of infidelity, but it also provided a platform for people who angrily denounced the phenomenon as a myth. 'It would be most unfortunate if an impression got abroad that the wives of servicemen were neglecting their duties in the home, had lost all sense of loyalty to their men abroad, and had sunk to a low and reckless standard of conduct,' said the *Daily Mirror*. 'These women are loyal and true, even better, perhaps, than some of their men deserve.'[65]

Acknowledgement that some wives had faltered did not always come loaded with condemnation. Even socially conservative organisations were willing to concede mitigating circumstances. 'The claims on our sympathy are very great for the soldier . . . who returns to find his wife has left him, and his home is broken up,' wrote Rosamund Fisher, the president of the Mothers' Union, in April 1946:

> But I think the woman who was left behind in the war alone, with perhaps only her small children for company, in the full prime of her life, with desire strong in her . . . needs sympathetic understanding too. Many women have been placed in positions of almost intolerable temptation . . . it seems to me therefore to be supremely important in dealing with this serious problem to help the husbands to realize more fully what their wives suffered through the sudden loss of their companionship, and through long years of loneliness.[66]

Commentators attributed the vulnerability of otherwise good and faithful wives to the unnatural circumstances that the war had created. Their loneliness after the prolonged absence of their husbands was stressed. Women, it was made clear, were not always in control of their own passions; the psychology of 'feminine nature' had to be respected and allowed for. 'The emotional life of the woman is an "all or nothing" business,' suggested Dr. David Mace, the chairman of the Marriage Guidance Council. 'She may pass in a moment from complete self-control to unconditional surrender. Then she is apt to suffer more than the man, to find the terrible burden of conflicting loyalties a very heavy load.'[67]

Given this natural fragility, relationships with members of the other sex, even those that began with the most chaste of motives, could end in unintentional disaster. '[As] the woman's latent needs grow nearer the surface, she becomes aware that part of herself, hitherto unknown and unsatisfied, is becoming insistent,' suggested Phoebe and Laurence Bendit, authors of *Living Together Again* (1946). 'She is sensitive to her man friend's sympathetic touch upon all her interests and problems. And so the relationship grows and expands like a plant turning towards the sun . . .'[68] 'It may be very easy to start anything, but very difficult to stop,' agreed Kenneth Howard in *Sex Problems of the Returning Soldier*.[69] This was all a little patronising, denying as it did the capability of adult women to make rational moral choices. Nonetheless, to say that a woman had sinned because of tragic circumstances beyond her control was rather different from calling her a whore.

Husbands were urged to take this into account in responding to the situation. Mary Grant, the agony aunt for *Woman's Own*, pressed her many ex-soldier correspondents to view their wives' sins in the context of war. 'She let you down shockingly,' she consoled one husband whose wife had had another's baby, '[but] she may have suffered a good deal in remorse and apprehension before your return . . . do try to put that memory behind you, just as I am sure she is trying'.[70] 'I take it for granted that she regrets the past and is prepared to do her utmost to make the future a success,' she counselled another. 'What other people say or think does not matter.'[71] Good faith on the part of the wife was seen as a given.

Husbands were told to accept their share of the blame for failing to provide emotional support to their lonely spouses. 'I am terribly sorry for you, but are you sure you didn't precipitate the ultimate disaster yourself?' Grant rebuked one man whose wife had left him during his absence overseas. 'In the Army you have lots of distractions, while a lonely wife often has nothing, and turns quite innocently for distraction to another man. Too often such an association ceases to be innocent . . .'[72] A willingness by wronged men to see some fault in their own behaviour appears to have survived the high passions of homecoming. A surprisingly large number of husbands who took part in a 1951 survey on adultery organised by the anthropologist Geoffrey Gorer were prepared to accept that wifely misconduct could be a shared failing: 'The blame rests on his own head,' chided one Doncaster man. 'If he gave his wife proper care and attention and praised her good points she would not go astray.'[73]

It is worth noting that when a serviceman behaved brutally towards his spouse without *any* mitigating circumstances, the public was willing to concede the right of the wife to take extreme measures too.[74] In May 1945 a Manchester jury took just eighteen minutes to clear a Stockport woman of the murder of her husband, RAF Squadron Leader Francis Chitty, despite strong circumstantial evidence that she had shot him during a violent row.[75] Two months later in Birmingham another wife was freed despite her admission that she had killed her husband, Flight Lieutenant Donald Allen, a former Bomber Command pathfinder, with a service revolver. In both cases the dead men were serial adulterers who had shown considerable mental and physical cruelty towards their spouses; acquitting Mrs. Allen, Mr. Justice Humphreys concluded that the accused 'acted in self-defence against a man who had been a brute to her for years'.[76]

The really unqualified villains in the press, people who deserved no sympathy at all, were not erring wives so much as busybody neighbours who tattled in poison-pen letters to absent husbands. 'The nosey parkers are still at work, dipping their dirty pens in acid to hurt the men who have dared and suffered so much for them,' chided Sally Andrew in the *Daily Herald*: 'The people who write these letters, so calculated to demoralize every servicemen who receives one, do not take the risk of being shot or hanged. Yet they are doing their best to undermine men on monotonous and dangerous work.'[77] The collaborationist theme was echoed by an army spokesman who described 'tittle-tattle busy-bodies' as 'Fifth Columnists of the worst order [who] should be punished severely . . . whenever a person in this country talks glibly about the misbehaviour of a soldier's wife and has no foundation for his facts, he should look in a mirror and say "I am a traitor". '[78]

Agony aunts dealt brusquely with relatives or neighbours who were considering sending 'helpful' information to husbands in the armed forces.[79] Although some critics of poison-pen gossip dwelt on the damage done to innocent reputations, others indicated that even accurate allegations were unjustifiable because they spoiled the chance for reconciliation.[80] J.B. Priestley made this point in his account of Eddie Sloane's homecoming in his 1945 novella *Three Men in New Suits*. The demobbed soldier's neighbours take delight in regaling him with salacious hints about his wife's activities during his absence, and Eddie responds with drunken violence. But ultimately he is more outraged by the unpleasant behaviour of his fellow townsmen and women than he is by the mistakes of his lonely and vulnerable wife, whom he eventually admits he would have forgiven had others not interfered first:

'Well, she didn't ought to have done it, y'know?' said Eddie earnestly, 'not with me out there, she oughtn't. Not right is it? But there was the kid and all that . . . I might 'ave given 'er a good talking to, an' then said, "Let's forget it". I might 'ave done that.'[81]

## Sleeping with the Enemy

In the six months that followed the end of the war in Europe, the popular press did not wholly concern itself with tales of demobbed soldiers garrotting, shooting and bludgeoning their wives. The British Occupation Zone (BOZ) of Germany was also serving up titillating scandals too good to ignore. Stories such as 'German Girls Rob Allied Wives of Happiness: Fratting Wrecks British Homes' became a regular Sunday staple.[82] British servicemen, it was claimed, were sexually fraternising – 'fratting' – with German women, taking up mistresses from amongst their former enemies and sometimes abandoning their marriages to boot. Led by the *People*'s correspondent Evadne Price, Fleet Street depicted occupied Germany as a vast bordello, poisonous to any decent sense of morals:

Germany is swamped in sensuality. Go into any of their deserted houses, as I have done, and examine their literature – ordinary houses. The man in the street type. You will find books in all of them containing pictures so disgusting you are stunned with horror. Pictures of degeneracy, sex perversion, abnormalities, tortures. The women of Germany understand nothing outside sex . . . they are deliberately contaminating our soldiers . . . Germany is like a foul octopus reaching out its destroying tentacles.[83]

Much resentment was stirred up by the apparent plethora of nylons, perfumes, cosmetics and other feminine paraphernalia in the BOZ at a time when goods like these were practically unobtainable at home. 'They are all feminine appeal,' insisted Price: 'Smiles. Silk stockings. Short skirts. Expensive make-up.'[84] Faced with a sophisticated erotic onslaught – one correspondent warned about the 'repulsive neatness' of girls with 'fine clothes and hearts full of hatred' – it was assumed that the naïve young British boys garrisoning the zone would be unable to resist.[85] Price's thesis was that these wily women were pouring propaganda into the ears of foolish Tommies in order to downplay German war guilt: 'They have done their job well . . . I tell you, I have heard more rubbish about our "injustice" to Germany in these past weeks from our soldiers than you would believe possible.'[86] It amounted to a 'slaughter of the innocents'.[87]

During 1945 the *People* received more than a thousand letters on the subject, many of them from women dumbfounded and contemptuous of their servicemen. Readers of other papers joined the chorus of disapproval. The girls of England, insisted one infuriated *News Chronicle* reader, were so disgusted with servicemen overseas as to leave them 'bereft of speech'.[88] 'Our boy has been a PoW in Germany since May 28, 1940, but if the price of his life and safety is to marry a German girl, then I hope he never returns,' declared another, in what was simultaneously a lament, a threat and a warlike boast.[89]

Some servicemen protested, naturally, at what one of them called the 'scurrilous myth' that Price was creating.[90] 'The cumulative effect of her articles,' wrote one, 'is to create the impression that every other man in the British Army of the Rhine has made an attachment with a German woman.'[91] Marriages, it was said, were being broken up on the strength of the fratting scandal. 'Six months ago we were the finest men in the world – the magnificent British Army,' wrote a soldier exasperated at the calumnies directed from Britain: 'Now we are black marketeers and sex fiends, out with a fraulein every night.'[92]

It has been said that infidelity by British servicemen during the war was expected, excused and ignored, that, as the historian Geoffrey Field has put it, 'masculine sexuality was tacitly assumed to be natural and inevitable . . . [and that] the sexual behaviour of soldiers, married and unmarried, was generally condoned'.[93] That there was a double standard seems beyond question. Women were scrutinised and judged for moral lapses far more often than men. But it would be a mistake to think that men always got away scot-free. As the fratting scandal shows, there were sins that were forgivable and sins that were not. Sleeping with the enemy was *verboten*.

British servicemen didn't take advantage of sexual opportunities in Germany alone. The ancient relationship between military camps and brothels had persisted throughout this war as with all the others. The armed forces wrestled with the medical and morale problems of prostitution.[94] Sexual opportunities, and opportunists, appeared wherever troops were stationed. The Berka, Cairo's notorious red-light district was said to entertain 90,000 clients a month.[95] By 1944 there were believed to be 42,000 full- and part-time *demi-mondaines* servicing soldier clients in Naples.[96] 'In Sicily and Italy we met a world sexually mad,' despaired RAMC venereal disease expert Douglas Campbell: 'soliciting and pimping were unbelievably prevalent and open'.[97] Later in the war, Brussels and the Belgian port cities became just as notorious for their sensual delights.[98]

Just how many servicemen were seeking out these sexual opportunities is unknown. It may be that a small number of enthusiastic customers made up the prostitutes' main clientele. The novelist

George MacDonald Fraser thought that the troops he knew were far more interested in talking about sex than actually seeking it out, belonging as they did to an 'inhibited, pious and timid generation'.[99] In fact, on active service it was not uncommon for servicemen to experience a reduced libido – a natural and predictable bodily response to stress and exhaustion. Indeed, the condition was so universal that, as a timeless army legend had it, all the NAAFI tea was being laced with potassium bromide, the 'passion killer'.[100] Barrack-room fables contributed to these fears of impotence and the popular belief that enforced celibacy damaged men's health.[101] In the Mediterranean theatre, it was held as axiomatic that sexual abstinence in a tropical climate caused sexual dysfunction.[102] Army psychiatrists reported that many men suffered depression because they believed they would no longer be able to make love to their wives after the war.[103]

Still, as the fighting ebbed away on the Continent and servicemen found themselves with more and more free time on their hands, so the casualties of Eros mounted up. The VD infection rate amongst occupation troops in northwest Europe shot up from 199 per 100,000 on the February 1945 ration strength to 1,064 a year later, more than five times the rate amongst home service troops.[104] This was judged to be an ethical as well as a medical debacle. 'In matters of sexual morality something is gravely wrong in the Army,' warned Seebohm Rowntree.[105]

There had been an important and enduring shift in feelings about the serviceman's sexuality. To the Victorians, military lust had been both natural and, within certain limits, commendable.[106] But that had been the era of Rudyard Kipling's grizzled old sweats who rarely married – certainly not into respectable working-class families, anyway – and whose behaviour could be overlooked precisely because they lived apart from the rest of society. By the Second World War, promiscuity in the ranks was being increasingly pathologised, the provenance less of the padre than of the unit psychologist. Those at risk were stigmatised as the 'neurotic and inadequate . . . the rejects, the neurotics, the cast-outs unable to get "a real woman" '.[107] Army studies depicted the typical VD patient as 'a selfish mother's boy, who shirk[ed] his responsibilities to comrades and country in his desperate search for comfort' – everything the self-controlled British citizen was not supposed to be.[108]

## A Man Who Can Forgive is a Real Man

By the end of the Second World War, attitudes towards masculinity had themselves shifted under fire. The old Victorian patriarch, brooding, physically sinister and unforgiving, was making way for the new 'temperate man' – gentle, rational, generous of spirit.[109] This temperate man was defined by his open-mindedness. 'A man who can forgive is in my opinion a real man,' suggested a 29-year-old from Durham. 'It is best to be a better man than the [cuckold],' agreed a Staffordshire pensioner: 'Tell her that she has gone far enough . . . [but] that with all her faults you love her still, and that all is forgiven'.[110] Almost half of all husbands accepted that 'talking it over' and self-examination were the best ways of dealing with unfaithfulness.

Those ex-soldiers who had returned and killed had let their passions overtake their rational sense. Like VD patients, they were failures as citizens and as men. Whatever sympathy they deserved was strictly qualified by their failure to exhibit proper self-control. Didactic tales of servicemen enraged by their wives' actual or suspected adultery always stressed that the good British male would act rationally and magnanimously, no matter what provocation he suffered. The old myth of British stoicism held as strong as ever.

In *They Are All Alike*, a short work of fiction published in *John Bull* in July 1945, Stan comes home with a Sten gun in his kitbag to confront and kill his supposedly unfaithful wife Becky. Primed for violence by his wartime career – 'he'd marched from Alamein to Hamburg and killed many a Jerry without a quiver' – Stan confronts Becky with his accusations, but is literally disarmed by his weeping wife's resemblance to the body of a boy comrade he had once seen die on an Italian battlefield. The pity of one combat memory cancels out the rage of others, and disgusted with himself

Stan abandons his plan, telling Becky to keep to herself whatever she was about to reveal.[111]

Similarly, in Olga Trim's *Double Journey*, published the following year, demobbed private John Brown has a recurring nightmare that his wife will confess her adultery to him on his return home and that 'a mad devil' will be released within him, with unaccountable results. But Brown is strong enough to take control of his own fate. When his wife does indeed admit her sin, he overcomes 'the scorching fear of himself, of what he would do' and forgives her.[112]

Fictional soldier-killers who could not control their murderous passions were invariably weak and pitiable figures. The murderous ex-serviceman portrayed by Peter Finch comes to a rather sticky end in the compendium film *Train of Events*, no particular surprise given the conventions of cinema in 1949. But his crime is depicted as the culmination of years of humiliation by his shrewish spouse. Violence was symptomatic of manly weakness, not masculinity: murder, the last resort of the pathetic.[113]

Indeed, according to Geoffrey Gorer's 1951 survey, only 14 per cent of married men felt that physically attacking their wife or her lover was a justifiable response to adultery any longer – a higher figure than one would expect today, but still a big shift from a half-century previously.[114] Gorer was struck by the gentleness and reasonableness that characterised the British outlook on life, despite the stresses of two world wars: 'Sexual jealousy is a comparatively uncommon emotion among the English,' he suggested: 'where anger is felt and expressed in such a situation it is more likely to be vindictiveness, a desire to hurt rather than a desire to avenge'.[115] Gorer also believed that a shift in the definition of honour was lowering the stakes in adultery. Honour was now generally understood to inhere in the personal characteristics and behaviour of the individual man rather than in the public actions of his family, so an 'honour killing' would no longer be understood as necessary or acceptable.

And when it came down to it, violence was *foreign*. By 1945 the British people had come to see themselves as citizens of a 'peaceable kingdom' characterised by restraint and respect for law and order.[116] It was for this reason that vengeful returning servicemen were so troubling. Their anger might be sincere; but what would come of it? There was great apprehension about the failings of women during the war, but on the brink of demobilisation there was equally great apprehension about the disruptive effect that military violence would have on British society. The nation was troubled by the prospect of a generation of soldiers returning home angry and resentful, their powers of self-control attenuated by wartime stress and the skills of violence fresh in their minds. Contaminated by foreign ideas, the demobbed veteran was a potential disturber of the peace. Perhaps his return home would cause more problems than it would solve.

# CHAPTER FOUR

# What the Hell Has Happened to This Country?

*One has the feeling that there is not much gratitude in England.*[1]

In February 1946 one of *Picture Post*'s readers offered 'a little advice and information' to servicemen like himself newly returning home for demobilisation. 'First of all,' he wrote, 'they should have replies ready for the following topical remarks':

(1) *Did you have a good time, old chap?* (This is asked with a frowning sort of look which says *I know you can't tell me in front of the ladies!*)
(2) *By Jove! You are lucky to have seen a bit of the world at the country's expense!*
(3) *You are looking jolly fit, old chap, but then of course you fellows in the Services had all the good food!*
(4) *You were lucky to have missed the fly-bombs and rockets!* (Now follows a discussion on fisherman lines as to the size and closeness of the missiles which affected the people in the room) . . .

'By this time,' he warned, 'you'll begin to feel what a coward you were to have joined up at all, and especially to have left the country in its hour of need.'[2] This wasn't an isolated case of malcontent.

Soldiers who returned home at the end of the Second World War expecting a hero's reception wherever they went were going to be in for a rude awakening.

During the worst of the fighting, the writer David Scott Daniell had found great satisfaction in imagining himself and his comrades telling their battlefield stories to their friends and family. He conjured up a vision of them, like King Hal's Agincourt veterans, rolling up their sleeves and showing their scars on Saint Crispian's Day: 'it would,' he predicted, 'be comforting and somehow compensating . . . we would describe it modestly, with salt-cellars and toast-racks for German positions'.[3] Old soldiers liked an audience.

But ex-servicemen who felt that they had anything unique to say about war were going to find themselves severely upbraided on their return to Britain. Sailors on the light cruiser HMS *Phoebe*, returning from the Far East at the end of 1945, were warned by an anonymous on-board poet that:

> Your folks will greet you with great glee
> And lavish hospitality
> But when the first three days have run
> No longer will they find much fun
> In tales how victory began
> Along the coast of Arakan
> Or how you sweated night and day
> Thousands of ruddy miles away . . .[4]

'Perhaps egoism or conceit on my part prompted me to imagine that on my return to England to be demobbed after six years spent abroad, a tumultuous welcome would be waiting,' thought Eighth Army veteran Maurice Merritt:

> It did not happen that way at all. . . . The reverse was often more apparent, for a soldier wearing his medals and a glorious tan, invariably seemed to annoy civilians. This was apparent if he entered a pub. Hostile faces would turn to him, and a bystander was once heard to say: *Lucky b——, look how brown he is, he's had a bloody good time.*[5]

'Do not expect,' warned the ex-Forces magazine *Civvy Street* in 1946, 'to see the bands playing or the flags waving, or even to see a crowd in the local pub keep silent when you open your mouth. *What? Let that chap have first pick in the leave list this year?* I heard a clerk saying. *Why, he's only just out of the army. Two days off every week and ten days' leave every three months! He ought to be at the bottom of the list.*'[6]

The novelist Anthony Burgess, newly returned from Gibraltar, also had the feeling 'of being derided in the streets' by civilians.[7] A Corporal D. Evans of the Royal Welch Fusiliers got back to Britain jobless and unwell after occupation duty in Germany, only to be told by one civilian that: 'You've had great experience. All that travel and excitement; we've missed all that.'[8] 'When you went in the pub you got the same atmosphere: *Oh here they are, here's the lad with the demob money*,' thought another ex-soldier. 'They seemed to feel a kind of resentment to the serviceman that was returning.'[9] A recurring grievance amongst demobilised men returning to Britain in 1945 was that civilians were jealous and dismissive towards them because of the perks they were supposed to have enjoyed in uniform.

To men who had been locked away for years behind barbed wire and bamboo stockades, sweated it out in the malarial jungles of Burma, been close to frozen on Arctic convoys to Murmansk, waded through Apennine mudslides, or dodged Flak 20,000 feet above Berlin, the British public's talk of 'pampered ex-soldiers who have had everything done for them'[10] appeared astonishingly unappreciative. 'Everyone looks at you as if you're a God-awful smell,' complained Lieutenant H.C.F. Harwood, newly returned to London after five years' imprisonment in Germany: 'What the hell has happened to this country?'[11]

## Nice War If You Can Get It

In the September 1944 edition of the literary journal *Horizon*, Cyril Connolly included a 'Letter from a Civilian' addressed to an overseas tank officer, 'Victor', who had seen little of Britain since

1939. Connolly's tone throughout is affectionate, yet he cannot help but notice the ironic gap between what Victor has gained out of the war and what he, a mere civilian, has lost. Victor has eaten quails and wild strawberries in Syria, skied in Beirut, inspected the ruins of Carthage, and tasted the nightlife of Sicily – enjoyed, in other words, a long and revivifying holiday paid for by someone else. The civilian Londoner, by contrast, has grown shabby and sordid, and benefited from none of the incidental rewards of travel and the outdoor life. 'The civilians who remain,' says Connolly:

> Grow more and more hunted and disagreeable, like toads, each sweating and palpitating under his particular stone. Social life is non-existent, and those few and petty amenities which are the salt of civilian life – friendship, manners, conversation, mutual esteem – seem more extinct than ever . . . never in the whole war has the lot of the civilian been more abject, or his status so low . . .
>
> Meanwhile, what about you Victor? Fighting as usual, making history, drinking calvados . . . you have won a Mercedes-Benz and a DSO in the field and now you are back in all my favourite [French] restaurants again. I die by inches; you live in continuous exultation, drunk with health and action, and rewarded for it by your grateful country. When the war is over you will be ten years' younger than you were when it started, and I shall be twenty years' older.[12]

As Connolly's letter suggested, a *lot* had happened to Britain during the war. Even the most solipsistic ex-serviceman returning after years of overseas duty couldn't have helped but notice how utterly transformed the British physical and mental landscape had become by 1945. It was so much 'smaller' and 'shabbier', as one former soldier put it, after six years of grueling attrition.[13]

The countryside was scarred and pitted by tank-traps and barbed wire. Shops and houses were dirty and unpainted; the windows still draped with heavy blackout curtains and criss-crossed with peeling sticky tape to prevent shattering in bomb blasts. Signposts had been painted over to thwart enemy invaders. Iron railings, long melted down, had disappeared from the parks.

Tom Harrisson, back after leading a commando unit in Japanese-occupied Borneo, was struck by the grim government propaganda posters 'offering three alternatives – venereal disease, diphtheria, or car-borne death'.[14]

The people, pasty and washed-out, had changed too. 'There was a tense, workmanlike atmosphere,' acknowledged Lieutenant Harwood: 'Everyone was setting about his or her business with utterly weary faces but with grim purpose.'[15] 'People looked more grey, shabby and worried than ever,' recalled Jean Crossley, who had spent the war working on technical translations of German documents: 'They smelled because so little soap was to be had.'[16] 'Civilians were shabbily dressed, the women mostly in head scarves, hair stringy and unwashed, lined faces plain without makeup,' noted servicewoman E.J.F. Knowles, while those in uniform struck her immediately as smart and well-fed.[17]

Thin, threadbare and exhausted, civilians were not, unsurprisingly, in the best or most generous of spirits. 'People are tired, strained and nervous,' warned returned servicemen S.C. Lawrence in *Civvy Street*: though the war tension had snapped, it had been succeeded, he thought, by 'a grey vacuum with little to fill it, either in the form of an increased supply of goods or of more leisure'.[18] The mood was not especially gentle or tolerant. 'We are suffering as a nation from some malaise – ill-manners, ragged tempers,' thought James Hodson, the war correspondent.[19] The *Daily Herald*'s Janet Grey agreed: 'Ask an ordinary polite question in a shop and you get a snarl of an answer . . . there's an aggressiveness about which seems to be affecting us all.'[20] Anyone expecting a hero's welcome was clearly pushing his luck.

But there was more to this than just fatigue and indifference. British civilians did have genuinely mixed feelings about the servicemen being returned to them. If demobbed veterans suspected that some of their countrymen were less than sympathetic towards their difficulties, they were right. It's not that civilians were unmoved by what the men in the Forces had accomplished. And there was relief and gratitude at the safe return of loved ones, without question. But there was confusion too, mixed with not a little suspicion and resentment. In the Second World War, the traditional moral economy of sacrifice had been unexpectedly complicated. Soldiers were the ones who were supposed to take all the risks, endure all the privations. But that hadn't really been the case in this war. Indeed, it seemed to many civilians, looking at the physical desolation surrounding them, that on the whole they had had as bad a time of it as anyone in uniform – maybe worse, in fact.

Consider this letter to *Picture Post* in April 1945:

'Blighty' is proud of, and grateful to, its fighting men, but its civilian population has had its share of war and privations. It therefore does not care for the loud protestations of *some* of the Forces men who expect priority in travel, plentiful leave, good food, pleasant accommodation after the war, gratuities, and an assured job. Contrast these desires, which the civilian is expected to finance, with a civilian's life for the past few years: constant anxiety about his children in the Forces, crowded trains, a few days' holiday a year if lucky, monotonous rations, blasted and ruined homes, high taxation, long working hours, and the possibility of losing his job when the Forces return.[21]

As this suggests, public complaints about servicemen during wartime were often couched with conventional nods of approval to their heroism. But private and unattributable comments were less polite. And with the end of the war this kind of self-censorship was increasingly set aside, as civilians openly aired the suspicion that servicemen – especially those in the fleshpots of continental Europe – were having a bit too much fun for their own good at the taxpayers' expense. It was sobering for the demobbed to discover that the gratitude they'd taken largely for granted was going to be rationed as ruthlessly as sugar and soap.

## Rumours of War

'The *din of battle*? Now you really cannot come home, angel, and imagine you can teach us in London anything about the noises of war,' the hero of *Punch*'s 'Home Chat' is brusquely informed by his wife in October 1945. 'That will make you most dreadfully unpop-ular.'[22] She had a point. The armed forces had maintained no monopoly on courage during the war. That is not to deny for a moment the great courage their men *had* displayed. Over 264,000 British servicemen paid the ultimate sacrifice. Another 277,000 were wounded, many maimed, blinded, or crippled for life.[23] The dangers of front-line service during the Second World War were real enough, and indeed often exceeded those of the Great War. In units that saw intense action the death toll was simply appalling: an infantryman in the First Battalion of the Royal Norfolk Regiment who landed in France on D-Day had a one-in-six chance of being killed by the end of the war.[24] It was more dangerous to lead an infantry platoon in Normandy in 1944 than it had been in Flanders in 1917.[25] The prospects for RAF aircrew who took part in the strategic bombing campaign over Germany were even grimmer; it's been estimated that only one in four survived a tour of operations completely unscathed.[26]

But overall, Britain was spared the bloodletting that it had endured during the First World War, when the national death toll had been almost three times higher.[27] It would be nice to think that the much lower casualty figures were the result of greater tactical acumen or generalship under Churchill. But the reason was simpler than that: the British Army just didn't play such a decisive part in Germany's defeat in the second World War. Its role in the victory this time, though less costly, also seemed more incidental.

From the first days of August 1914 until the final hours before the Armistice, the Western Front was the principal battleground of the First World War, and the British Army remained in contin-uous contact with the enemy's ground forces from beginning to end. Indeed, in the final year of that war it was Field Marshal Haig's troops who broke the Hindenberg Line and finally smashed the long stalemate of the trenches. By contrast, the Second World War had a very different course. After the disaster at Dunkirk in June 1940, the bulk of the British Army remained in the United Kingdom for the next four years. Indeed, in the mid-period of the war, it seemed to be performing little obvious military function at all. Large numbers of soldiers were garrisoned indolently across the country, and those few troops who were employed against the enemy in North Africa and the Mediterranean did not seem to be accomplishing much – an unfair assessment, perhaps, but not under the circumstances a surprising one. What, the British public asked with some impatience, was its army *for*? According to a September 1941 Mass-Observation survey, no one was quite sure: 'At the moment they have nothing but victorious withdrawals to their credit,' said one interviewee. Added another:

> Although I can readily believe that most serving men want to play their part in winning the war, I can't resist the taunt that joining the Army is about the quickest way to forget all about it.[28]

Another Mass-Observation survey the same year asked whether soldiers ought to be required to do fire-watching duties and help with the clear-up of air-raid debris. The response was mixed, but some civilians were unafraid to voice their opinion that the army was a haven for timewasters. 'They need something to do . . . they just play at it'; 'Keep them busy'; 'Make them work for their pay.'[29]

The British public might have been more impressed by its soldiers at this time had it not been in the firing line itself. Between 1939 and 1945, 62,464 civilians would die from war operations in Great Britain, most the victims of the *Luftwaffe*'s aerial bombardment, and another 86,000 were seriously wounded.[30] These casualties were not proportionately distributed across the country; city-dwellers were overwhelmingly more vulnerable than those in rural counties, with about half of all deaths and injuries on the mainland suffered by Londoners. But civilian men, women and children in places as far apart as Hull, Bristol, Belfast and Clydeside were all targeted at one time or another. The worst period of the bombing was from September 1940 to May 1941, and it never resumed the same intensity again. But the psychological stress persisted. 'There was seldom a day in five years when enemy aeroplanes or flying-bombs or rockets were not over some part of Britain,' commented the official historian of the home front, Richard Titmuss:

Between the first bomb on Britain and the last, 2,019 days elapsed – a long and wearisome period during which, for the most part and for most people, nothing happened. But all the time there were threats; of bombs, of gas, of sabotage, of invasion and, at the end, of new and unsuspected horrors. At no time did the workers in the post-raid evacuation and hospital services know when the next attack might come, whether it would be by night or day, what form it would take, which city would suffer, how severe destruction would be, or how long it would last. In these sectors, the enemy held the initiative almost to the end.

London was on duty for most of the war. Between the first and last incident, the alert was sounded on 1,224 occasions. If these are averaged, it may be said that Londoners were threatened once every thirty-six hours for over five years, threatened at their work, having their meals, putting their children to bed, and going about the ordinary business of their lives.[31]

Between the Battle of Britain and the end of 1942, the weight of the enemy's blows fell predominantly upon Britain's civilians, not its servicemen. Anthony Weymouth noted in his journal in early 1941 that the war had become 'a paradoxical affair' in which most of the men in the ostensibly 'fighting' forces had, since Dunkirk, experienced little more danger than civilians: indeed, in London's heavily bombed East End and the Midlands industrial cities it had been the worker and his wife, not the soldier, who had suffered most.[32] In a strange inversion of gender roles it was often the soldier who fretted and waited for news of his loved ones while he sat out the war in comparative safety. A mass-observer serving in the army commented that the war had brought about 'a reversal in the current of anxiety. The soldier is worried whether his wife is alive more often than the wife worries if her husband is alive. She is in the position of the greatest danger.[33]

Most British soldiers stationed in Britain were garrisoned in isolated rural areas a long distance from the *Luftwaffe*'s urban and industrial targets. This did not improve their reputation amongst civilians. In June 1941 the Weekly Home Intelligence Reports compiled by the Ministry of Information noted that the army was increasingly viewed as a 'cushy number': 'As long as he remains in England, the soldier is thought [by civilians] to have few worries.'[34] Alan Wood, himself a serviceman, suggested in his book *Bless 'Em All* that 'the soldier has lost a great deal of his luster in the changed atmosphere brought about by air raids ... in contrast to the bombed civilians, the idea [has grown up] that soldiers [are] having a safe, easy time of it in the country'.[35]

In Sheffield in 1942, civilians were said to feel contempt for soldiers who (albeit under orders) had disappeared from the city centre within a few minutes of the air-raid warning being sounded in order to disperse their vehicles safely. This scorn was associated with the army's poor performance fighting the Afrika Korps in North Africa: 'they're practising for when they meet Rommel'.[36] It was only the army's victory at El Alamein in November 1942 that began to dispel the reputation it had acquired of being 'effete'.[37]

Eventually, British soldiers did return to the European Continent, first in Italy in September 1943 and then as part of the Anglo-American expeditionary force sent to liberate France in June 1944. But by then the war's outcome depended almost entirely on the apocalyptic battle between Nazi Germany and the Soviet Union. The Western Front was, at least in manpower terms, a sideshow. At El Alamein, Montgomery had faced four German divisions. That same month the Red Army was fighting 179 of them. It was Stalin's troops who overwhelmingly broke Hitler's *Wehrmacht*. Even British servicemen themselves were overawed by the Soviets. The ordinary soldier, chafed a War Office morale report, 'often regards our Russian allies as the sole saviours of Europe, and is inclined to assume that while we owe everything to them they owe little or nothing to us'.[38]

Britain's military contribution to victory came to be overshadowed by the United States too. In the closing months of the European war, General Dwight D. Eisenhower had three times as many American as British troops under his command.[39] It was much the same story in the Pacific. South East Asia Command

(SEAC), the only theatre in the Japanese conflict in which British and Commonwealth forces predominated, eventually dwindled to a strategic afterthought.

In any case, even in the bloodiest of campaigns, only an unlucky minority of British soldiers ever actually became regularly exposed to enemy fire. During the Second World War the 'teeth' of the armed forces shrank drastically in comparison to their 'tails' – the support arms that supplied the fighting vanguard with equipment, communications and mechanical assistance. For every British Army division of about 15,000 men sent into combat there were another 45,000 men supporting it from the rear. In each theatre of war there was, beyond the front line, a vast network of camp followers: base and training depots, repair workshops, field hospitals, reception units, convalescent depots, rest camps, transit camps, leave camps, education and information centres. Armies had become mobile cities, with baggage trains of astonishing size, diversity and sophistication. The teeth-to-tail ratio in the RAF was even more lopsided: out of every twenty airmen, seventeen never so much as left the ground.[40]

Front-line soldiers were frankly contemptuous of the soft life supposedly led by their support comrades. George Millar, an officer in the Rifle Brigade, compared the 'infinitesimal minority' of front-line servicemen to those in uniform giving 'the minimum of effort . . . [clinging] greedily to comfortable jobs at home, or even abroad'.[41] They were 'the chairborne troops', according to J.L. Hodson.[42] The indiscriminate distribution of campaign medals at the end of the war was a particular source of ire to men who had risked all at the 'sharp end'. It is ironic that the Burma Star, which was to become the symbol of Fourteenth Army veterans, was originally dismissed as the 'Chowringhee medal' (Chowringhee being the name of Calcutta's commercial high street) by fighting soldiers in the Far East. Men who had spent barely twenty-four hours east of the Brahmaputra river were, it was said, eligible to receive the medal.[43]

That doesn't mean that their life was necessarily either happy or fortunate. Without the fear, excitement and distraction of battle, the monotony and petty disciplinary restrictions of the service existence could seem all the more pointless.[44] The vast service corps placed little emphasis on *esprit de corps*: in some technical depots, one or two officers might be responsible for the welfare supervision of 500 or 600 men.[45] Sprawling and anonymous, such camps could be breeding grounds of frustration. It is not difficult to imagine how a sentry guarding an airfield in the Scottish Hebrides or a bored pay clerk in Khartoum might have wondered what possible difference he was making to the war effort.

Still, it was a life with little mortal risk. Indeed, for most men in the 'tail', the war was 'as remote as the top of Snowdon', as correspondent Philip Jordan put it.[46] Their day-to-day work, however important, was safe and mundane, their time spent on tasks that were largely indistinguishable from civilian labour. J.L. Hodson, who accompanied the troops across northwestern Europe, suggested that perhaps three-quarters of the men in the Forces ran less risk during the war than the average Londoner.[47]

To be a typical ex-servicemen returning to Britain in 1945, then, especially if you had been a former member of the 'tail', was to experience the uncomfortable suspicion that you had missed out on the 'real' war. And civilians were not going to let you forget it.

## Mufti

On the day of their demob from the Royal Navy, Nobby Clark and Pincher Martin, the eponymous ex-ratings of Arthur Barker's 1950 comic novel *Nobby and Pincher in Civvy Street*, parade down Portsmouth High Street in the splendid finery provided for them by a grateful nation. Like all demobilised British servicemen,[48] Nobby and Pincher have each been fitted out with a 'demob suit' – a complete civilian outfit, from cufflinks to shoes. Yet neither man feels particularly at ease in his new attire. Quite the contrary:

> It was the first time they'd worn civvies for donkey's years, and instead of being touched for luck by everybody – including kids with jammy fingers – were stared at and passed by, with the under-toned remark *just demobbed* . . .

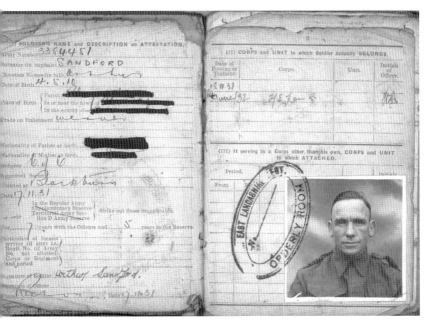

**1** The Service and Pay book of Arthur Sandford, who enlisted in the East Lancashire Regiment in November 1931. Like many regular soldiers, Sandford's discharge from HM Forces was postponed indefinitely by the outbreak of war in 1939. By the time the war ended, his 'short-service' enlistment had lasted fourteen years.

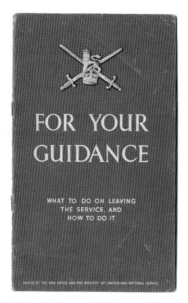

2 *For Your Guidance* and *Release and Resettlement,* two of the mass-produced booklets distributed to all servicemen in the spring of 1945 to explain the demobilisation scheme. Most men were discharged according to their Release Group Number, which they could calculate on a table by looking up their age and the number of months they had spent in wartime military service.

3  Labour Party general election poster, July 1945. The vast majority of servicemen who voted in the first postwar election supported Labour, mainly because they hoped for speedier demobilisation under the People's Party. But the new Labour government's unwillingness to release more men from the Forces after Japan's surrender in August was bitterly disappointing.

**4** Demobilisation notice board at RAF Mauripur, a giant transportation and maintenance base near Karachi. By January 1946, frustration at the slow repatriation of wartime conscripts and complaints about squalid living conditions and pedantic discipline brought the men at Mauripur and dozens of other RAF stations in the Far East out on strike. Over 50,000 men are believed to have taken part in the protests, one of the largest acts of indiscipline in the history of the British armed forces.

**5** A brass band at Southampton Docks welcomes home troops of the 2nd Army, returning from Germany, in November, 1945. With millions of men trickling home one by one over the eighteen months of demobilisation, most homecomings were less colourful. 'There was no excitement,' wrote one soldier: 'we had come full circle, not with a bang, but a whimper.'

**6** With their bomb-damaged windows draped with bunting, one couple awaits the return of a soldier son. Many servicemen who had been abroad since the outbreak of war were shocked on their repatriation to see the condition of blitzed cities such as London, Liverpool, and Coventry.

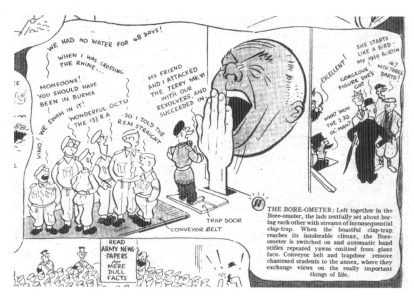

7 'The Bore-ometer', as described by *Soldier* magazine in January 1946. Returned servicemen were disappointed by the apparent lack of interest their families showed in their war stories. 'Nobody asked how we were – nobody said anything,' complained one ex-soldier bitterly.

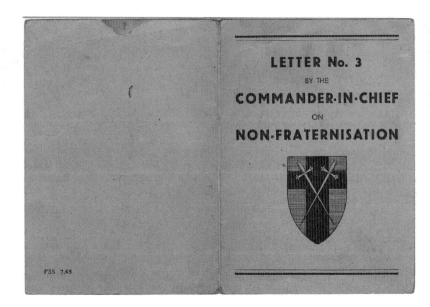

**8 & 9** Pamphlet issued by Field Marshal Montgomery's headquarters warning British troops in occupied Germany not to fraternise with civilians. In practice, however, illicit 'fratting' with locals, especially girls, was rife. Back in Britain, a hysterical press campaign in autumn 1945 alleged that the British Army in Germany was being subverted by female fifth columnists. Sexual jealousy and suspicion on the part of both husbands and wives was inevitable after years of separation.

**10 & 11** An RAF airman selects his demob suit at the vast clothing depot at Wembley. Although many ex-servicemen complained about the bad fit and garish style of the suits they were issued, they didn't always appreciate how lucky they were to have new clothes at

all in austerity Britain. Service life was sheltered from the rigours of civilian rationing and shortages, as this NAAFI counter laden with sweets, tobacco, and cigarettes suggests. Adjusting to life outside the 'khaki cocoon' could be a trial.

**12 & 13** A spokesman for the neo-fascist British League of Ex-Service Men and Women delivers an oration in 1948. Despite being banned during the war, Oswald Mosley's Blackshirt party reorganised itself in the postwar years by recruiting disaffected ex-Forces men. To disrupt the Mosleyite revival, demobbed Jewish soldiers formed the 43 Group, which launched commando-style raids on British League meetings. The clandestine military-style atmosphere of the conflict (secret memos were circulated amongst 43 Group volunteers) attracted ex-servicemen bored by peace.

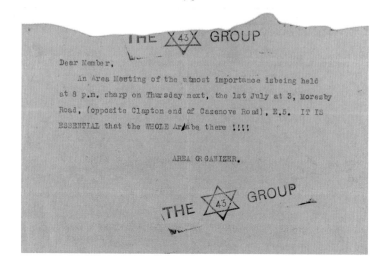

THE ✡43✡ GROUP

Dear Member,

An Area Meeting of the utmost importance is being held at 8 p.m. sharp on Thursday next, the 1st July at 3, Moresby Road, (opposite Clapton end of Cazenove Road), E.5. IT IS ESSENTIAL that the WHOLE Area be there !!!!

AREA ORGANIZER.

THE ✡43✡ GROUP

**14 & 15** An anti-looting notice on the outskirts of Ravenna. Despite the best efforts of the Royal Military Police, trafficking in millions of pounds' worth of 'liberated' goods took place in every theatre of war. Much contraband ended up being fenced by servicemen in black market bazaars such as 'Loot Alley' (Cutler Street) in East London. By the end of the war it was commonly alleged that military service was an apprenticeship in crime.

**16 & 17** Former prisoner-of-war Clem Morgan (Trevor Howard) dodges the law in the 1947 noir thriller *They Made Me a Fugitive*. The brutalised ex-serviceman wreaking violence on the home front was a stock figure of postwar British cinema. Neville Heath, hanged in 1946 for the sadistic murders of two women, was the real-life archetype: 'If ever a man seemed like a gallant young officer of World War II,' suggests Heath's biographer, 'it was he.'

**18** Dustjacket of the children's novel *Gimlet* Lends a Hand (1949), by Biggles creator W.E. Johns. Unlike his dashing aerial predecessor, the ex-commando Gimlet is a cold-eyed maverick with scant regard for the niceties of the law – a perfect illustration of the ambivalent public attitude towards Britain's special forces veterans.

**19** Bill Bates, telegraphist on the destroyer-escort HMS Goodall, the last ship of the Royal Navy to be sunk by a U-Boat in the Second World War. Bates was one of the few survivors pulled out of the icy arctic water after Goodall was torpedoed on 29 April, 1945. He suffered years of post-traumatic stress disorder (PTSD) as a result of his harrowing experiences.

**20** Liberated prisoners of war catch up on news of the Japanese surrender on Sumatra, summer 1945. By war's end, over 40,000 British servicemen had spent more than five years in captivity. Prolonged imprisonment left profound physical and mental scars; of all the Britons who returned home at the end of the Second World War, ex-POWs faced the most difficult adjustment to normal life.

*Everybody seems to know our history sheets by these 'ere togs. Pity the government didn't rig us out in plus fours and sports suits. Might just as well 'ave put a broad arrow on our backs instead of a chalk stripe in our flannels. Marked men, that's what we are in this rig.*[49]

Many real-life demobbed men grumbled about this conspicuousness. One recalled the unmistakable sight of fellow ex-soldiers at Manchester station: 'You could pick out the people who'd been demobbed – there with their raincoats, all with trilby hats, and a big brown box tied up with string.'[50] 'It was strange to walk around a lot of young men your age wearing virtually the same suit,' agreed Eric Feakins, who had just returned from Palestine.[51] 'You looked like bookends – everyone looked the same,' recalled Tony Cameron, who'd been with the Durham Light Infantry in Austria.[52] The demob suit, others agreed, was simply 'one uniform received in exchange for another'.[53]

Ironically, that all too conspicuous demob suit – the universal badge of the ex-servicemen in the late 1940s, and one of the best-known artifacts of twentieth-century British material culture, as iconic as the tailcoat or the miniskirt – had been dreamed up in order to help ex-servicemen blend imperceptibly into the crowd. Before October 1944, any man who left the Forces had to trade in his uniform for an ad hoc package of civilian clothes of austerity pattern. The result could be embarrassing. One disabled Scottish ex-serviceman complained to *John Bull*:

I was given a brick-red overcoat, a brown suit, a grey cap, an Army shirt with a collar that was mauve in colour and two-and-a-half sizes too big, one blue and silver tie, a pair of Army socks and a pair of Army boots. I had to travel in this hideous outfit from Durham to Glasgow and I don't think it was my crutches that drew so many looks of pity.[54]

The spectre of a generation of homecoming heroes returning to civilian life looking like beggars had worried Major-General W.W. Richards, the War Office's Director of Clothing and Stores.

'After the last war,' he explained to the *Sunday Express*, 'when I saw people lining up for jobs it was easy to pick out the ex-soldier. He wore the issue suit, Army greatcoat, hobnail boots and a cap! His clothes were often his biggest handicap in job hunting and he knew it.'[55] Richards sought to prevent this humiliation recurring. He obtained approval for a generous clothing gratuity to be awarded to every demobilised ex-serviceman. Most importantly, all garments would be non-utility. Made of the highest available quality material by professional tailors – some even hailing from Saville Row – demob suits were the first high-quality men's clothes to be produced in Britain since the early years of the war.

Not that every demob suit was necessarily a sartorial master-piece. Some servicemen complained about their ferocious patterns and unflattering cut. Reactions were often far from complimentary: 'obviously a pre-war seventy-five-bob effort. Not any sort of suit I would buy . . . foul.'[56] 'Gaudy.'[57] 'It fairly screams at you.'[58] 'A ghastly garment of stiff brown serge with purple stripes which made me look like an old-time gangster.'[59] 'Like walking around in a pair of pyjamas.'[60]

Yet what returning ex-servicemen didn't always appreciate at first was how fortunate they were to be getting any clothes at all. By 1945 the British civilian male was a sorry-looking specimen. The possessor on average of four shirts and two or three pairs of trousers, none likely to be in good condition, he was patching the holes in his shoes with spare bits of cardboard and paper.[61] Prewar wardrobes had been cannibalised to destruction. Scruffiness was an unavoidable fact of life. By contrast, the demobbed man was a prince amongst paupers – literally 'a cut above the rest of us', as J.B. Priestley put it.[62] No wonder, then, that he looked so conspicuous.

The ex-servicemen's good fortune was paid for by everyone else. By October 1945 demand for demob suits was so great that tailors were churning out 75,000 a week, and production of other civilian garments had to be scaled down to save cloth.[63] The dearth of materials, warned manufacturers, might make it impossible to honour coupons, and thus one of the early acts of the incoming Labour government in the summer of 1945 was to cut the clothes ration by

25 per cent, forcing civilians to eke out thirty-six coupons for a year.[64] By the following April the Board of Trade was receiving 1,200 letters a week from people petitioning for an extra ration.[65]

Not only did each ex-serviceman receive a suit, but he also got ninety bonus coupons to re-accoutre himself above and beyond his basic outfit. With these he became a source of patronage. A government survey in December 1945 found that four in ten demobilised men were contributing at least some of their coupons towards a family pool from which other relatives could draw.[66]

Even receiving one's suit involved a series of luxuries ordinarily denied the common man. 'From the moment that I entered the dispersal centre until, laden with a complete civilian outfit, I emerged from the clothing store, I met nothing but quiet efficiency and outstanding courtesy,' reported an ex-Lieutenant Colonel of the Irish Guards to *The Times*:

> Soldiers hurried to show me the way; officers and NCOs, obviously masters of their subjects, explained clearly and patiently the intricacies of ration cards, new identity cards, and gratuities: experts helped me to choose my clothes, socks, and shoes: and NAAFI attendants took infinite pains to ensure that I was supplied with the cigarettes that I like.[67]

These were not privileges accorded merely to the exalted ranks. 'Wing Commanders smile at you, Squadron leaders bow to you and Flight Lieutenants open doors for you,' reported Leading Aircraftman Brian Poole, ordinarily a student of cynicism, in a letter to his American penpal.[68] For one demobbing sailor, 'the Place of the Civvy Suit' was a veritable Aladdin's Cave:

> This is still in the barracks, but like nothing else in the barracks. Rooms tastefully painted in cream and green. Large lists of the civvy clothing to which we are 'entitled'. Shop windows with examples of the civvy garments which we can get: and good stuff too. A polite gentleman (in civvies), eager to measure us, to show us his goods, to hear our choice, to fit and please us in the good old

way. This raincoat or that? A suit – or sports coat and grey flannel trousers? What colour coat? . . . we are back in the land of freedom – of choice.[69]

Choice! Courtesy! Entitlement! What precious commodities these had become in a land where retail had become synonymous with rudeness and petty tyranny, and where people joined queues even when it was unclear what they were queuing for – half a pound of liver, perhaps, or a cooking apple, or nothing.[70] And as many newly demobilised servicemen were about to discover to their shock, in a lot of other respects they'd had an easier existence in uniform than they were going to have out of it.

No one disputed the authentic sacrifices of the military life, which, as Captain Raymond Blackburn put it in the *Daily Herald* in December 1945, were not so much the dust and danger of battle as subtler psychological ordeals:

> The pain of prolonged separation from family and the frustration and boredom . . . the growing terror of nothing to think about . . . the constant invasions of privacy: the petty irritations of day-to-day Service life . . . [during the war] one sensed the suffering of those who endured silent agony through the restraints on individuality which group life imposes, seeming almost to turn a man into an automaton.[71]

Yes, military service even far from the 'sharp end' was dreary, frustrating, sometimes degrading. But it was also a shelter – a khaki cocoon – from many of the practical problems of civilian life: rationing, shortages, the day-to-day scramble to make ends meet in wartime. 'If you look at it one way it could be said that we were thoroughly molly-coddled,' admitted one former sailor in his postwar memoirs:

> No rent, no rates to pay. No maintenance or repairs to see to . . . all your food was provided free . . . no need to worry about money . . . no fear of redundancies, of the firm going bankrupt or being taken

over. Plenty of companionship, plenty of card games on the mess-decks on evenings onboard, free cinema shows, free postage for letters (and free French letters if you wanted them), free medical treatment . . . free lighting, the advantage of living only a few yards from your place of work . . . put that way, what a cushy way of life it seems to have been.[72]

Life in the Forces had been financially subsidised. British troops had complained bitterly about their pay during the war, and indeed their basic daily rate was much lower than that of industrial war-workers at home. But a much higher proportion of the British serviceman's income was available for discretionary spending, since so many of the essentials of life were taken care of for him. 'When I was away, I heard about youths in Britain earning £10 and £15 a week,' reported a demobbed veteran of the Fourteenth Army:

It had made my blood boil while we were sweating in a jungle on a few shillings a day. Now I'm beginning to see how impossible it is to live on present-day civilian wages – let alone pre-war pay. The value of money is topsy-turvy. With free keep, free clothes, free travel, family allowance, cheap cigarettes and entertainment, I was much better off in the Army.[73]

By comparison, civilian workers were expected to pay for every-thing out of their wages. Conscripted miners – the 'Bevin Boys' – received about the same amount of 'pocket money' a week as soldiers but had to buy their own clothing, even their own shovels.[74]

So the demobbed were about to develop a new and unwelcome acquaintance with all the annoying practical concerns that they'd been able to ignore in the Forces. Responsibilities that had previously been the job of others were abruptly returned to the new civilian. 'I'm bothered by minor jobs I never had to worry about in the Services,' moaned one ex-corporal to *John Bull*:

I have to take the laundry, and calculate so that I have enough to wear before I can collect it again. My shoes want mending and I have to find a cobbler, take them, fetch them, and incidentally pay about 7s 6d. I have to watch not to get my suit dirty, and I can't spend my money on one grand night out because I have to eat at the end of the week too . . . I'm more harassed by small worries than I have been for five years.[75]

*Punch* had great fun with the idea of a former army officer demanding the same conditions of employment at his new job that he had enjoyed for the last six years:

The bulk of salary allotted as income-tax-free allowances;
Seven day's holiday every three months with paid fares both ways;
Free meals;
Free clothing and footwear;
Free medical and dental treatment;
Free or subsidized entertainment, laundry and haircuts;
A car, chauffeur, and domestic servant on call;
Complete security and freedom from dismissal no matter how badly you conducted yourself.[76]

'There's a lot of truth in the joke that the Army will need a toughening course to fit the troops for civil life,' suggested the *Daily Express* in October 1945. It was going to take time for men used to the largesse of the quartermaster and the cookhouse to plan out their own lives for themselves: food, clothes, fuel and quarters were no longer going to appear miraculously through the energies of the War Office.[77]

Indeed, there were serious suggestions that the Forces had sapped British men of any willingness to exert themselves. 'At one time an idler was despised by his workmates,' complained one reader of the *News Chronicle* in September 1946. 'Now it is with pride that a man announces that he isn't going to lose much sweat for this firm . . . I have been sorry to note that a large minority of recently demobbed ex-servicemen take this line. Service life has turned them out maladjusted.'[78] Cracks about 'stripes disease', 'pippitis', 'air crews' chest', 'storeman's clutch', 'ranker's dodge' and other debilitating medical conditions peculiar to service life began to do the rounds. Ex-servicemen, it was alleged, were refusing to 'demean themselves by doing manual labour any more'.[79]

It was widely believed that military service was a schooling in sloth, with 'scrimshanking' – the deliberate avoidance of work whenever possible – a difficult habit to shed. Ex-servicemen were stigmatised as shiftless. 'The effect of army life on a normal young man is generally deplorable, rarely beneficial,' grumbled two NCOs in a 1946 letter to the *Daily Herald*: 'The Army is the easiest of jobs . . . as a result the soldier is unproductive and lazy'.[80] Some servicemen admitted that they had indeed developed bad work habits in the Forces. 'Adapting yourself after a life in the services is very hard,' admitted Victor Morrison of the Fleet Air Arm. 'You get terribly lazy – always too many people to do too few jobs. You could wander around with a piece of paper in your hand pretending to do something and no-one would question you.'[81] Awaiting demob, airman Brian Poole complained that: 'I'm lazy now and haven't the will to do things like I used to do.'[82] Some were less troubled by this languor. One of the respondents to Seebohm Rowntree's 1951 study of *English Life and Leisure* looked back on his army days with great nostalgia: 'Plenty of grub and nothing to do.'[83]

Returned ex-servicemen seemed so clueless about the difficulties of ordinary postwar life back in Britain that civilians weren't sure whether to mock them, condemn them, or pity them. 'We completely misunderstand [their] point of view if, when they voice surprise at life's threadbare quality, we assume they are complaining,' suggested *Woman*. 'Their shocked exclamations are genuine astonishment at a state of affairs which produces in the rest of us a numbed, accustomed acceptance.'[84] The *Daily Mirror* lent a conciliatory shoulder to cry on:

> Those of us who have been at home have of course got used to the social asperities of daily life which war conditions produced, but men and women coming out of the Forces after several years' absence abroad appear to be depressed at the atmosphere in which

they find themselves. Setting out gaily to make a few purchases, they soon come up against, not merely the absence of the goods they want, but of a frigid, half contemptuous manner on the part of the exponents of the eternal 'No'. This makes the returned warrior wonder what has become of the warm-hearted Britain he used to know.[85]

## Military Corpulence

'There must be a racket on somewhere,' wrote Royal Artillery Bombardier Arthur Harris, after he arrived in occupied Germany in December 1945. 'Not only do we get too much to eat but everything in the canteen seems to be issued free. Even the beer is free, as much as you want.'[86] By January he had settled in nicely to the holiday conditions. 'It is a home from home this unit, with practically no discipline as the army knows it, and plenty of Germans to do anything that wants doing for a cigarette or two.'[87] Harris found daily life at his barracks almost absurdly undemanding. 'It is like living in a hotel here, there are so many people to wait on you.'[88]

Soldiers such as Harris arriving in the British Occupation Zone (BOZ) for the first time were often surprised at what they found. Cities such as Hamburg had been laid waste by bombing or ground combat. Many German civilians were living pitiful lives amongst the rubble, homeless and starving. But some areas seemed virtually untouched by war; indeed, the quality of life there was far better than in Britain. 'The first feature to strike the eye of the newcomer [is] the beauty and prosperity of the German country-side,' reported Lieutenant-Colonel John Sparrow to the War Office in May 1945: 'The farms were well kept and well stocked; in the country districts there was certainly plenty of food; and the average German peasant (at any rate in Oldenberg and Hanover) seemed to have gone about his business without being appreciably affected by the war . . . this certainly impressed itself on the troops.'[89]

As rumours of this prosperity grew back in Britain, they were accompanied by claims that the British Army was wallowing in a private island of sordid plenty while those at home lived lives of cheerless asceticism.[90] The publisher Victor Gollancz, who toured the British Occupation Zone of Germany shortly after the war to research his book *In Darkest Germany* (1947), was outraged at the luxury enjoyed by the occupiers: 'Our officers' messes are at worst pleasurably comfortable,' he wrote:

> And such of the senior ones as I visited were, for the most part, quietly and discreetly luxurious. Every time I entered such a mess before dinner the atmosphere reminded me very vividly of Singapore in 1918: there was the same sense of happy relaxation, the same feeling that you belonged to a privileged caste.[91]

Army literature exacerbated suspicions that Germany was a gigantic holiday camp for its soldiers. 'Hun Luxury Town For BLA' read the *Daily Mirror*'s headline at the announcement that Bad Harzburg, a tourist spa in lower Saxony untouched by war, was to become the occupation zone's main troop rest centre.[92] 'There is a fair chance,' suggested the information booklet provided to soldiers, 'that you may be the lucky one to have French windows opening onto a balcony overlooking the mountains.'[93] Soldiers could apparently also enjoy:

> A stableful of horses . . . excellent lawn tennis courts, a clay pigeon shoot, fishing trips, swimming . . . pleasantly exhausted by all this exercise, stroll down to the café in the town and repair the tissues with tea, cakes, and ice-cream; visit the shopping arcade and buy cigarettes, pipes, and tobacco, perfume, cosmetics and brilliantine; have your tunic pressed by the valet service; get your nails mani-cured at the friseur and your hair cut, trimmed, singed, dyed, restored or permanently waved . . . fit an excellent dinner anywhere in this programme and you'll all be set for the cinema, a symphony concert, or dancing at the Kurhans ballroom . . .[94]

Not all of this should be taken at face value. Away from the delights of Bad Harzburg, British servicemen complained about the lack of entertainment in garrison towns.[95] But a few lucky servicemen truly, if briefly, found themselves living out the fantasy. After a road traffic accident, sapper Edward Kirby recuperated in a swan-shaped bedroom at the baronial schloss in Ostenwalde, which was being used as Montgomery's 21st Army Group headquarters.[96] Dennis Middleton's demobilisation was peremptorily deferred because he was needed to run a ski club in the Harz mountains ('there's the Army for you,' he later noted); among those on the piste were Douglas Sutherland and other members of the Allied Liaison Group, who also enjoyed the 'horsey events' and other splendid opportunities to relax for which 30 Corps became well known.[97]

Ian Harris, a Jewish refugee from Austria who had served in the Royal Marine Commandos and whose language skills eventually found him a place as an interpreter with the British Control Commission, enjoyed himself immensely. 'It only served to ruin me even further for any normal civilian life,' he admitted. 'While everyone else was getting on with resettlement courses I was busy driving Goering's light-blue Mercedes around Berlin.'[98]

British civilians, bewailing their 'tobacco famine', particularly resented the flood of cigarettes into Europe. By autumn 1945 over 350 million were being distributed gratis by the NAAFI in service canteens every week, with another 200 million shipped to the Continent duty-free because of a loophole in the customs and excise regulations.[99] It was widely assumed – and not without reason – that these massive shipments were fueling the Continent's black-market economy. Tobacconists in Lincolnshire refused to serve RAF men because of the widespread belief that cigarettes were being smuggled into Europe from the numerous local air stations.[100]

But it was the amount of food available to the Forces that provoked the most shock back in Britain. 'We had as much meat for one day's dinner as we get in a week at home,' admitted a former captain in the Allied Control Commission in Italy after his return to his old civil service job in Britain.[101] During his final week in Belgium one soldier about to be demobilised claimed to have eaten fifteen new-laid eggs.[102] By 1945 ex-servicemen were coming home from the war literally too big for their britches, thanks to the bolstering power of high-calorie military rations. In May 1946, despite reductions during the previous summer and autumn, home service soldiers were still receiving thirty-five ounces of meat per week compared to fourteen for civilians; more than double the amount of bacon; twice as much cheese; and five ounces more sugar.[103] Servicewomen were getting more meat and bacon than coal miners.[104]

Many working-class personnel, particularly those on home service or in support branches, experienced a much better diet in the Forces than they had ever enjoyed in prewar civilian days. The army had once been notorious for its rotten food, but thanks to the introduction of the specialist Catering Corps in 1941, meals available to soldiers had greatly improved by the end of the war.[105] The vast network of NAAFI and Women's Voluntary Service (WVS) canteens also supplemented the serviceman's diet with free or heavily subsidised tea, sweets and other snacks.[106] 'Military corpulence' was a common problem for ex-soldiers who had lived well on army-strength rations.[107] For example, demobbed former jockeys were sometimes too large to compete any more, so Newmarket was faced with a shortage of riders.[108]

Adjusting to home-front levels of consumption could be hard after such largesse. One careless demobbed soldier finished off his household's weekly fat ration in two meals and drank all the tea in the house in three days.[109] Maggie Lanning remembered her father digging hungrily into the cheese on the dining table and asking her mother whether there was any more: '*no dear, you've just eaten the family's ration for the week*'. Afterwards 'he was very quiet'.[110]

Many servicemen became embarrassed at the profligacy of their own rations. 'Every time I come home on leave I realize forcefully that in the camp dining hall I get more meat daily than the rest of the family at home get in a week . . . the waste of bread is often shameful,' wrote one soldier.[111] Aldershot's food committee reported that soldiers who were doing very little were buying seven or eight chocolate bars a night at a time when children were lucky to receive any.[112] 'In the base areas of the continent there are many thousands of staff officers, many of them little more than clerks, eating three great meals a day, while liberated townspeople are scrabbling in their dustbins for scraps,' complained one soldier. French and Belgian civilians were manifestly starving in front of men eating beautifully cooked meals unimaginable even back in England, let alone in the shanties of the Continent's malnourished refugees.[113]

As the pace of discharge remained sluggish throughout the winter of 1945, gossip spread at home that some men were deliberately avoiding release from the Forces in order to enjoy the benefits of their continental lifestyle. 'I hear of generals and air-marshals settling down in castles which have been converted into palatial headquarters, with enormous staffs, apparently for a lifetime,' wrote the Conservative MP Robert Boothby in the *News of the World*: 'A number of people have dug themselves into "cushy" jobs, from which they are in no hurry to be ejected.'[114]

In April 1945 the *Manchester Guardian* stirred up a minor public scandal when its Rome correspondent suggested that British soldiers enjoying a life of luxury in Italy would find it hard to adjust to life in grey austerity Britain. How would demobbed officers and NCOs face up to the mundane existence back in England without their servants, their white-coated waiters bringing up their morning tea, their chauffeured jeeps and their opera boxes?[115] The *Manchester Guardian* was forced to apologise after a stream of invective from the readers of *Union Jack*, the newspaper of the Italian occupation forces. But one demobilised officer fully endorsed the original claim: the spoiled elite of occupied Europe would find its repatriation to drab civilian reality traumatising. 'The article . . . could be duplicated elsewhere – in Belgium, Holland, Germany, and the Middle East,' he claimed:

> There is little to defend the level of extreme luxury which is now being supplied. It is not easy for the demobilized man, especially the officer, to come down to present-day civilian earth, but it is made far more difficult by the standard of living he has had to leave. I venture to say that in Brussels (to give one instance) more champagne is drunk nightly in officers' clubs than in the whole of London . . . the temptation of the black market looms on all sides.

But this easy money is fatal to the real work one must face on demobilisation. Already many Service men, especially officers, dread being demobilized because they do not want to give up this luxury living.[116]

## Some of These People Make Me Feel Like Murder

For most ex-servicemen, the suggestion that military life was one of pampered idleness was, not surprisingly, infuriating. 'As one who has had five years holiday in foreign lands at public expense,' wrote a seething veteran to *Picture Post*, 'I feel that it is high time I turned my hand to honest work and civilian life while some over-burdened civilians are given the chance of rest and recuperation in the Forces. Why should the delights of a camping holiday in sunny Burma or a cruise to Japan be denied these jaded people?'[117]

To men who had seen want and destitution many times worse while abroad, complaints about austerity could seem like carping. Compared to, say, rural India, even wartime Britain was a land of plenty. When flying over rural Somerset in the summer of 1945, Harold Scull remembered vividly the 'great big fat sleek brown cows', very different from the 'skinny scrawny things you were used to seeing' in the Far East.[118] Soldiers who had undergone horrors far greater than anything experienced in wartime Britain were, not surprisingly, contemptuous of civilian complaints. 'Frankly, the moans in the UK about shortages made us sick,' remembered ex-prisoner of war Howard Baker, who after a month's hospital treatment still weighed under six stone. 'The mass doesn't know or care what starvation or privation is; they've seen a few grisly pictures in the Daily Comic. They want the portion due to them and are the most wasteful people we've seen.'[119]

'People who had been in England through all the war told me what a terrible place it now was,' wrote another returned prisoner:

This made me angry. When you have been really hungry, and know that there are millions who still are, it is not pleasant to hear people talking about a food shortage when what they really mean is a shortage of the things they particularly like to eat. When you have known discomfort, not for minutes or hours but for years on end, it is not easy to sympathize with people who complain about having to stand in a queue. When you have seen a society completely smashed in defeat it is absurd to hear someone talking about 'the intolerable curse of being unable to get a taxi'.[120]

'People at home should try living on compo rations for a week,' complained a *John Bull* reader. 'Contrary to some newspaper stories, the boys out here [in the Far East] do not get fresh eggs and fruit whenever we like.'[121] 'Some of these people make me feel like murder when they tell me what a good time I'm having, and how hard is the life of a civilian,' raged one aircraftman. 'I know that service life has many things to recommend it but what these people do not realize is that it is also BONDAGE!'[122]

Still, some servicemen were willing to concede that a khaki cocoon existed. 'Why treat us servicemen different from anyone else?' wrote one airman in Greece to *Union Jack*. 'Many of the people back home have seen more action and suffered more injuries than a lot of fellows in the Services, so why make a fuss about us when we come back?'[123] A fellow soldier in Italy agreed:

> To build up a country worthy of our efforts in this war, we must all – civilians and service folks alike – learn to appreciate the outlook of our fellow countrymen. We in the Services must remember that the people who stayed at home did not just have a life flowing with milk and honey . . . let us each and all forget what we individually did in the war and get together to keep Britain in her rightful place.[124]

'We must,' David Scott Daniell warned his fellow repatriates, 'be prepared to be less wonderful than we think we are.'[125] There was wisdom to that, of course. But it seemed like an odd kind of an epitaph to six years of blood and tears. It had been a funny old war, hadn't it?

# CHAPTER FIVE

# Clocking On

*Could you really imagine me going back to being a junior clerk?*[1]

On the night of 11 September 1943, as the minesweeper *HMS Circe* lay offshore of Salerno, Italy, taking part in the furious naval bombardment of the Allied invasion beachhead that had been established so precariously two days earlier, Royal Navy coder K.B. Huntbatch wrote up his daily diary entry as usual. His concerns that night had nothing to do with the furious battle raging within a few miles of *Circe*, however. Huntbatch was thinking about the future:

I'm afraid I want to do too many things, I am too moody. My greatest desire is to be a farmer in England, but I sometimes wonder if I shall be able to stick in one spot day after day, year after year. I have only seen small parts of the English countryside and there are still hundreds of places there which I want to visit besides these foreign countries. If I become a farmer then I shall just have to stay put. The ideal way, of course, is to wander while I am still young and then when I get tired of it, settle down to farming. The only trouble is money. The only way to obtain that is by work and plenty of it so how can you obtain it by wandering around as a tramp. Farming and capital as well as experience ... oh! What's the use of wondering about all these things.[2]

Three months earlier and thousands of miles away, somewhere on the Moulmein Road on the border between Thailand and Burma, Sergeant W.M. Innes-Ker, a slave labourer on the Bangkok to Rangoon 'Death Railway', had written an imaginary letter to his wife back in England. Like Huntbatch, Innes-Ker was dwelling on the problems of peace:

There are two main plans I have for the future ... *Plan one:* At South Walsham with Aunt Agnes, raising hens, bees, hiring the meadow below the paddock and having a few calves and pigs. All this, according to expert Norfolk smallholders here might net us £200 a year. Possibly writing short stories in the winter. *Plan two:* With what little capital will fall due to me, and this I estimate at £200 army pay, £300 gratuity and possibly £100 from HG and Co., equip a small cake shop in London (or Yarmouth) and bake our own stuff. I could take a course in cake-making and feel sure could make a success of this.[3]

For Huntbatch and Innes-Ker, in their different ways, the end of the war did not simply mean a return to the old job and the old routine. They were looking for something new: a clean slate and a fresh start.

It is a little astonishing that the return to work of over four million such men in the space of just two or three years, after the traumatic interruptions of military service, should have been regarded by historians as so inconsequential. Yet there's little or no mention of the demob experience in accounts of the postwar British labour force.

It is not that men like Huntbatch and Innes-Ker couldn't find jobs. Britain's problem at the end of the Second World War turned out to be an acute manpower shortage, not a surplus. And both Labour and the Conservatives were publicly committed to a full-employment policy by the May 1944 coalition white paper. Postwar Britain would be a bleak and austere place in many ways, but few who wanted work were left idle. In March 1946 only 24,500 recently demobilised men were drawing the dole. Disguised within that figure were some sub-groups, such as older ex-officers with acute problems; still, most ex-servicemen were finding some kind of job.[4] Veterans were not left on street corners selling matches.

But that does not mean that the return to civilian work after the war was a seamless transition. 'Men will find factory life monotonous and office conditions lonely after the tempo and companionship of the Forces,' *Soldier* magazine presciently forecast in March 1945. 'They have learned new crafts and techniques, and will feel frustrated if they are merely put back on their old jobs. In no way can they be considered the same individuals who left benches and stools to go to war.'[5]

And so it proved. After coming back from Italy, ex-fusilier Bert Scrivens had trouble settling back into his job in an advertising agency. 'I couldn't get used to being stuck in an office, at a desk. I'd been too used to being out – free to do as I wanted to do my job, no-one overseeing me most of the time.'[6] The drudgery and physical toil of factory work could be hard on minds and muscles adapted to a simpler outdoor life. Vic Emery, who had just returned from Palestine, was released to return to work twelve-hour shifts as a machine operator at a cardboard mill in Bristol. The suffocating physical conditions of the work – the vast drying cylinders churning out steam, water and hot air – knocked a stone off him in three weeks. 'I'd just spent four years out in the open air, never been indoors at all.' He worked seventy-one hours for £7 1s.[7]

Fred Hazell, who had returned to work in a draughtsman's office after serving as a sergeant with the Royal Norfolk Regiment in the Far East, was another man who found himself struggling to readjust. 'Having gone abroad for the first time and gotten away from the family, going back to civilian life was most difficult to get into. Once I left the office at the end of the day my head was buzzing so much that I was likely to walk out the door and walk under a bus by mistake.'[8] Hazell found that he 'still had the sergeant-major attitude towards everything'. Younger employees who had not served in the Forces were undisciplined in comparison: 'I threatened to throw them out of the jolly old window.'[9]

Bert Wolstenholme, a former wireless operator on a Lancaster bomber, had a similar problem when he got back to work on the railways in Manchester in 1946: he couldn't stop hitting his bosses. 'The inspector walked in and wanted to know what I was doing . . . he kept on and on at me and the next minute I'd just put one on him. And I was sacked.' He then went to work for Crown wallpaper and promptly did the same thing. 'Things were so mundane . . .'[10]

## Back to the Old Firm

Not all men agonised over what to do when they left the Forces. Leslie Westcott, who had served in India and Burma since 1939, got home from the Far East one Sunday. The following morning he was back at work on the railways.[11] For men like Westcott, reassimilation boiled down to one simple request: *Let me have my old job back*.

Many ex-servicemen, looking back to the dark days of the 1930s' slump and the dole queues, prized stability over ambition. In his 1943 study *Post-War Employment*, E.S. Conway claimed from his informal survey of serving soldiers that the great majority of servicemen were thinking conventionally about their future: 'To most soldiers,' he thought, 'the end of the war means no more than the continuation of a life which had been suddenly and unpleasantly disturbed.'[12] 'All I want is what I'm going to get,' one orderly told his officer the night the Germans surrendered in Italy: 'A nice little council house in Ruislip and a job on the council.'[13]

The 1944 Reinstatement in Civil Employment Act was the first major piece of demob legislation. It required employers to rehire ex-workers who had served in the wartime Forces for at least six to twelve months, depending on the length of their prewar service. To guarantee this right, ex-servicemen had to approach their old firms no more than a month after their demobilisation, and they had to be available for work within a further month. This meant, amongst other things, that returning men needed to get in contact with their former employers before their fifty-six-day paid discharge leave ended – a nicety that may have been lost on many men enjoying the carefree Indian summer of their military career.[14]

The 1944 Act left much unclear, however. Some vacant jobs were filled by men who had then been called up in their turn. Which ex-serviceman had the legal right to the job? The man who originally held it or the man who took his place? Many firms had reorganised during the war and had changed the nature of their business entirely. Did they still have to re-employ men whose workplace experience was now irrelevant? Bottlenecks in reconstruction meant that some prewar jobs were not yet viable: for instance, there was, in 1945, little work for salesmen in the retail and distributive trades, for production was still tightly controlled. But under the terms of the Act did these ex-employees have to be taken back on to the payroll anyway?[15]

And how should returning employees be graded and paid compared to their co-workers who had stayed on and perhaps prospered in their absence? Reinstated men were entitled to jobs with terms and conditions, including pay, no less favourable than those that they would have hypothetically received had they remained at their posts instead of joining the Forces. On the other hand, employers were only required to accommodate demands that were reasonable and practicable; if a job vacancy no longer existed, they could discharge their legal responsibility by offering an alternative, which it was up to the returning serviceman to accept or decline.[16] All of this made for some delicate negotiations. 'Once more we have the problem of a youth returning from the services,' fretted Sheffield accountant George Taylor in his diary, September 1946, in what must have been a typical employer's predicament:

He ha[d] left us as a junior of eighteen, and now returns as a man of twenty-two. During his four years' absence his little experience of accountancy has rusted away, and yet now he will want a man's wages. We decided to give him a 100% advance on the wages he received before going away, but I do not know whether he will be satisfied.[17]

Ex-servicemen who were not satisfied with the terms they were offered could turn to one of the local Reinstatement Tribunals that were set up by the Ministry of Labour to arbitrate grievances between employers and returning employees. Of the 4,782 claims taken up across Britain by the end of 1946, 2,033 ended with an order for reinstatement and 1,374 for compensation – in many cases, both. In Leicester, a son brought his own father before the local Reinstatement Committee after he was denied his old job back in the family textile firm. He won.[18]

But not everyone was left happy. Overall, more than half of the appeals were dismissed.[19] And even a successful claim was a double-edged sword. 'An employer . . . holds the whip hand in the long run,' warned *Union Jack*. 'An employee may stand on his rights. But if he does he will always have the ill will of that disgruntled employer hanging over his head. It is an awkward position.'[20] Many thousands of otherwise legitimate claimants must have chosen not to take their cases to tribunal rather than run the risk of antagonising their bosses.

In any case, the reception that men received from their former bosses and colleagues was not always a welcome one. Wartime had disrupted the generational hierarchy at work. Having to report to former peers or subordinates who had been promoted during the war – sometimes men young enough to be their children – could be galling. After commanding a gunnery school in occupied Austria, Royal Artillery officer Raymond Child found himself back making tea at his bank branch in rural Oxfordshire.[21] Cecil Wareham discovered that he was treated like an office boy by colleagues who had stayed at Cambridge University Press during his absence as a Royal Marine Commando.[22] Alan Hay discovered that commanding a battalion of the Durham Light Infantry in Italy didn't mean anything back in his old accountancy office.[23]

'I'd been away all this time – when I left them I was a rookie,' remembered Walter Harris when he was reinstated as a fitter at a car dealership. Harris was a former sergeant in the Royal Electrical and Mechanical Engineers who had won the Military Medal for meritorious service in Belgium. But when he returned 'they were treating me as if I was the young bloke that was with them those years before'.[24] Duncan McNie had left his bus garage as an inexperienced trainee and returned a fully trained fitter. 'I was a sergeant with twelve men under me who did what I told them,' he remembered, 'but I had to come back under another boss who had got the job not by what he knew but who he knew.'[25]

When Ron Ayers asked to be reinstated in his old job as a sales engineer for an electrical manufacturers:

> I was offered the same money as I was earning when I left. . . . I negotiated an increase with very subtle overtones of *you're very lucky, you know – people who've been here all through the war have earned their positions, blah blah blah* . . . and I began to realize that there was a very big gulf between those who went to war and those who didn't. I found that very difficult.

> I might as well have come from another planet. My time in the services had changed me tremendously. For somebody who'd never been further than London in his life, I'd been to the Mediterranean, America, West Indies, up to Russia – all these people had been going on doing the same old job; their life hadn't altered one whit in the past four years. I felt a bit disgruntled about that. Those who'd been in the services were carrying a penalty like a jockey who'd run too many races.[26]

In June 1946 the British Legion complained that some exservicemen were being accused of having 'let the firm down' by enlisting voluntarily rather than seeking reserved occupation status.[27] 'I visited my old employer,' wrote one demobbed veteran of the Far East campaign to *John Bull*, 'and his attitude knocked me cold . . . employers seem to be put out by [reinstatement]. The work of reshuffling staff is too big for them. I am not looking forward to returning to work in the atmosphere I sensed.'[28] Some bosses made it clear that they intended to fire any reinstated men once the regulations allowed them to. At a tribunal in Leeds a rent collector's office was fined for having paid a returned ex-serviceman £5 10s per week to sit in a chair doing nothing, waiting out his time until redundancy.[29]

Perhaps the reluctance to rehire ex-Forces men was because they were supposed to be difficult. After all, the Ministry of Labour's own postwar guide for industrial managers was cautioning that ex-servicemen might show very little initiative in the workplace, 'because they will have gotten into the habit of waiting for orders'.[30] Other experts warned bosses to expect friction and discontent from ex-service employees. According to Reg Ellery's *Psychiatric Aspects of Modern Warfare*, published in 1945:

It is not easy [for an ex-serviceman] to settle down to study or to apply himself to constant work. The life he has led in uniform has unfitted him for steady application; he is easily distracted by trifles. He looks instinctively for diversion or becomes apathetic and a little bewildered at the tasks which confront him. His routine is broken; he can neither pick up his tools nor open his text-books. He cannot concentrate. His emotions are disturbed by the impact of his new surroundings; and he often finds it difficult to control them. Life, no longer governed by army discipline, now presents problems he is ill-prepared to face, being thrown [back] on his own resources.[31]

It's true that the unquestioning rote system of learning in the army – best remembered now in Henry Reed's 1942 poem 'Naming of Parts' – did not encourage much critical thought. The evaluators of an experimental teacher-training programme for ex-servicemen at Goldsmith's College, London, commented that the students, though otherwise exemplary, 'were rather inclined to regard the lectures, which were meant to be provocative and conducive of discussion, as medieval dogma which could hardly be questioned'.[32] Even the Forces newspaper *Union Jack* suggested that 'several years of Army life have dulled [soldiers'] sense of appreciation and their ability to think things out for themselves'.[33]

Lieutenant-Colonel R.A.C. Radcliffe, who was the army's demobilisation liaison officer at the Ministry of Labour, suggested that foremen should be flexible about work discipline because new ex-service employees were liable to resist attempts at regimentation.[34] All this advice was no doubt well meant, but one wonders how many employers decided after this barrage of warnings that ex-servicemen were more trouble than they were worth.

## A Fresh Start

As *Union Jack* reported in August 1945, some servicemen weren't interested in going back to the old factory floor. They had developed fresh ideas about what to do after the war:

A mine-filler at a blast furnace, now a Regimental Sergeant-Major having disciplinary control of 1,400 men, asks for a more responsible post . . . a blast furnace labourer, now a lieutenant, would like an administrative post . . . a junior wages clerk, now a captain in the Pay Corps, expresses a desire for administrative work . . . a labourer, at present a staff-sergeant air-gunner, said: *unless wages are good, I will emigrate to the Dominions* . . . one former employee does not want to go back to his pre-war occupation as a miner. Now a driver-mechanic, he says: *I have got to have plenty of fresh air.*[35]

After three years as a wireless engineer in the Royal Navy, Ken Bean did not see the prospect of returning to his job at the Inland Revenue in the least bit appealing: 'I think I suffered from feelings many people had that I didn't know what I wanted to do.'[36] 'What job?' wondered Captain A.M. Bell MacDonald in a letter to a friend in May 1944: 'Solicitor, for which I'm trained on paper but after five years will be a trifle rusty? Strike out on a new note? The BBC? Interior decorating? Writing rather bad novels? International law research?'[37]

After all, men such as these had had their parochial prewar lives transformed beyond recognition by military service. Victor Bell, who took part in the ferocious Salerno landings in September 1943 as driver of a Humber reconnaissance scout car, had been a plumber in Civvy Street.[38] Joe Kidger, a milkman and apprentice painter and decorator, found himself searching for U-boats on a hunter-killer frigate in the Western Approaches.[39] Birkenhead schoolboy Harry Morrell became the navigator of a Beaufighter torpedo bomber, strafing Japanese transports on the Irrawaddy river in Burma.[40] John Gray, who had started the war as an errand boy for the Co-Op, drove a Honey light tank in Normandy.[41] Trevor Timperley left his Coventry insurance desk to train as a gunner on heavy bombers in Georgia and Alabama in the United States, before joining one of RAF Bomber Command's Pathfinder squadrons in the devastating firebombing raids on Hamburg and other German cities.[42]

Hundreds of thousands of men such as these had been plucked from workaday jobs and dusty offices to perform complex and exciting tasks in places they would once have been unable to locate on a map. Not every serviceman had regarded overseas duty as a burden; some relished the opportunity to travel. On his return to England in 1946, Dr. Robert Lees wrote wistfully about his experiences as a medical officer touring stations in Africa and the Near East:

> Many are the memories evoked: the absolute quiet of the moonlit desert: the stench and heat and noise of Baghdad; the beauty of Tehran; the heavy perfume of the Palestinian orange groves; the historical miracle of Jerusalem; the incredible beauty of spring flowers in the Jordan Valley; the bazaars of Damascus and Aleppo; the beat of drums at night in Khartoum at the feast of the Prophet; trout fishing on the slopes of Mount Kenya; Pretoria smothered in jacaranda blossom; the beauty of Capetown seen from Table Mountain; Vesuvius in eruption; Rome; Florence. All these, and a thousand more, were worth the fatigue and frustration, the heat and smells and flies.[43]

Other servicemen, who had not necessarily travelled across the world nor undergone the hazards of the front line, had nonetheless received rank, training and responsibilities far beyond anything they had ever enjoyed in civilian life, benefiting from all the perquisites of promotion as well as the emotional satisfaction of command. Little wonder, then, that the relief they shared at their return home at the end of the war was tinged with regret and unease at the prospect of resuming safer, but smaller, civilian lives. 'How are we to give the young men whose war work is adventurous and dignified a peacetime job they'll enjoy?' worried James Hodson in 1943. 'Thousands of young men and women whose pre-war jobs were not worth tuppence either in pay or dignity or true service have now got all three things.'[44]

How many servicemen decided to strike out on their own? It's impossible to know for sure, though there are some intriguing hints. When wartime demobilisation effectively ended in December 1946, one quarter of employees of the 'Big Four' railway companies – GWR, LMS, LNER and Southern – who had served in the Forces during the war, had not reported back to work.[45] More than 1,700 of the 3,700 former employees of the iron and steel manufacturer Dorman Long didn't respond to the company's questionnaire asking about their postwar plans in the summer of 1945. At least some of these men, presumably, must have had other plans in mind.[46]

Individual veterans had their own idiosyncratic motives for changing careers. John Frost, a clerk in the 11th Armoured Division, abandoned the idea of returning to his City firm because he wanted to stay mobile and wear a uniform; so he decided to become a bus conductor.[47] George Bell could not stomach the thought of going back to his old job at an ordinance factory after all the bloodshed he'd seen as an ASDIC sonar operator on a destroyer sub-chaser, and tried teaching instead.[48] After his years of captivity, life as a bank clerk held little remaining attraction for ex-POW Corrie Halliday, who planned to travel to New Zealand to work as a rancher instead. 'I wanted to be active. A labouring job – sheep farming – gave me the opportunity of getting physically tired and forgetting all the mental strains and stresses.'[49]

The plans of others may have been shaped by the new skills they had learned while in the Forces. Thousands of men had been taught to drive, operate heavy machinery and repair electrical equipment. By the end of 1944, 881,000 soldiers were classified as tradesmen, and around a quarter of a million of them taught in the army's technical training groups.[50] RAF personnel at home and abroad in the last month of the European war included hundreds of thousands of fitters, drivers, communications specialists, wireless and radar maintenance technicians, armourers, electricians, instrument technicians, machinists, metalworkers, clerks, instructors, meteorologists, medics, and so on.[51] More than 120,000 RAF officers and airmen were qualified aircrew, with another 20,000 in training.[52] The Royal Navy, too, had its thousands of gunners, torpedomen, engineers, telegraphists, artificers, mechanicians and shipwrights. Many of them wanted to carry on this sort of work after the war. By 1944 almost half of all soldiers wishing to change their careers once they left the army were looking for jobs in engineering, transport and communications.[53]

But not all trades in the Forces, however hard-earned, had a civilian application. Able seaman J.B. Lindop arrived back in Britain at the end of 1947, after two years in Ceylon, and was demobbed a month later. He had picked up no end of skills during his time in the Royal Navy: 'I was an expert on various types of Search and Warning radar, a good shot with a twenty-millimetre Oerlikon cannon, excellent on gunnery and torpedoes. But I had an uneasy feeling that there was not a lot of call for attributes of that sort in civvy street.'[54] He was right.

Ex-RAF aero-engine fitters were soon chagrined to discover that their experience did not qualify them to work on the heavy-vehicle motors serviced in bus depots and garages.[55] One veteran sergeant-fitter had spent years working on experimental jet-propelled engines and had passed all the air force's aero-engine instructional courses with flying colours. 'But when I interviewed with a civilian employer,' he complained to *John Bull*, 'he could offer me nothing more than a job as a lorry driver.'[56] A former corporal with the Royal Corps of Signals who wanted to work in engineering or radio found himself back in his old place on a grocer's counter, earning £3 a week.[57]

The spectre of the trade-union worker, who had supposedly shirked behind the lines while better men had sacrificed their lives, and who was now jealously guarding all the best jobs, was suspected of being behind all this. 'It would appear from my observations that conscientious and hardworking employees are of no consequence in this "brave new world",' complained Eric Horn at the end of 1946: 'trade unions to ensure that nobody works seems to be the order of the day!'[58] The unions were completely hostile to ex-service vocational schemes, according to one *John Bull* reader who had attended a public lecture on the subject: union members in the audience 'swore to oppose the entry of any government trainees . . . and considered the whole thing a conspiracy to flood their trades with cheap labour'.[59]

In any case, there was a definite limit to the number of skilled tradesmen that postwar British industry could absorb. As wartime manufacturing wound down, so manpower in the engineering, metals, chemicals and shipbuilding sectors was inevitably shrinking. Already by the summer of 1945 firms advertising positions for drivers and engineers were being bombarded with far more applications from ex-servicemen than they could ever hope to satisfy.[60]

The government tried to help. The Ministry of Labour's Resettlement Advice Service was intended to assist men like these find a new place for themselves in the workforce. Over 370 dedicated centres were created, with many more operating from existing government buildings, all staffed by serving officers seconded to the Ministry of Labour. By early 1946 they were dealing with 40,000 enquiries a month; by the end of that year, there had been two and a half million visits by ex-servicemen to these centres across the country.[61]

Numbers like this speak well of the service, and it must have done much useful work for thousands of ex-servicemen. But some came away less than satisfied. The Ministry of Labour went to great lengths to distance the public's perception of these offices as much as possible from the foreboding prewar labour exchanges. But ex-servicemen complained that the offices were more about eye-catching presentation than content; the 'flowers and nice posters and comfy chairs' were all very well, but the advice was often vague, contradictory, or just plain wrong.[62] Some staff were alleged to be less than understanding. 'I could have taken it better if the pompous ass had been sympathetic,' remembered one man who went unsuccessfully seeking information about apprenticeship schemes: 'But he was most supercilious, wanting only to be rid of me so that he could enjoy his sinecure of a job in peace.'[63]

Many servicemen asked about teaching jobs. They had had a brush with education during their military service and saw being a schoolmaster as an attractive postwar career opportunity. The need was certainly there. Britain's primary and secondary school system was in a state of chaos at the end of the war. Inner-city schools had been evacuated to the countryside in 1939, many never properly re-establishing themselves until after the war. About one in five school buildings had suffered some kind of war-related damage. An estimated 70,000 new teachers were required to fulfil the ambitious demands of the 1944 Education Act, which called for the school leaving age to be raised to 15 by 1947, creating at a stroke 391,000 new students to instruct.[64] With the demand for new instructors so great, the Ministry of Education and the teachers' unions were willing to place greater emphasis on experience and character in the selection of teacher trainees than on the paper qualifications that before the war had restricted the profession to grammar-school alumni with a school certificate or better.[65]

The Emergency Teacher Training Scheme was the Ministry of Labour's flagship resettlement programme. Where it stumbled was not owing to a lack of interested candidates, but to the completely inadequate means with which to train them. By November 1945, 5,000 new applications were being received every month. Yet only five emergency colleges were operating throughout Britain, with space for just 850 trainees.[66] Candidates from the armed services might have to wait eight to twelve months for a place. 'Kicking one's heels for a year or so is not what the demobilized soldier likes,' bridled the *Manchester Guardian*.[67] A number of demobbed servicemen were left on the waiting list for so long that they regretfully had to take other jobs.[68]

Another possibility for ex-servicemen was self-employment. For men who had laboured under the strict hierarchy of the Forces, the attraction of having no one to answer to was obvious. Ex-servicemen across Britain began to establish small retail and service businesses such as tobacconists, grocers, wireless repair shops, goods hauliers and filling stations. Cafés and boarding houses were also popular as small businesses.[69] The war had seen a huge improvement in the stability and prestige of the small retailer. The 1930s had been locust years for Mr. Polly; almost half of all bankrupts in 1937 were shopkeepers.[70] But with competition effectively at an end owing to postwar rationing and controls, small retailers were in their element.

There was plenty of capital flowing around for new investment. The government offered a commercial resettlement scheme that by the end of 1946 had distributed £1.5 million in grants to 15,000 would-be small businessmen.[71] And ex-servicemen had gratuities, postwar credits and back pay due to them. These could add up to a tidy sum. An unmarried private released in June 1945 who had served for five years, including three years overseas, could expect a total of £109 (half of it tax-free) on his demobilisation – worth about £10,000 by today's standards.[72] Some senior officers had accumulated enormous sums. One general who spent most of the war in a POW camp left the army with £15,000 in savings (£1.4 million nowadays).[73]

What money could not buy was the right to trade legally. A retail business licence had to be awarded by the local price regulation or food control committees of the Board of Trade or the Ministry of Food, and the crucial petrol coupons needed to run cars, taxis and lorries were only obtainable from the Ministry of Fuel. Licences were hard to get. Priority went to the 16,000 persons listed on the Registry of Withdrawn Traders, former retailers who had had to close their businesses because of the war. Some provision was also made for disabled ex-servicemen. The able-bodied were usually out of luck. Three out of four ex-Forces applicants who applied to the Board of Trade for retail licences in November 1945 were refused.[74]

Some ex-servicemen made rash investments in their new businesses before working through the red tape. Flight Lieutenant

John J. Brown, a veteran of the Battle of Britain, took on a fourteen-year rental of a hardware shop in Westgate-on-Sea in Kent, only to discover that he was forbidden to open it up.[75] It was alleged that members of the local regulatory committees, who often had vested business interests in the areas under their jurisdiction, were deliberately blocking ex-servicemen so that they could prevent the establishment of commercial rivals.[76] Even with licences, many ventures failed. By 1951 new competition brought on by the winding up of rationing had whittled down the number of small shopkeepers in Britain to 312,000, which was 50,000 fewer than there had been in 1931.[77]

When ambitions sputtered out, wives were typically blamed. Ex-servicemen complained that their spouses had talked them out of dramatic career changes. 'Am I to give up being happy in my work for safety and security? My wife urges that I should,' fretted one of Ann Temple's readers, who had 'thoroughly revelled' in the work he had performed in army administration, 'the reorganizing, building up, having an aim in life'. But his wife wanted him to return to his old job as a bank clerk.[78] Ann Temple and other press commentators tended to side with the unheroic but level-headed. In her 'Wanderlust Warning' she cautioned: 'The last thing I want to do is to damp enthusiasm, or clip the wings of initiative, but it is just as well to face the fact here and now that the greatest expansion of openings in jobs in this particular post-war period is going to be in office work.'[79] 'Too Many People Try to Reach for the Moon', agreed *The News of the World* in an article urging ex-servicemen to be conservative in their career choices.[80] It wasn't unreasonable, of course, for wives to want security after years of hardship and uncertainty. One ex-serviceman's spouse described her mixed feelings to Ann Temple:

My husband has been a physical training instructor in the RAF and wants to carry on with the work in schools . . . I am begging him to go back to his job as a boot and shoe [shop] manager. Our home has been in store for five and half years. I do so desperately want to settle down. I am terrified of this chasing round after something that may never materialize. But is it wrong to discourage him?[81]

## Risen from the Ranks

Messrs. Grub & Gadgets,
The Emporium, Church Street,
Tithington, Slugshire.

Dear Sirs – As I may, I am told by the War Office, properly anticipate my release from the Forces . . . I write now to inform you of my intention of applying for reinstatement in my former peace-time occupation. Yours faithfully, Arnold Suggs, Major-General.

Dear Sir – We are in receipt of your letter of October 30th and would like to say how proudly we shall welcome home to the emporium a member of our staff who has such a distinguished war record as yourself. We feel, however, a little hesitant about acceding to your request about reinstatement. Perhaps you will remember that when you went into the Army your occupation was, if you will forgive our mention of it, that of delivering groceries on a tricycle, and we thought perhaps that a position of greater trust would be more acceptable to you now . . .

Dear Sirs – I am afraid you misunderstood my previous letter. My application is for reinstatement in my former employment. The only favour I should like to ask is that I should not be given the tricycle without the bell. All the other boys had bells on theirs. Yours faithfully . . . (etc.)[82]

Men like Major-General Suggs really did exist. In 1942 Thomas Evers, an orphan with no secondary-school education, had left the Yorkshire town of Dewsbury as a bus conductor. Rapidly promoted while in the army, he ended the war a lieutenant-colonel in charge of welfare services for hundreds of thousands of soldiers across the Middle East.[83] Sydney Wigginton, a former Nottingham City Transport clerk, reached the same rank after illustrious service behind the lines in occupied Yugoslavia.[84] A former junior porter at Shenton railway station also became a lieutenant-colonel while in India.[85] A yard sweeper employed by the London Gas Light and Coke Company returned to his employer a captain.[86]

The 'temporary gentleman' – the demobilised ex-officer of modest background left socially *sui generis* by war – was a stock character in the literary dramas of the interwar years. Oliver Mellors, the deracinated blacksmith-turned-subaltern-turned-gamekeeper of D.H. Lawrence's *Lady Chatterley's Lover* (1928), is perhaps the most famous example.[87] The Second World War also produced such men. These were the 'Hoopers' so despised by Charles Ryder in *Brideshead Revisited* (1945), the unromantic, passionless commercial men who, in Evelyn Waugh's view, refused to take the army (and their officerial duties of *noblesse oblige*) seriously enough.

Under the influence of its progressively minded adjutant-general, Sir Ronald Adam, the wartime army developed a system of 'scientific' officer selection from the ranks, with all candidates required to pass a War Office Selection Board – a 'Wosbie' – before advancement to an officer cadet training unit. This process broadened the social range of would-be officers; as early as 1941, three out of four newly minted second lieutenants had been educated outside the public-school system.[88] The wartime Royal Air Force, more technically demanding and less traditionally hidebound than the army, with fewer concerns about man-management, promoted more Hoopers still. But it was unclear what expectations these temporary gentlemen would or should have for the postwar world.

Industrial tribunals were not necessarily sympathetic to the plight of some returning servicemen. In September 1946 former Captain John Dare, who had been responsible for the rations of 20,000 men while stationed in Madagascar and had enjoyed an army salary of £800, sought unsuccessfully to force his employer, a meat market in Harborne, near Birmingham, to reinstate him in a better position than his old job as a distributor earning £6 11s a week.[89] Employers argued that the military promotion system was too arbitrary to apply back in civilian work. The London and Home Counties Joint Electrical Authority pointed out, for instance, that many of its returning staff members had been prisoners during the war. Had these men not been captured, they too might have attained high rank. Were they to be disadvantaged in their postwar careers because of simple misfortune?[90]

Ex-officers striking out on their own might find the labour marketplace unexpectedly bleak. 'I wish to draw your attention to a serious crime in this brave new world of ours,' wrote one to the *Manchester Guardian*:

> I refer, of course, to the appalling stupidity of being an ex-officer – and confessing to it. In the past eight weeks I have applied for more than twenty posts. Not one advertiser has paid me the courtesy of a reply . . . in vain I protest that I want no more than a living wage of about £5 weekly, that I am keen and a hard worker.[91]

A vast number of ex-officers were jostling for the humblest of openings, complained one demobbed man to *The Times*: 'A staff controller whom I know has told me that he receives as many as three hundred applications for any post which he advertises in the daily press, and that to give consideration to every application is impossible.'[92] A *Spectator* reader wrote that: 'My tally so far since demobilization has been 43 applications, 14 replies, one interview – and no job yet.'[93] When the London Orphan School for Boys advertised for a new headmaster in the summer of 1945, its treasurer noted that among the 260 applicants were two Royal Navy lieutenant-commanders, three lieutenant-colonels, five wing-commanders and an air vice-marshal.[94] Arthur Vizard, whose major's salary had been 43 shillings a day, had no choice but to take a £400 pay cut and 'a tremendous drop in living standards' in order to get a job.[95]

The Ministry of Labour did attempt to make special provision for men of high rank. In conjunction with private industry it offered a range of general and specialised business training courses in which several thousand demobbed men eventually took part.[96] It also established an appointments department to handle recruitment into more senior professional and executive positions. But this was the butt of much criticism from ex-officers who complained about its 'meandering machinations' and supposed lack of energy.[97] 'I was demobilized in early November, 1945,' griped one former squadron leader:

> In the six months that I have been on the appointments register my name has been submitted for two jobs – an average of one every three months – and so far I have not been accepted for interview by a single prospective employer. Like many others I fought my way out of a reserved occupation to serve with the RAF . . .
>
> As the only alternative left open to me, at the age of 40, is the frightening prospect of life on the dole at 45s a week, I naturally begin to question my sanity in choosing to serve my country in an active capacity and so reducing my family to a state of comparative destitution. I am not unique: there are 10,000 unemployed ex-officers on that register alone . . . members of a half-forgotten fraternity – a post-war detritus – the 'submerged ten thousand'.[98]

A persistent problem was lack of business experience. Many officers had taken it for granted that their man-management responsibilities in the armed forces would count for much amongst employers back in Britain. But in 1945 ex-servicemen with leadership experience were two-a-penny. Practical commercial skills were what employers were looking for. Few ex-officers had any. 'In the minds of most business men there does not seem to be room for an intelligent conception of experience,' grumbled one jobseeker.[99] 'Men who without "previous experience" have administered khaki businesses under circumstances which would have caused despair in many a City firm . . . find that in the eyes of industry they lack the training and experience necessary for the most humble appointments,' seethed another.[100]

The public was divided about the merits of these complaints. There was some feeling that temporary gentlemen should be given a chance to build on their wartime success. 'Give the lads who have "made good" in the Forces a worthwhile job when they come back to civil life,' insisted the *People*:[101]

> They want a job. A real job. Something they can get their teeth into as they got their teeth into helping to win this war. They have no intention of being pushed around by some superior elder clerk who hasn't lived one tenth as much as they. Neither of them is going to pick up the threads of his pre-war living just where he dropped them.[102]

The *Manchester Guardian* agreed, though more cautiously: 'The ability, enterprise and aptitude for responsibility that raised a young man to major or colonel will not have evaporated on demobilization. Given the chance, those qualities should have something to say for themselves in civil life.'[103]

But the old working-class antipathy towards social climbers was still strong in the 1940s. Its culture was deeply conservative. As historian Ross McKibbin argued, it was 'ruled by group opinion, seemingly without ambition, and deeply suspicious' of change.[104] The psychological security provided by working-class life demanded strict conformity in its turn. Social drifters were not tolerated.

Ex-officers who had 'forgotten their place' were scorned. A district secretary of the National Union of Enginemen and Firemen complained that temporary gentlemen were coming home with 'high falutin'' ideas about pay.[105] One *John Bull* reader lambasted:

> people who evidently consider themselves supermen because they have been officers in the Forces. I would enjoy watching some of them earning their £800 and 'handling large numbers of men' without the backing of King's Regulations. They would find the little dictatorial methods acquired in the Services would not cut much ice in business.

'Not one officer in ten has more than a boy's idea of organiza-tion as it is understood in the business world,' suggested another. 'A knowledge of firearms and a parade-ground voice are not enough.'[106] 'In the Army an officer can very often get by on what his underlings know – not that the average officer is required to know a lot when you get down to brass tacks,' wrote a third:

> No wonder, then, that many ex-officers are finding civilian life a bit hard to face. May I suggest that these gentlemen swallow their pride and come down to earth a bit? Let them start off in a job they can do (even if it is only junior clerk) . . .[107]

' "Ex-officer" is [not] synonymous with "lotus eater" . . . we are not all idle monsters looking for directorships,' insisted one ex-officer.[108]

This may have been true. But it could be genuinely difficult for temporary gentlemen to return to humbler lives. Working-class wives and parents worried about whether their ex-officer husbands and sons would now be embarrassed by them.[109] Some evidently were. 'I am back in this country after some months in the services, where I had to mix with people whom in the ordinary way I would not meet socially,' wrote one concerned ex-serviceman to the *Daily Mail*'s Ann Temple. 'Now I find that in my mind I am criticizing my friends from the point of view of class and education. I know it's poisonous. I know I have become a snob.'[110] One young husband who had enjoyed military rank and prestige now thought of his wife as 'rather common,' reported *Woman*.[111]

The split personality of the temporary gentleman was subtly caught by Rayner Heppenstall in his 1946 short story 'Local Boy'. Broadbent, a lieutenant on leave in his small industrial home town, finds himself embarrassed and socially awkward in front of his family and old neighbours. When he spots Toothill, another working-class lad who had received a commission in the Forces, the dilemma becomes explicit:

> They smiled. Broadbent's mind searched quickly for a clue to the language the two of them should employ with each other, the

language of the neighbourhood and the engineer's yard or that of the officer's mess. Toothill hesitated too as if occupied with the same problem, and then he plumped for the language of the mess. *Arthur, old boy*, he said. *What are you drinking?* Broadbent replied in kind. *Got one, thanks, old boy*, he said. *What's yours?*

Broadbent bought two pints of bitter, and, the conversation accepted, the two little officers sat down and compared notes, cautiously at first and then more open-heartedly, about their sergeant-majors, their batmen and the chaps in the mess. Two local boys who had made good in the army, they took poor and dim views of this and that, exhorted each other to turn it in and fortified their statements with *actually* and *I say*.[112]

Which of the two mental worlds Broadbent and Toothill ultimately came to inhabit on their demob would probably be decided by the sort of job they were able to get. Some fortunate temporary gentlemen would rise permanently into the middle classes; others would slip back into their plebeian past.

## Lost Opportunities?

In Zachary Gold's short story 'The Way Back', published in May 1945, Mr. Benson, the accounting manager of a small novelty company selling powder-puffs and trinkets, introduces his new demobbed employee, Sergeant Harry Reid, to the office. Reid is a former commando who has won the Distinguished Conduct Medal in Normandy, and Benson – well-meaning but awkward and tongue-tied – is embarrassed by the triviality and monotony of the paper-pushing job he's about to assign Reid. Both men want to talk about the tension in the air but cannot quite find the right words. 'Look,' Benson finally says:

'I got in here after the last mess, but I was out of work for months before I landed any job at all. I had four years in France and when I got back all the best jobs were gone. I was pretty fed up about that for a long time. I know how it is. They say they're going to do things better this time. You fellows aren't having any trouble about jobs?'

'No. Not much.'

'You can get on here if you want to,' Mr. Benson said. 'It's a good firm.'

So 'The Way Back' is a story with a happy ending – of a sort. But both men share an unspoken though unarticulated sadness. They have won the war. The sergeant is home, safe and solvent. It is surely better to spend one's life manufacturing knick-knacks than fighting and killing on a battlefield. But something has been lost, nonetheless.[113]

This sense of a great unspoken lacuna in the lives of ex-servicemen was identified by the sociologist Ferdinand Zweig, who in *Labour, Life and Poverty* (1948), his study of British working-class life in the late 1940s, was struck by the number of demobbed men he met who could not settle back happily into civilian work. Many ex-servicemen, he observed, had made ambitious plans during the war years but afterwards had 'had no alternative but to accept what they regarded as dull and uninteresting jobs'. They were frustrated men, 'carried away by too great an ambition, which they [did] not see any prospect of satisfying'.[114] Work was central to the self-image of British men: such disappointments cut deep. Amongst Zweig's case studies were ex-soldiers such as:

Case 39: A joiner, employed on making window-frames, thirty-six, married . . . he spent four years in the Army, and was demobbed last May, but even now he feels restless and unsettled. He misses the companionship in the Army, the freedom and lack of responsibility. If he could, he would sign on again. One of his friends – a married man with children – has signed on for a further period after six years in the Army.[115]

Case 54: A coachbuilder, thirty-two, single, an ex-Serviceman . . . he left the Army a year ago after six years' service, and when he started work he felt so restless and wretched that he had to leave the firm after the first week before he could settle down properly. He still feels unsettled, and says it is the excitement and companionship that he misses. Companionship in the Army is different from that in Civvy Street. Life is now drab and monotonous. When he came back he couldn't find his old friends, and he was lonely.[116]

When one reads such stories of spent ambitions, one is left wondering that if the return to work from the Forces after the Second World War wasn't a failure as such, it was, nonetheless, a lost opportunity.

In the United States the Servicemen's Readjustment Act of 1944 – the 'GI Bill' – made demobilisation a vast engine of social mobility, as millions of blue-collar veterans were propelled by college education into the prosperous middle class. Of the fifteen and a half million US veterans eligible for education benefits, almost eight million took advantage of them, and more than two million attended two- and four-year colleges.[117] Most ex-servicemen who used the Readjustment Act's educational provisions would later characterise this decision as a critical turning point in their lives. The GI Bill, it has recently been said, 'stands as a premier example of how government can, through public policy, provide social opportunity and promote active citizenship'.[118]

Britain had its higher-educational opportunities for ex-servicemen too, but they were simpler, cheaper and (crucially) far, far less ambitious. Between 1945 and 1950, 83,000 Further Education and Training Scheme (FETS) grants were made to demobbed men and women, 43,000 of which were used at universities.[119] Although by 1950 this did help to increase the nation's tiny student population by roughly two-thirds, the initiative only encompassed one in a hundred of all returning ex-servicemen.

After turning in their uniforms, four in five of the demobbed returned to the industrial working class from which they had come, their intelligence and talents as unrecognised, untapped and underutilised as they had been before the war.[120] The expansion of higher education in Britain, with its concomitant effect on class mobility, would have to wait more than a decade. A chance to shake up Britain's sclerotic mid-century social system was crucially delayed, perhaps with important consequences for the country's subsequent economic and political history. One can only wonder how some form of British GI Bill might have transformed the lives of the bored and frustrated ex-servicemen chronicled by Zweig.

Psychologist Reg Ellery suspected that these men would never completely get over their sense of loss. 'War makes and mars such men,' he wrote:

> It raises them up only to cast them down again in civil life when the exhilaration of campaigning has departed. In war they served their country; in peace they are needed no longer . . . men will not spring to attention when they pass. Words of command perish on their lips unuttered. The great days have passed like a dream; yet all their lives they will try to live in this dream.[121]

But some disgruntled ex-soldiers had an answer. If civilian life would not give them the excitement, money, and opportunities that they craved, they would take them anyway. The injustices of demob would be settled by crime.

# CHAPTER SIX

# They Made Me a Fugitive

*SITUATION WANTED: Advertiser with wide knowledge of tank warfare; indomitable, mettlesome and stubborn; twice decorated . . . seeks post where violence, severity and impetuosity required.*[1]

March, 1946: Maccabi House, Hampstead. A group of forty-three people, most of them obviously ex-Forces – their tanned, muscular bodies squeezed awkwardly into brand-new demob suits – have assembled at this, the London headquarters of the international Jewish sports organisation, to discuss the re-emergence of an old and hated enemy. Veterans of Oswald Mosley's anti-semitic British Union of Fascists (BUF), banned in 1940, have begun to reorganise now that the war is over as the 'British League of Ex-Servicemen and Women'. Though Mosley himself is keeping a low profile for the time being – he has only just been released from house arrest – one of his former deputies, Jeffrey Hamm, has been speaking to thousands in Hyde Park, and is actively recruiting demobilised men to begin BUF-style rallies and marches in London's working-class boroughs.

The atmosphere at Maccabi's is tense; feelings are raw. Belsen, Dachau and the Nazi extermination camps in Poland were liberated less than a year previously. Many of Hitler's factotums responsible for carrying out the Jewish Holocaust in Europe are currently on trial. The thought that fascism in Britain might be re-emerging just months after the Third Reich's fall enrages these veterans of Monte Cassino and Falaise. 'Anger was rising and spreading,' one of the organisers of the meeting, ex-sailor Morris Beckman, later recalled. 'These ex-servicemen [were filled] with emotion ranging from choleric anger to a cold hard desire to kill the perpetrators.'[2] The decision is made to create a street-level counter-movement to Hamm's League: the 43 Group. A 'a new mood of excitement' fills the air.[3] By the following month 300 ex-servicemen have enlisted.

For the next three years the 43 Group is the home of men like Beckman, ex-paratrooper Gerald Flamberg (winner of the Military Medal at Arnhem) and Leonard Sherman, a former Welsh Guardsman and martial arts expert. The Group is explicitly modelled on the army's wartime commando brigades; its 'outdoor activities teams' are trained to operate as efficient fighting units, disciplined and ready for action at a moment's notice. Coordinated by a military-style intelligence network, the teams mount pinpoint assaults on British League meetings, Ridley Road in Hackney being a key field of battle. Hamm's fascists respond to the 43 Group by assembling quasi-commando units of their own. Rival ex-servicemen fight it out across the bloodied alleyways of East London, street corner by street corner.

The violence worsens; fists are fitted with knuckledusters or replaced by coshes, steel-capped boots and knives. Potatoes with razor blades stuck in them become a gruesome form of artillery. But the 43 Group veterans seem inured to the possibility of injury. 'Many had seen active wartime service in which they had accepted the possibility of being wounded or killed,' notes Beckman:[4]

Seemingly nerveless, they actually looked forward with relish to the prospect of 'having a barney', as they put it, with the fascists. Even when bound over by the courts [and forbidden from breaking this by the Group] there were those who ignored the sentence and returned to the fighting; it became an addiction. The more they fought the Blackshirts the more they wanted to, as if they knew it was to be a passing phase and they wanted to enjoy its excitement to the full.[5]

The Group is condemned by the Board of Deputies of British Jews and other mainstream Jewish organisations for being in their view 'a bunch of heavies seeking their kicks in going out and having violent punch-ups'.[6] The families of some of the young men try to persuade them to stop. But the men are undeterred; their blood is up. 'I see this fascist in front of me and I think of the newsreels,' one young commando told Beckman. 'I automatically put the bastard into a Nazi uniform in my mind and I go mad. I just want to hurt him!'[7]

By the spring of 1949 the Mosleyites' brief renaissance is visibly fading, and though Mosley himself will continue to drift along the fringes of British politics for the next two decades, the threat of a mass fascist resurgence in London is over for now. With no meetings for the 43 Group to disrupt, ex-servicemen face a second demobilisation. Some have already had to leave the fray because of visible signs of battle fatigue; others will decamp to join the Israeli Defence Forces and fight in the wars of the Middle East. Many will look back on their postwar military career with as much nostalgia as their wartime one. 'It had been a great adventure,' remembered Beckman. 'The comradeship engendered was so staunch that it hurts just to recollect it.'[8]

What went on in the streets of north London during those three years was an intense political struggle. This was no aimless yobbery; the men on both sides felt that real principles were at stake. But seen in the context of demobilisation, the battles of Ridley Road and other flashpoints of the Mosleyite revival take on another complexion. It is evident from their testimony that ex-servicemen joined quasi-military organisations such as the British League and the 43 Group not just because of their politics. Fighting fascists – or fighting anti-fascists – was a continuation of the Second World War by other means. The British Army may no longer have required your services, but that didn't mean that you couldn't carry on playing soldiers. The demobbed were drawn to these groups because of ideology, to be sure; but their mental atmosphere also appealed. Peace, it was turning out, could be a bore. So why not give war another chance?

### Trained in Lawlessness, and Decorated for Doing It . . .

'Too much energy, that's your trouble Clem – too much animal spirits. What you need's an outlet.' Clem Morgan (Trevor Howard), former RAF pilot and POW, now an unemployed barfly lacking money and purpose, is a casualty of war in Alberto Cavalcanti's 1947 *noir* thriller *They Made Me a Fugitive*.[9] Bored and broke, Clem has 'found life a bit tame since he's been demobbed' according to Narcy (Griffith Jones), the sadistic teenage spiv who recruits him into his ration-busting black-market ring. The outlet he needs, it transpires, is another war. 'Can I help it if I've got too set in my habits?' asks Clem.

Accepting the job on the toss of a coin, Morgan treats racketeering as a lark, a break from the dullness of postwar British austerity, until he discovers that Narcy is peddling drugs as well as legs of lamb. This inspires an eleventh-hour burst of moral outrage, and Narcy decides to remove the troublesome Clem by framing him for the killing of a policeman. Reprising his wartime breakout, Morgan escapes from prison and after a convoluted series of adventures confronts Narcy, who is accidentally killed. Clem is unable to clear his name and so returns to jail. The wartime hero is crushed by a postwar world that cannot successfully reabsorb him. His real crime? 'I went on doing what the country put me in a uniform to do after they'd taken it back.'

The following year ex-commando Captain Dick Tarleton (Denis Webb) nearly meets the same fate as Clem when he's tempted into crime by the heartless moll and racketeer Paula Danvers (Colette Melville) in *The Flamingo Affair* (1948). Hard up and missing the glitzy life he enjoyed as an officer, Tarleton – back to being the garage mechanic he was in 1939 – is seduced by the prospect of punishing civilians who he believes haven't paid him the respect he's earned. 'You told me you were once respon-sible for the lives of hundreds of men,' purrs Danvers: 'What are you responsible for now? You don't owe them a thing the way they've kicked you around.' The resentful veteran plans a military-style operation to rob his boss, and is only provoked back to his law-abiding wits when another gang tries to break into the garage and he has to use his commando training to stop them.[10]

We tend to regard the gentle, measured world of the Ealing Comedy as synonymous with British film in the late 1940s. But *They Made Me a Fugitive*, *The Flamingo Affair* and other largely forgotten *noir* thrillers of the same period hint at an altogether different kind of Britain emerging from the Second World War – a nervous, angry country, pulsating with aggression. The protago-nists of these films are not the mild-mannered naïfs of *Passport to Pimlico* (1949) or *The Lavender Hill Mob* (1951); nor, for that matter, are they the square-jawed heroes who in the classic 1950s war epics will bomb the Ruhr dams (*The Dam Busters*, 1955) and tunnel out of grim Nazi fortresses (*The Colditz Story*, 1955).

No, Clem and Dick and their other demobbed comrades are warriors of an altogether different and more worrying type, prod-ucts of an anxious cultural mood. These are men left adrift by peace, jaded, sullen, and capable of startling acts of violence. '*Civvy Street seems strange to some of the boys*,' muses the police inspector who investigates the murder of Tobruk veteran Dave Robinson in the seedy palais of postwar Soho in *Dancing with Crime* (1947). Such twisted ex-servicemen seem to have lost all moral bearing, their characters now 'pungent' (as the *Spectator*'s film critic Virginia Graham put it of Clem Morgan) with 'brutality, liberally spiced with sadism, harsh, ruthless, and unpleasant.'[11]

By the year *The Flamingo Affair* was released, Britain seemed to be a country in which law and order had completely broken down. In 1938, the last full year of peace, 283,200 indictable offences had been reported in England and Wales.[12] In 1948 there were nearly 523,000. This increase was bad enough, but the types of crime being committed were even more worrying. In 1938 there had been approximately 57,700 indictable offences involving violence;

in 1948 there were 130,000. Sexual assaults rose from 5,018 to 13,185 between 1938 and 1950. Crime was not only rising but getting uglier.[13]

'We are reaching a situation where the ordinary citizen feels he is no longer safe in his own home,' warned the criminologist Leo Page. 'Ten years ago such a statement would have been regarded as an absurdity,' he added, 'but in July 1948 at the Stafford Assizes the Lord Chief Justice said that he had found cases of old people trembling as they went to the door to open it at night.'[14] Just six months after V-E Day, the *Daily Mail* had already been lamenting that 'gangsterism on the Chicago model has taken root in London . . . murders, stabbings, beatings-up of both men and women, gang fights and every kind of Black Market activity are sweeping through the Victoria area'.[15] *John Bull* was similarly despondent. 'Crime marches on almost unhindered. Now it has reached the stage where jewellers and their assistants are being waylaid by gangsters . . . when innocent traders and private citizens marked out for robbery are being beaten up.'[16]

As the postwar horror stories began to pile up, worried Britons sought an explanation. Perhaps the nation as a whole had fallen by the ethical wayside? Sir Gerald Dobson, Recorder of London, suggested that a 'distemper of dishonesty' had infected the British: 'people have lost sight of the difference between right and wrong. Morals have been weakened to the point of becoming extinguished.'[17] Sir Harold Scott, chief commissioner of the Metropolitan Police, also blamed the crime wave on 'a certain laxity' produced by wartime conditions, 'a slackening of moral fibre'.[18]

But perhaps there was another impulse involved here – the same impulse that had drawn demobbed soldiers back into knife fights on Ridley Road. Perhaps brutalised ex-servicemen were the ones creating havoc. Perhaps – and this was seriously proposed by criminologists at the time – Forces life was inherently corrupting, encouraging theft and wearing away at self-restraint. As the *Daily Mail* suggested, perhaps the rise in violence was due to men 'trained in the use of lethal weapons [losing] some of their normal inhibitions against the taking of human life'.[19] 'They've been trained in lawlessness, ordered to behave like thugs, and decorated for doing it . . . what do you expect?' was (as the *New Statesman* suggested) by 1946 becoming conventional wisdom.[20]

Maybe the crime wave was the demobbed soldier's private revolt against civilian life. It could be that ex-servicemen were breaking the law not because they needed the money, but because they *enjoyed* it – because criminality, with its risks, its excitement and its disdain for bourgeois respectability, felt comfortingly familiar to the world of war from which these men had just emerged. Perhaps the ex-serviceman was a misfit, his moral constitution fatally corrupted; perhaps he was lost to law-abiding Britain.

## Anticlimax

'I want danger and excitement. And I am not alone in this. There is quite a little minority of fellow-sufferers. What is there for us? There seems to be nothing but the dull prospect of a pre-fab, raising the family, the 8.30 up and the 5.15 down . . . the prospect appals me.'[21] This ex-paratrooper, writing to *Civvy Street* magazine in August 1946, was not alone; there were men like this all over Britain, restless men who advertised their willingness to do almost any job so long as it was sufficiently thrilling. 'Ex-commando, capable, willing, requires situation any part of the world.' 'Three Australian officers . . . seek any adventurous undertaking or occupation . . . little regard for personal safety.' 'Ex-naval officer, intelligent, fit, able, aged 24, seeking any hazardous occupation.'[22] A perilous job opportunity for six volunteers to work in a remote Chinese province received 600 applications, half of which were from men about to leave the Forces.[23]

As he returned home from Borneo in 1946, Mass-Observation's Tom Harrisson already sensed in his demobilised comrades 'a pathetic nostalgia for those days of comradeship, discomfort, and at least the *feel* of masculine adventure'.[24] The sense of a vital spirit slipping away was felt by many men about to be demobbed. Awaiting his discharge at Woolwich barracks, Eighth Army veteran John Guest found himself unexpectedly dejected: 'There was no excitement, no farewells, and – I felt then – nothing to look forward to. We had come full circle, not with a bang, but a whimper.'[25] At RAF Transport Command's 'X' Squadron; airman F. Warburton was one of two crew members still remaining out of a former wartime complement of 500. 'We live now in a centrally heated room fitted with wash-hand basins and steel wardrobes,' he wrote to the *Manchester Guardian*:

All the things we wished for in the days when the east wind found every crevice in our ill-jointed corrugated dwellings and our own Arctic Circle began a bare yard beyond the glow of slow-combustion stoves we now have . . . [yet there is] a sense of loneliness and a nostalgic yearning for the Nissen huts . . . something that in the earlier days made Service life almost an adventure has gone.[26]

Royal Marine Cecil Wareham found his repatriation amongst strangers at Chatham in Kent curiously unmoving. In moments of despair during the war he and his comrades had often talked of the moment when they would receive their 'one way ticket to freedom', and the almighty booze-up they would have, yet when the day of his discharge came he could not conjure up the slightest excitement.[27] Able seaman J.B. Lindop arrived back in Britain at the end of 1947, after two years in Ceylon, and was demobbed a month later. He, too, found the moment unexpectedly flat. 'For years I had looked forward to this event,' he wrote in his memoirs, 'but now it was actually here there was a severe anti-climax':

Only moments before I had been a proud member of the Royal Navy . . . now, in those few brief seconds a vast, almost uncrossable gulf had opened between me and [his former comrades]. That great privilege of being in the RN had gone forever . . . I suddenly felt a great sadness and very much lost; a strange longing came over me to get back through that door again to meet my old oppos with whom I had enjoyed great comradeship, excitement and danger.[28]

To be sure, many men had found wartime service dull and dispiriting. And not every veteran who had had an 'exciting' career wanted to continue the adrenalin rush in peacetime. Reconnaissance pilot Charles Crichton found that as a result of the war he had entirely lost any desire 'to hurtle around at great speed' in a car any longer; he'd had a 'basin-full' of it in his Spitfire.[29] But others had been galvanised by their experiences. The war had provided men from the most humdrum of backgrounds with opportunities for thrill-seeking: bomber aircrews flying nightly sorties through flak-infested skies, paratroopers dropping headlong into enemy territory, submariners stalking merchantmen from beneath the waves. There was terror, but also exuberance.

Indeed, for some men the war's dangers had clearly been addictive. 'Mad' Jack Churchill of the Manchester Regiment, who won the Military Cross in 1940 for holding back an enemy advance with two machine guns and a bow and arrow, would later in his military career lead commando raids in a full-dress kilt, a broadsword in one hand and a set of bagpipes in the other. When he was finally captured fighting alongside Tito's partisans in Yugoslavia, the Germans had to chain Churchill to the floor of his prison cell to stop him escaping, though he did eventually get out and walked across the Alps to Italy. After the war he took part in the counter-insurgency campaign in Palestine, became a parachutist, took up motorcycle racing and surfed up the Severn estuary.[30]

Then there was Sir Adrian Carton de Wiart, widely regarded as the model for the impetuous Brigadier Ritchie-Hook in Evelyn Waugh's *Sword of Honour* series.[31] Already a holder of the Victoria Cross owing to his courageous actions as a junior officer in the First World War, Carton de Wiart was missing his left hand and had a black eyepatch, and he resembled nothing so much as a mustachioed pirate. He took part in the Norwegian campaign in 1940, and was later shot down over Libya and imprisoned by the Italians, attempting to escape from his captors five times. He ended the war on the Dutch East Indies coast, sitting on a deckchair on the bridge of the battleship HMS *Queen Elizabeth* as Japanese fighter planes buzzed over him. Such men were extreme examples of military enthusiasm, of course. But even soldiers with less emphatic tastes for danger had still found much to enjoy in war. How would the tedium of everyday reality compare?

In October 1945 a columnist for the *New Statesman* took a hair-raising train journey with a boozy clique of RAF officers, one of whom casually climbed out of the compartment window at full speed: 'I gathered he felt that a railway journey had not been sufficiently exciting unless he had run this particular risk,' he wrote later. 'What are all these young airmen, with their highly specialized training, their terrific sense of adventure and their complete lack of earning power, going to do in postwar England?'[32] To psychologist R.S. Ellery, frustration for this lost generation was inevitable. Wartime heroes unable to accommodate their heroism within the narrower scope of civilised society were, he wrote, 'lost – hamstrung by inactivity, palsied by their inability to conform. . . . No longer [do] they have a kitbag in which to pack-up their troubles – a bayonet to brandish – a dixy to deliver – a palliasse to unfold. Peace gives them no scope for their bravery.'[33]

In his 1948 sociological survey *Labour, Life and Poverty*, Ferdinand Zweig found many 'recruits of secondary poverty' to be ex-servicemen, bored and frustrated with the monotony of civilian life, who were falling prey to vice – alcohol, gambling, and what he called 'exciting [motion] pictures'.[34] Seebohm Rowntree, the veteran social campaigner, similarly complained in 1951 that what he described as 'the thriftless element' of the ex-service population had 'blued' away its wartime gratuities and savings at the horse and dog tracks.[35]

Sensing the potential danger, some altruists wanted to direct all the chaotic pent-up energy of ex-servicemen to the benefit of humanity. The celebrated bomber pilot Leonard Cheshire, winner of the Victoria Cross, had a short-lived plan to commission 'Commandos for Peace', an organisation that would send 200 war-toughened men to conduct dangerous scientific expeditions on the uncivilised periphery of the empire. 'You cannot,' he wrote, 'expect a man to screw up his courage day after day for year after year and then to take his uniform off and be just a normal citizen, content to catch the same train at morning and night and live a quiet life immediately.'[36]

Indeed, it was this kind of hollowness that was going silently to haunt men who were beginning to realise that the most exciting moments of their lives were over. As ex-serviceman Raymond English put it in his 1947 book *The Pursuit of Purpose*: 'It is more than strange that in a civilization in which much of our popular entertainment is full of violence, adventure, risk and escapism, there should be so little sense of high adventure in ordinary life.' English called it 'the absence of the heroic'.[37] And, as the American criminologist Perry Wagley warned, this absence might trigger 'nomadic behavior' and conflict with the law in the ex-serviceman whose needs for excitement and adventure could not be found through normal outlets.[38] How else to explain, for instance, the respectable Royal Navy veterans who, 'face[s] and hands blackened in Commando fashion', had embarked on new careers dodging customs officers as they smuggled liquor and luxury goods across 'Rum Row' between Cherbourg and the Hampshire marshes?[39] It must be, *The Times* thought, 'the search for adventure . . . the whole affair a manifestation of what is loosely termed "unsettlement due to the war" '.[40]

### One Thing the Army Taught Me is How to Nick

In the autumn of 1945 any savvy Londoner looking for a watch or jewellery with no questions asked was being steered towards places such as Cutler Street, Houndsditch – 'Loot Alley' as it had become popularly known. In this blitzed cul-de-sac just around the corner from Liverpool Street station, the purloined goods of occupied Europe were being fenced at hugely inflated prices. It was largely a Forces affair. A *Daily Express* investigative reporter saw soldiers and sailors, 'their jackets stuffed with strapless watches', openly selling stolen goods along Cutler Street: 'men walked around with their £50 rings shining in the morning sunlight on their fingers asking all comers: *like to buy a nice ring?*'[41]

By the end of the war, lamented HM Customs and Excise, smuggling by homecoming servicemen was becoming endemic.

Soldiers returning to the United Kingdom on leave or for demo-bilisation were spiriting through their loot – cameras, jewellery, spirits – without paying duty on it. In one case a homecoming private was found to have nineteen watches, fourteen rings, four pairs of silk stockings and a clock hidden on his person. A lieutenant-colonel with the Distinguished Service Order was amongst those arrested.[42]

Smuggling was just one of the rackets fostered in the cigarette economies of the European occupation zones. Counterfeiting and the fencing of stolen goods such as penicillin from military hospitals (the background to Graham Greene's celebrated 1949 screenplay *The Third Man*) were widespread across the Continent. The army estimated that in the year after the war was over £20 million in military property was stolen, largely by its own soldiers. Another £60 million was swindled by British troops in fraudulent currency exchanges.[43] Crime was so widespread on the Continent that soldiers grew blasé about it. After one private was arrested robbing the supply depot he was supposed to be guarding, he was asked whether he felt any sense of remorse: 'No, everyone was doing it . . . we had no fear of being caught, because all the officers were in the swim as well.'[44] In its quarterly morale reports the War Office admitted ruefully that soldiers' letters home were 'remarkably frank' about the success they were having stealing and fencing.[45]

Some soldiers felt that this open larceny was breeding a rancid atmosphere in the garrisons of Europe.[46] 'I have observed with increasing dismay,' wrote one, 'the rapid disintegration of moral standards amongst the troops. What do the Germans think of an army which destroyed the big gangsters only to replace them with widespread petty racketeering?'[47] In a 1947 article for the *Spectator*, the Reverend Cuthbert Bardsley, who had been touring British regiments in Germany, quoted a letter from a conscript: '*I am faced now with what appears to be a simple way out of the continual tension, and that is to break all the rules which you and others have taught me and to become what I have always looked upon as a bit of a swine.*' Bardsley concluded that naïve young boys were in danger or returning to their homeland as a menace to society:

'Germany today is diseased; she is not normal . . . we seem very lightly to be exposing [our young boys] to a country where there is moral and spiritual paralysis.'[48] 'It is difficult to believe that the racketeering mentality will disappear when we all return to civilian life,' warned another soldier.[49]

Perhaps military service was inherently corrupting, as some people worried. After all, the Forces encouraged an unconventional attitude towards private property. Servicemen tended to think of clothes, food and equipment as objects arbitrarily distributed by the quartermaster, not as personal belongings that had identifiable origins and owners. In 1940 the criminologist Hermann Mannheim was already predicting that this belief might become a lifetime habit. Soldiers during the First World War had relied upon 'the state's provision of every necessity of life'; little wonder, then, he thought:

> that some of them became embued . . . with the idea that the state was under a moral obligation to supply them with everything they needed. If the state failed to fulfil this duty, they had the right to help themselves . . . from such disregard of state property it is only one step to the corresponding attitude towards other impersonal bodies, as railway companies, collieries, banks, etc.[50]

Military practice only hazily defined the divide between stealing and 'requisitioning'. Soldiers got used to walking away with supplies that they had a less than watertight right to possess. They routinely appropriated civilian goods, sometimes with only the vaguest promises of compensation. It was only a short step from that to 'liberating' the property of enemy prisoners, or the contents of abandoned buildings – something that the Forces officially condemned but often, in practice, overlooked or even encouraged when done with sufficient imagination. 'In the Army,' admitted *Soldier* magazine, 'the moral code and accepted regulation is not so much *thou shalt not* as *thou shall not be caught doing*.'[51] The novelist Anthony Burgess met a demobilising private who had taken the lesson to heart: 'A job? Me? What does the likes of me want with a job? One thing the army taught me is how to nick. I look forward to a life of nicking.'[52]

And by 1945 it did seem that British soldiers had a knack for nicking. Throughout the war the Special Investigative Branch (SIB) of the Military Police struggled with the daunting and thankless task of trying to check the worst of the army's banditry. Thefts of stores and equipment in transit were rife, with everything from iron rations to Mosquito fighter-bombers (sold to Jewish guerrillas in Palestine) finding their way on to the black market. The hashish-smuggling route from Lebanon to Alexandria, operated by army drivers of the Middle East Force, took years to smash. In Italy, probably the single most crime-ridden theatre of the war, the SIB made over 38,000 arrests.[53]

## Someone Is Going to Die Tonight

When Private R. Jameson baldly announced out loud that 'someone is going to die tonight', it sounded like a line from a bad B-movie. None of his comrades in the company canteen in Eschle, Baden-Wurttemberg, took the threat particularly seriously that evening in July 1945. Jameson had been complaining that one of the NCOs, a Sergeant Major Arundel, had admonished him earlier in the day for not having his cap badge on, but the incident seemed too trivial for anyone to get worked up about. It was probably just the drink talking. So when Jameson went into the company billet a little after ten o'clock that night and borrowed a rifle, no one thought to raise the alarm.

Ten minutes later Jameson walked into Arundel's room with the rifle butt at his hip. 'So long, chum', he said, and put a bullet through the sergeant major's chest. They found Jameson in the street shortly after Arundel died. 'You know what you have done?' an NCO asked. 'Yes,' replied Jameson calmly, 'I have had it in for him before.' At his trial, prosecutors could shed no more light on the 20-year-old private's decision that night. He was in many respects an exemplary soldier with just one minor entry on his charge sheet. The whole business was a tragic mystery. Jameson was found guilty of murder and given a mandatory death sentence, but the court recommended mercy – partly because of his age, and partly because 'after nearly a year of active operations as an infantryman [Jameson] was more easily inclined to resort to the use of arms'. His sentence was commuted to life imprisonment.[54]

The assumption that saved the young private's life – that military service made men volatile and trigger-happy – was particularly ominous in a continent awash with guns and ammunition. Too many servicemen were walking about with too many weapons. Even in the absence of malice, this could be dangerous; in the summer that followed the end of the European war, 146 British soldiers in Austria alone were accidentally shot by their comrades. Forty-seven died.[55] But what was more frightening was the steady flow of rifles, pistols and machine guns returning to Britain. In a postwar amnesty arranged by Scotland Yard, 17,000 weapons were handed in – more than had been collected at the height of the invasion scare in 1940.[56] Many of these were simply souvenirs from the battlefield, looted Lugers and the like which would have otherwise just gathered dust on ex-servicemen's bookshelves. But some firearms were being sold on, inevitably into criminal hands. By September 1945 a revolver on the black market in London could be picked up for as little as £5. Concealable, pocket-sized Biretta automatics were apparently the weapon of choice amongst the capital's criminal cognoscenti.[57]

Just as worryingly, the Jameson case suggested that the armed forces had permanently reprogrammed boys into killers. Was 'habit' going to be responsible for a wave of reflexive homicides? The month before Sergeant Major Arundel's murder, demobilised paratrooper William David Williams had shot his wife dead with a handgun lying by his side when she woke him suddenly during the night. 'Perhaps,' the coroner proposed, 'all the years of training in the army made Private Williams grab the pistol.'[58] On other occasions post-traumatic nightmares might trigger a deadly reaction. A few weeks later, the 'noise of radio and aircraft [filling] his head' was said to have driven Flight-Lieutenant Pablo Salkeld, a wartime pilot recovering from neurotic strain, to shoot a random victim at a Loughborough dance.[59]

Most notoriously of all, there was the pilot and serial killer Neville Heath. 'If ever a man seemed like a gallant young officer of World War II – the finest of the "Few" – it was he,' suggested one of his biographers: 'The fair wavy hair and the clear blue eyes, the easy laughter softening the strong line of mouth and chin . . .'[60] Heath, a drifter, deserter, part-time crook, full-time sexual psychotic, and pathological liar, had joined the South African Air Force at the beginning of the war and risen to the rank of captain (though he later promoted himself to group captain). While doing the rounds of West End nightclubs in the summer of 1946, he had picked up two young women and savagely tortured them to death. His trial proved to be one of the sensations of the year, with a frenzied mob of spectators straining to get into the public gallery each day.

As part of his criminal defence, Heath's lawyers cited the effects of his bailing out over Holland on a bombing mission in October 1944. It was not an especially plausible justification for his behaviour: he had clearly had a deeply unstable personality long before the war had even begun. But while on remand Heath wrote to one of his friends that 'I honestly don't give a damn what happens to me. I've faced death too often in the last six years to worry about it.'[61] He seems to have believed his own story of war trauma right up to his death by hanging.

The veteran-as-madman was to become the inspiration for several postwar novels. In 1949 Elizabeth Taylor wrote *A Wreath of Roses*, in which Camilla, an ageing spinster-schoolma'am, strikes up an awkward flirtation with Richard, a handsome but brooding young man (loosely based on Heath). He claims to be an ex-group captain who conducted dangerous behind-the-lines missions during the war, and is now living an itinerant life drinking away his service gratuity. It later becomes clear that Richard is a fantasist and liar, but the novel suggests that whatever the true circumstances of his wartime past, Richard is battling demons acquired somewhere on the battlefield. 'I suddenly feel I can't stand anything any more – the boredom – hopelessness. I miss the war,' he complains: 'I need excitement, I need things crashing against me, violence; the quiet will kill me.'[62] Death comes in the end not just to Richard but to a girl he casually picks up and strangles, his only motive being (as he confesses to a horrified Camilla) a detached fascination for cruelty.

Fears that the war would churn out maladjusted men originated in its earliest years. In November 1941 the military correspondent of *The Times* had visited a military camp to see a demonstration of infantry battle drill. He reported back with approval that 'the students' blood was up', and he was particularly impressed with a burly subaltern of the London Irish, 'his shirt torn to ribbons and brandishing a fighting-knife at the heels of the pack', who conducted what he called a 'private hate campaign' at anyone who would listen, including two solitary cows.

Six months later the same reporter was pleased to discover that this appeal to hatred had been formalised within the pedagogy of one of the infantry's new 'Battle Schools' for advanced training. Students at the School were given lectures on German atrocities in Poland in order to stir their emotions, and were shown footage of *Wehrmacht* soldiers in action with a chorus of 'hate' superimposed on the soundtrack. So effective were these methods at stimulating raw passions, according to *The Times*, that students were sometimes in danger from their own comrades on the firing range; a soldier whose 'blood was up' was liable to forget the nearby presence of his fellow trainees once a gun was in his hands with potentially fatal consequences.[64] The BBC Home Service gave a similar report on a Battle School the same day as *The Times* article, 27 April 1942, adding that students were doused in animal blood and taken to a slaughterhouse to watch butchers at work.

The public was not happy. 'It is plain that a state of hysteria has developed [at the Battle Schools] which, if not checked, may spread and do much harm . . . all this hating, and spraying men with blood, is a form of neurosis,' wrote one former infantry officer.[65] Labour MPs pressed for an explanation in the House of Commons; the Archbishop of Canterbury made his concerns known.[66] 'When [the army] seeks to make "killers" it not only ceases to make soldiers, but it seeks to make something essentially un-English,' suggested *Time and Tide*: 'something spawned by a vicious Hollywood out of a perverted Freudianism.'[67] Chastened by this criticism as well as by a damning internal report by an army psychiatrist, the Battle Schools abandoned 'hate training' after a few weeks.[68] But its brief notoriety helped to implant the troubling idea that the army was in the business of manufacturing murderers.

Such anxieties intensified as the war neared its end and the prospect of millions of ex-servicemen returning to civilian life drew closer. James Hodson, writing in September 1944, noted that 'paratroops have been trained as all-in-wrestlers and boxers, and Dacoits who can kill by the quick twist of a cord. Yet,' he mused, 'we shall expect all these lads to be well-behaved and docile post-war.'[69] *Good Housekeeping* magazine warned its readers that their homecoming husbands had been transformed into 'mechanized men, trained to do one thing only – kill the enemy'.[70]

Even Lieutenant-Colonel T.F. Main, one of the army's most senior psychiatrists and a man who devoted his career to a sympathetic understanding of service and ex-service neuroses, felt that many postwar 'problems of aggressiveness and despair [were] the result of the exhibition of aggression in wartime'.[71] Martin Dempsey, author of the 1947 Catholic pamphlet *Back in Civvy Street*, complained that the war had prodded 'the placid . . . into ferocity, the peace-loving into the ferocious . . . [the reader is] not, I hope, one of those who are now showing themselves capable of acts of brigandage and a lack of moral values most disturbing in a society that is supposedly at peace.'[72]

## The Criminal in All of Us

It is 1947, and Duggie Brent is on trial for his life. A former commando, Brent has openly killed the man who taunted his sweetheart; his guilt is not in question. But he is being defended by Major Carter, a barrister who trained him in knife-fighting during the war, and Carter's strategy is not to dispute the material facts of the case but rather to question whether Brent can be truly held responsible for deadly instincts that were honed into him by the state. 'For many months, by the delegated order of the King executed through his officers, this immature young man has learned deadly crafts,' Carter tells the jury.[73] And he sums up his case with a question that many people were evidently asking themselves in the late 1940s:

> Where is this thing to end? You may say, the Army is training men in the dire arts of homicide and training them to kill at sight without thought, mercy, or compunction. The Army euphemistically describes this as a 'toughening' process. You may well ask, how are these killers that the Army has created to be controlled if the Law be not strained and twisted to convict them? . . . how is the public to be protected from the homicidal crafts that he has learned in the years following the war?

But Carter reassures us that these fears are unwarranted:

> When Corporal Brent walks out into Civvy Street, all those dread arts will be sloughed off like his uniform. In three months after that you will find him thinking only about motorcycle races or the wallflowers in his garden, and when at times he is reminded that he once killed men in brutal physical assault, he will be filled with wonder that the same man was he.[74]

Carter wins his case. But the readers of Nevil Shute's 1947 novel *The Chequer Board* may nonetheless have felt less than sanguine about the long-term prospects of men like Brent. If any ex-serviceman exemplified the mixed feelings of the British public toward their homecoming servicemen, it was the commando – the soldier who, as Betty Miller suggested in her 1945 novel *On the Side of the Angels*, appealed to 'the criminal in all of us . . . the anti-social impulse'.[75]

The British had pioneered the modern concept of 'special forces' during the early years of the war. Lacking the manpower to launch a full-scale assault on Hitler's Fortress Europa, they had picked around its edges instead, creating what Churchill called 'butcher-and-bolt' teams of highly trained volunteers who would launch airborne and amphibious raids on the coasts of France and Norway. Eventually, four brigades of army and Royal Marine commandos were formed. In North Africa, the Long Range Desert Group (LRDG) and the Special Air Service (SAS) performed similar hit-and-run raids behind Field Marshal Erwin Rommel's lines. The secret agents of Special Operations Executive (SOE) were another special forces prototype.

The military utility of these tiny private armies remains in dispute. Though dramatic, their missions rarely had any decisive effect. John Sparrow, the War Office's morale expert, thought that the elite units were a waste of manpower; they drained regular infantry companies of good men and stole away prestige from the ordinary soldier.[76] But they caught the public's imagination at home. The commando, his face blackened with boot-polish and a knife clenched grimly between his teeth, became one of the inspirational icons of Britain's war. Indeed, by the end of the war, the word 'commando' had become synonymous with a particular kind of power, efficiency and ruthless skill. It was a label that others were eager to appropriate. The Ministry of Labour was calling for 'commandos of industry';[77] 'crime commandos' trawled London's West End seeking deserters.[78]

What was fascinating about the commando was that he exemplified the revival of ancient warrior traditions in the midst of robotic, industrialised destruction. The Second World War's race for technology had resulted in the atomic bomb, the V-2 ballistic missile and other impersonal weapons of the future, yet the commando, trained in brutal hand-to-hand fighting tactics that would not have been out of place in Homer's *Iliad*, seemed strangely modern too. War appeared to be taking a step backwards as well as forwards. 'Able to scale cliffs like a Pathan, to live like a Boer with no transport columns and no cookhouses, and to disperse and break away like an Arab before he could be pinned to the ground' was how *Soldier* magazine admiringly described the commando.[79]

Yet just as the martial races of the empire – the fearsome dyaks of Borneo, the ruthless Thuggees of India – had been admired for their military prowess but feared for their savagery, so the commando provoked apprehension as well as respect. He was brave and skilled, but his style of fighting was unsportsmanlike, 'dirty', suspiciously un-English. The name connoted a flirtation with illegality, an impatience with mere rules, a willingness to mete out justice with direct action regardless of the methods employed. The commando was a bit of a brute. He brought gangster values to the battlefield. Would he bring them home as well?

This clash between traditional military virtues and the commando creed – the antiquated pitted against the anarchic – was examined in Michael Powell and Emeric Pressburger's controversial 1943 comedy-drama *The Life and Death of Colonel Blimp*, which famously provoked Churchill's ire precisely because it suggested that fighting 'dirty' was the only way of defeating the Nazis.

One can detect the cultural ambiguity of the postwar commando in the 'Gimlet' series of children's adventure stories written by W.E. Johns, more famous as the creator of Biggles. Between 1943 and 1959 Johns wrote ten full-length books about Commando Captain Lorrington 'Gimlet' King and his team of Combined Operations raiders. Only the first two stories are set during the war itself; with the exception of one prewar tale, the rest take place after demobilisation and follow Gimlet and his comrades as ex-servicemen working informally for the Foreign Office on special overseas missions.

Although the Biggles and Gimlet stories share certain conventions of plot and setting, the personalities of the two heroes could not be more different. Whereas the Great War flying ace is full of chivalric *joie de vivre*, Gimlet is cold, humourless, steely: the violence in his adventures is much more graphic, and there is a sardonic attitude towards killing that won the cautionary label 'for older boys' on the books' dust jackets. Gimlet is not a criminal, but as a civilian he and the other members of 'King's Kittens' do display traits typical of the brutalised ex-serviceman. They find it impossible to settle down on Civvy Street after the excitement of their wartime careers. They show little concern for the niceties of the law when dealing with enemies in their usual ferocious manner. They are a little frightening even as they aspire to be role models for clean-living middle-class British boys.[80]

The belief that the commando was a sort of latterday pirate seems to have been widespread even within the British Army. There were early suggestions that commandos should be recruited from the criminal underclass of American and British slums, and that convicts and warders should create a special prison commando brigade.[81] 'In the early days,' wrote Major General Robert Laycock, postwar Chief of Combined Operations, 'much stress was laid, especially in the press, on the "toughness" of the Commando soldier . . . he was invariably depicted as a rather scruffy-looking man with a blackened face and a murderous-looking knife.' The propaganda value of this characterisation was obvious, but regular officers sceptical of the whole concept thought that commandos were 'a mob of unshaven thugs . . . an undisciplined rabble'.[82]

Commandos on field exercises routinely stole from civilians with the tacit approval of their commanders.[83] The commando ideal resembled what General Archibald Wavell would describe as the 'seasoning of devilry' necessary in all good soldiers – a combination of cat-burglar, gunman, poacher.[84] He had been taught 'how to enter buildings, crack safes, use small explosives, and live as [a] fugitive'. Trained to kill quickly and silently, would he (as *Picture Post* put it delicately) use these techniques 'less usefully' in civilian life?[85]

One who did was George Jackson, a former army commando sentenced to a five-year term for larceny at Parkhurst prison, Newport, on the Isle of Wight. In June 1946 Jackson escaped, and the public response to the news encapsulates how ambiguously people felt about his unorthodox military calling. For nearly two weeks Jackson remained at large on the island, living secretly off the land in the manner taught him by his wartime instructors, as an increasingly large force of police and armed troops scoured the countryside looking for him.[86] He was peacefully recaptured on the thirteenth day of his liberation, by which time he had become a minor press celebrity as Parkhurst's most successful escapee ever. Many press commentators did not try to disguise their admiration for Jackson: 'Never once in those twelve days did [he] forget the fieldcraft which he learned with the Commandos ... [it was] a great feat of self-discipline,' wrote the *Daily Herald*.[87] When Jackson arrived back at Parkhurst a large crowd, mainly women, turned out to cheer him on – a 'stupid exhibition [which] almost makes one despair at the complete lack of any social conscience,' one irate newspaper reader complained.[88]

But the Newport sightseers could have been forgiven for seeing in Jackson a close resemblance to the escaped prisoners of war whose stories had already become part of the core British memory of the conflict. After all, in the next column to the *News Chronicle*'s account of Jackson's recapture was a story about RAF aircrew receiving MBE's for their breakout attempts from Germany. 'These Men Would Not Be Caged', the headline read – and the article went on to celebrate men who had 'tunnelled their way out of German prison camps, picked cell locks, sawed window bars, forged papers, jumped trains'.[89] If the nation was a little confused about rebels such as Jackson, was it really any wonder? For wasn't their wartime heroism quasi-criminal to begin with? Feared and admired in equal measure, the commando was *the* quintessential soldier-villain.

## Compensations

In 1944, the same year in which Mass-Observation published its demobilisation prospectus *The Journey Home*, the author Robert Quixano Henriques published a novel of the same name that gave the ominous but vague forecasts of a wave of returning Calibans a frightening specificity.[90] Henriques's story follows a group of ex-servicemen from the Mediterranean arriving back in Britain for demob. Throughout their journey across the country the soldiers express varying degrees of scorn, contempt and rage at the civilians whom they encounter, stewing over a long list of grievances against a society that they claim has exploited and betrayed them. One of their number, Charlie, has been traumatised first on the battlefield and then by the vindictive treachery of his wife, who in his absence has taken up with a well-paid factory worker.

Men like Charlie are the natural pawns of 'David', a charismatic war hero with a head wound that has had a disturbing effect on his personality. David has rejected his carefree prewar dilettantism and now yearns to lead an English *Freikorps* of disaffected veterans, playing on demagogic themes of fear and resentment. At the close of the novel he orates an undisguised fascist appeal to a generation of front-line warriors disgusted by homeland decadence and yearning to see the purer virtues of military comradeship enforced in what is rightfully 'their' country:

> The best of England, the choice of the land, were away in the Forces. Those who remained behind were rotten in spirit and wouldn't fight, or rotten in body and couldn't get taken. They aren't fit to be masters with us as their servants . . . they shan't be . . . millions of men already organized, already enrolled in a great company, bound by common experience, common understanding, and a common way of thought.

> The rest is easy. You'll have your soldiers' guild, your soldiers' candidates, your soldiers' party, your party headquarters . . . this time it's going to happen – the soldiers' party! You'll sweep the country and no-one will dare oppose you. You'll march through the streets of the cities, you'll line the road to the polls . . .[91]

But of course this turned out to be pure fantasy. No murderous *Freikorps* led by a would-be *Führer* like David marched on Buckingham Palace in 1945. Which raises the question: to what extent, if any at all, did ex-servicemen really contribute to the postwar crime wave? Were soldiers really coming home unable to contain their predilections for violence, morally contaminated by the corrupting temptations of life in uniform?

No statistics exist to show the proportion of convicted postwar criminals who had served in the Forces. However, given that both groups consisted predominantly of able-bodied young men, it would be surprising if there was not *some* correlation between the two. But in 1954 the criminologist John Spencer researched the question thoroughly, and was unimpressed. Spencer found no compelling evidence at all of a postwar 'veteran problem', other than that conjured up by the press. In his many interviews with ex-service convicts, Spencer offered, and indeed encouraged, his subjects to use military life as an excuse for their behaviour: the suggestion, however, was never taken up.[92] He also noted that the vast majority of violent criminals were not bloodthirsty front-line fighters, but rather men who had done dull and menial service behind the lines. In the 1980s the criminologists Dale Archer and Rosemary Gartner revisited the British postwar crime wave as part of their much larger investigation into the links between social violence and crime, but they found that war tended to produce proportionally similar increases in lawlessness amongst women and older men as it did amongst men of conscription age: 'The image of the violent veteran,' they concluded, 'may be more myth than reality.'[93]

Crime in the armed services was supposedly connected to the problem of desertion. In February 1946 the government estimated that 14,270 army deserters were at large somewhere in Great Britain, with perhaps 1,000 or so more from the navy and air force as well as several hundred Americans, Canadians and other foreign servicemen.[94] Deserters were drawn to crime by the very act of fleeing the Forces: at the very least, a deserter needed to obtain false identity papers, and at worst he might turn to theft as a way of life, stealing in order to survive. The idea grew that a small army of deserters were responsible for much of the crime wave, and that these men were becoming a permanent criminal underclass. Arthur Harvey, Tory MP for Macclesfield, claimed in the House of Commons, also in February 1946, that one in ten of all crimes in London was being committed by deserters.[95]

Yet it turned out that the deserter problem was not nearly as important a source of crime as journalists and politicians had insisted. In the winter of 1945–6 civilian and military police conducted night-time sweeps of pubs and dance halls across

London's West End, cordoning off large areas of the city and bringing traffic to a halt to check the papers of pedestrians and drivers. But the resulting hauls were trifling – of 15,000 people who were stopped and searched in one clampdown, only thirty-two were found to be deserters.[96] At least half of all putative deserters had given addresses in the Republic of Ireland when they enlisted, which suggested that rather than living incognito in Great Britain they had simply returned home at the end of the war rather than waiting to be formally demobilised – technically a breach of military law, but hardly a sign of rampant domestic crime.[97] When the Metropolitan Police circulated an internal inquiry about the deserter problem amongst its divisional inspectors in 1946, most agreed that deserters were playing a small role in the crime rise.[98] In 1953 the few remaining wartime deserters were granted a general amnesty as part of the Coronation celebrations.

As for the brutalised soldier-Caliban, throughout the war senior officers had been more concerned that British soldiers were not brutalised *enough*. As Field Marshal Montgomery put it: 'The trouble with our British lads is that they are not killers by nature.'[99] Alex Comfort would go further in his 1950 book *Authority and Delinquency in the Modern State*, arguing that servicemen had been *less* brutalised by war than civilians. 'It is essentially the socially maladjusted civilian who is happiest in wartime,' said Comfort: 'armies lack the intense group psychopathic traits of wartime civilian populations.'[100]

In retrospect, the postwar crime wave itself is less mysterious or shocking than it seemed at the time. Wartime shortages had made goods that were previously too trivial to thieve worth pilfering. As Home Secretary James Chuter Ede pointed out himself, 'No-one would have thought of stealing second-hand shirts in 1938 . . . today [in 1946] the sight of a shirt on a clothes-line has become a temptation. Everything is worth stealing, and everything is much easier to steal.'[101] The police force remained enervated by the military service of its men; the regular constabulary did not return to its prewar strength until 1949. Local communities took several years to cohere after the mass migrations and residential transfers set off by the war. Crime was easier to commit within an anonymous and shifting population. Postwar Britain remained, by today's standards, an astonishingly law-abiding country. Indeed, by 1952, *The Times* admitted that it was no longer credible to suggest that 'tough ex-servicemen' brutalised by their combat experiences could be held responsible for postwar crime.[102]

The fear of the ex-serviceman at the end of the Second World War was, if anything, not a specific response to unique historical circumstances but a resurgence in a longstanding national prejudice against old soldiers. At the end of the Napoleonic Wars, middle-class households had bought up weapons at inflated prices in anticipation of a wave of robber-gangs formed from the demobilised redcoats of the Duke of Wellington's army.[103] In 1919 writers had fretted about the return of the brutalised masses from the trenches: the journalist Philip Gibbs had suggested that such men were 'subject to queer moods, queer temper . . . bitter in their speech, violent in opinion, frightening'.[104] The 1920 Prison Commission *Report* warned that a wave of sheer lawlessness had broken out across the country: 'normal restraints of conduct had been banished by the stress of war'.[105] By 1952, another scare had simply come and gone.

But if the soldier-villain was largely mythical, the wistful regret that many bored ex-servicemen took into civilian life was not. 'How many times, in the late Forties and Fifties,' recalled the novelist George MacDonald Fraser in his memoirs, 'did one see a sober citizen in his office throw aside his pencil and stare at the window and exclaim: *Oh, God, I wish the war was still on!*'[106] The escape for such men was not felonious but fictional. In 1953 the ex-operations planner of the commando formation 30 Assault Unit, codenamed '17F', published his first novel, *Casino Royale*. It was through such surrogates as Commander James Bond that bored and wistful men like Ian Fleming would spend the postwar years vicariously reinhabiting the mental world of wartime.

# CHAPTER SEVEN

# Something Has Gone Wrong
# Inside My Head

*The war doesn't only kill bodies – it kills minds and souls as well.*[1]

HMS *Goodall*'s war ended at exactly 19.35 hours on the evening of Sunday, 29 April 1945, in the frigid waters of the Kola Inlet which snakes between the port of Murmansk and the Barents Sea nine miles to the north. *Goodall*, a 1,100-ton Captain-class frigate, had just left Murmansk earlier that Sunday as part of the Nineteenth Escort Group, its task to protect the twenty-seven merchantmen of the homecoming convoy RA-66 which was about to sail en route for the Clyde. For almost four years British sailors had been navigating the perilous 1,400-mile journey from Scotland to the Kola Peninsula and back, carrying badly needed supplies and munitions to the USSR.

The journey through freezing fog-bound waters covered with drift ice was hazardous enough even in peacetime. But because of Germany's control of the west coast of Norway the Arctic convoys were continually harassed by land-based bombers, mines, surface raiders and submarines. Eighty-five merchant ships had been sunk. By the spring of 1945, with the war almost over, Russia's need for further Western aid was diminishing. But Stalin insisted that the sailings continue nonetheless, and in the interests of coalition solidarity the British continued to dispatch them. The Germans, for their part, remained determined to sink every ship they could. Lying in the Kola Inlet that Sunday evening was a 'Wolfpack' of fourteen U-boats.

It was just before 19.00 hours when one of *Goodall*'s escort partners, HMS *Loch Insh*, signalled that her ASDIC underwater detection equipment had picked up a suspicious contact beneath the Inlet. She and two other frigates began an attack run, charging ahead and firing their 'Squid' three-barrelled mortars and depth charges. A U-boat broke to the surface and was promptly torn to pieces by the frigates' guns and cannons. As *Loch Insh* rescued a handful of soaking, terrified survivors from the shattered submarine, the other escorts resumed their cautious hunt. They swept back and forth across the strait in wide zig-zags, their ASDIC operators straining to hear the giveaway 'ping' of reflected sound that would occur when striking a U-boat's hull.

At 19.29 hours *Goodall* reported a contact and began an attack run, her mortar crew standing by to fire. Six minutes later a final signal was received from her telegraph room: *sub definite . . .* it was never finished. At the same moment there was, as the Admiralty's official report later said, 'a tremendous explosion' right below *Goodall*'s bridge superstructure:

> This appeared to be caused by a torpedo hit on the port side which detonated a magazine. When the smoke cleared, the after section of the ship abreast to the funnel remained afloat, with the funnel and part of the bridge folded back on to the superstructure, and fires commencing to break out in the fore end.

Able seaman G.A. Roy was at his cannon station on the funnel deck when the torpedo slammed home. 'There was a terrific flash followed by flying debris,' he later recalled. 'Something big slammed into my gun shield . . . I was left hanging by the [cannon] straps spitting blood due to a rap on the head, plus a busted right ankle. My mate was lying beside the gun platform, his head missing.' Roy struggled to his feet and clambered across the deck, strewn with body parts, before throwing himself into the oily water. George Halliday, another gunner, was trapped when his cannon mounting collapsed on top of him, but managed to make his way to a raft overloaded with fourteen other survivors. The sea, though freezing, had caught fire as exploding ammunition ignited the diesel fuel haemorrhaging from *Goodall*'s tanks. Another frigate escort swept past the raft on an attack run, her bow wave tossing Halliday and the others back into the water. Eventually they were picked up by a Russian motor torpedo boat.

Some men on board *Goodall* that night simply disappeared, their exact fate never known. Leading Signalman John Rawlinson had only just joined the crew as a replacement before the ship sailed for Murmansk on her last voyage. A veteran sailor, he had a low Release Group number and was looking forward to an early demobilisation. He had left behind him a bride of three months, pregnant with a son he would never meet. The Admiralty did not have an up-to-date address for his next of kin and so contacted Rawlinson's father instead of his wife. She didn't find out until her father-in-law wrote to her, assuming she already knew.

Of HMS *Goodall*'s 156 crew, 98 died along with her on Sunday, 29 April 1945. Within minutes their assassins, the 51 men of submarine U-286, were themselves dead, their vessel smashed to the seabed by depth charges. Within twenty-four hours Adolf Hitler, the grand instigator behind all this destruction, was dead too, thirteen hundred miles away in his besieged Berlin bunker. Within nine days the war in Europe was over.

The encounter in Kola Inlet on 29 April was the last convoy battle of the Second World War, and *Goodall* was to have the grim distinction of being the final Royal Navy warship sunk by the German *Kriegsmarine*. She and her young sailors fought and died in the best traditions of the Senior Service. But she was sunk almost at the moment of victory. Her destruction did not alter the outcome of the war in the slightest. Her killers drowned in the freezing darkness without having delayed their country's defeat by a minute. These were deaths with a peculiar madness to them.

Even as the final minutes ticked away the war consumed lives, driven along by nothing more than its own insane momentum.[2]

But it was not only *Goodall*'s dead who were the victims of U-286. After the explosion telegraphist Bill Bates found himself trapped in pitch darkness in the three-feet-square emergency wireless cubby, the door jammed by debris. Bates clawed in the darkness at the access hatch as freezing water seeped into the tiny compartment and acrid fumes from the radio's leaking batteries saturated the air. Finally the hatch gave way and he staggered on to the deck, the sinking vessel now listing violently to starboard. He found his best friend outside the door, but when Bates tried to pick him up he literally fell to pieces, 'his left side went one way and his right side went another. He was almost in half.' Unidentifiable arms and legs were scattered everywhere.

Bates jumped into the water and clung to a cork float net, his eyes raw from the diesel oil. 'As we struggled to keep ahead of the flames we saw men who were on bits of rafts drift into the blaze . . . I was dimly aware that I was now alone and voices were screaming, the whole world seemed to be in a red glow.' He lost consciousness and awoke to the stench of smoke and vomit on board HMS *Honeysuckle*. Nine days later he arrived back in London, just in time for V-E Day. He was 'home' – but his real home was a thousand miles away, submerged forever beneath the arctic waters of the Barents Sea. The dancing and singing and cheers left him unmoved. 'Gone were the laughs and catcalls' he remembered from *Goodall*'s wireless office:

> Gone was the warm cosy mess-deck and getting ready for a run ashore . . . it was as if I had come home to London again during the Blitz to find the house gone. All those precious moments that had gone into making a home had been taken away. There was a great empty space within me.

Within a month of his return to Britain, Bates was posted to the Far East – 'the sun will do you good', they said – but he could not leave the Kola Inlet behind. The heat and diesel smell from the engine room of his new ship disturbed him. There were dreams, terrifying dreams of men trapped beneath the freezing sea, of the ship's bell tolling beneath the water. 'I'd get very emotional about old shipmates,' he recalled: 'you'd go out ashore to have a drink or go to a dance and you'd come back and you'd think: *here I am in bright sunshine, everything's nice and clean, I've had a good evening, and my mates are laying out in the Kola Inlet. And I might have been with them.*'

He returned to Britain and was demobilised in November 1946. That was when the shaking started. 'I went to drink a cup of tea and found I couldn't hold it.' He didn't want to leave the navy – it seemed like breaking faith with his dead comrades – and he was scared of what would he find in Civvy Street: 'I had no trade, no education as such, no substantial cash.' But the Admiralty wasn't interested: the war was over and he was surplus to requirements. Bates had always had a knack for wiring, so he went to work for an electrical company run by his uncle. But he had a panic attack on his first job when the lights failed and he found himself in the dark. 'I was completely shattered by that.'

The everyday routines of life were seeded with reminders of *Goodall*. The smell of diesel when a car went past in the street gave him 'collywobbles'. Relatives of crewmen reported missing from the lost ship came to see Bates, desperately seeking any glimmer of hope that their loved ones might still be alive. The burden of their grief on top of his own was unbearable. He was diagnosed with agoraphobia and anxiety neurosis. Eventually, he got a job as a housing officer with the Greater London Council, but the nightmares never really went away. He took early retirement in 1978 on medical advice. Bill Bates did not receive a war pension until 1993, forty-eight years after HMS *Goodall* sank to the bottom of the Kola Inlet, taking his youth and his peace of mind with it forever.

## Impertinent Survival

'It is strange that I am still alive, when so many better men are already dead,' wrote journalist J.L. Hodson the day after the war ended in Europe.[3] Men like Bill Bates who found, often to their amazement, that they had survived the war were confronted by this unforeseen combination of puzzlement and guilt. The moral problem of taking life had been anticipated, prepared for, and to a large extent, overcome. The problem of survival was more unexpected.

Francis McGovern, a Lancaster mid-upper-turret gunner with Royal Canadian Air Force 6 Group, was badly wounded in a raid on Leipzig in October 1943, and had to be grounded for treatment of shrapnel wounds in his hand, leg and eye. In his place another gunner, Tom Hastings, joined the crew. Two months later, while McGovern was still recuperating, the plane and its crew were lost over Frankfurt. Hastings was married with two children. McGovern found it hard to forgive himself for the death. 'I should have been in his place. I carried a guilt complex about that for a long time.'[4]

A year later driver-mechanic Robert Dare went through a similar cycle of remorse when his Churchill tank drove over a mine near Overloon in the Netherlands. Though badly injured himself, he tried and failed to rescue two of his comrades from the burning vehicle. 'They were such good friends,' he recalled years later: 'we'd been together for such a long time.' Afterwards he found that his ears were ringing and that he had lost the ability to speak. He continued to suffer psychosomatic symptoms for several years after the war, and only recovered his voice with great difficulty. Even in 1999 he felt guilt: 'I still think I should have made another effort to [rescue them].'[5]

Death in the Second World War was arbitrary, fickle, sometimes perverse. Men were killed and others spared for no particular reason. One attracted the sniper's attention, the other didn't. One stood at the precise spot where the bomb landed, the other found himself miraculously shielded from its blast a few feet away. Death was no respecter of talent, courage, or merit. Fortune favoured some and took others. But the audacity of survival could seem as though it were disrespect for the dead.

When the poet Vernon Scannell, who had fought and been wounded with the Gordon Highlanders in North Africa and

France, heard he was being discharged in 1947, his initial response was 'wild exhilaration . . . almost unbearable excitement'. But his joy subsided as he thought of his friends and comrades, 'with as much to live for as I', still lying in the Libyan sands and the Normandy countryside:

> However clean they kept their noses, no board would give them their discharge. . . . They accused, and [writing in 1983] they accuse me still. Pity for the dead is a wasted emotion, or so my reason tells me, but the heart is deaf to such counsel and it grieves for those young lives brutally and prematurely ended . . . the grief is poisoned with guilt and an obscure fear that in some way and some time full payment for one's outrageous good fortune will be exacted.[6]

Some officers felt obliged to keep faith with the dead. In three and a half years of service in North Africa and Italy, Arthur Vizard's infantry company lost seventy-three men. After the war he was able to track down fifty-eight of their families and went to visit all of them. 'They'd got over the initial shocks but there was a lot of sadness – going over the ground again and explaining how it all happened.' He gave as truthful an account as he dared, but there were no stories of agonising deaths. 'I always told them it was clean.'[7]

Impertinent survival in the midst of such grief could gnaw away at men already unsettled by their wartime experiences. When Group Captain Leonard Cheshire VC was relinquished of command in January 1946 diagnosed with psychoneurosis, it was vaguely assumed by the public that this had something to do with the atomic bombing of Nagasaki four months previously, on 9 August 1945, which he had witnessed as an official RAF observer. But Cheshire always defended the mission as militarily necessary. His nervous exhaustion at the end of the war was not difficult to understand. He was surrounded by ghosts. Of the aircrew he had flown with on his 102 missions, hardly any were still alive. Families of dead friends wrote to him looking for consolation. He had become, as his biographer puts it, 'a proxy for dead sons . . . a councillor for heartbroken parents'. It was all too much. He had a nervous breakdown.[8]

## The Breaking Point

'I am holding a packet of Woodbines, then there is a noise like thunder. It's right on my head, there's a high-pitched whistle in my ears, at first I black out and then I see red. . . .'[9] So Lance Bombardier Spike Milligan, 56th Heavy Regiment Royal Artillery, recounted in his famous postwar memoirs the exact moment when his gun position was hit by German mortar fire just south of Monte Cassino, Italy, one morning in January 1944. Milligan was already jittery; a few days earlier he had seen four of his comrades turned into blackened stumps when exploding ammunition had set fire to their tent. Now, at the dressing station where he was being treated for shrapnel wounds in the leg, he could not stop shaking and crying. The medical officer prescribed hot, sweet tea, a handful of barbiturates, and told him to get back into the line. But when Milligan returned to the battery he ran terrified for cover as soon as his own guns began firing. He was brought before his commanding officer, stripped of his stripe, and sent down to a military hospital in Caserta, near Naples, officially suffering from 'battle fatigue' and surrounded by other official 'loonies'. His active combat career was over; a lifetime of manic depression was just beginning.[10]

Milligan was just one of the better-known psychiatric casualties of the Second World War. He was far from alone. In some theatres of combat, up to one in three of all British servicemen evacuated from the battle area were diagnosed as suffering from mental trauma.[11] Its treatment received commensurate priority. In September 1939 the Royal Army Medical Corps (RAMC) had only two psychiatric advisers on its staff.[12] But within three years a Directorate of Army Psychiatry had been set up, and psychiatric advisers recruited from civilian practices were being attached to all army commands both in the United Kingdom and overseas. The 'trick cyclist' had become an important and permanent fixture of military medicine.

During the First World War the correct treatment of what was then known as 'shell shock' had been highly controversial. Many RAMC doctors had refused to recognise psychoneurotic complaints as legitimate wounds, and accusations of malingering and cowardice had hung over men whose nerves had broken in battle. The official 1922 government report on the problem could not quite make up its mind whether it was studying a medical or a moral phenomenon; although it admitted that the ultimate cause of shell shock was a mystery, it insisted that 'loss of nerve' was never an honourable escape from front-line duty, and that well-trained, well-led soldiers would rarely if ever succumb to it.[13]

In many respects the attitude towards war trauma in the Second World War was a lot more sympathetic. Shell shock disappeared as an official description of the condition, replaced from 1942 onwards by the less censorious euphemism 'battle exhaustion', which framed the trauma in a language that made it sound both natural and (it was hoped) temporary. RAMC psychiatrists were now emphatic that nervous strain in a soldier was an inevitable result of prolonged stress, and that all men, no matter how brave or conscientious, would begin to show symptoms of nervous strain if they were exposed to intense danger for as few as five days.[14] Since the death penalty had been abolished for cowardice and desertion in the 1930s, there was in any case less resting on the doctor's diagnosis.

Nonetheless, the old stigma had not disappeared entirely. Older RAMC doctors remained bewildered by psychiatric problems, and had what one psychiatrist described as an 'almost obsessional' reluctance to accept that non-physical causes might be to blame for their patients' behaviour.[15] The director of the British Army's medical services, Major-General E. Philips, regarded psychiatry as 'a new form of witchcraft'.[16] Churchill remained deeply suspicious of the discipline, suggesting in a December 1942 Cabinet memo that psychiatry in the army could 'easily degenerate into charla-tanry'; he regarded its practitioners as 'hangers-on and camp-followers', disturbing otherwise healthy men with odd questions.[17]

The Royal Air Force and Royal Navy were even less welcoming toward psychiatric methods. From the spring of 1940 onwards the RAF characterised aircrew psychologically incapable of continuing to fly as suffering from LMF, or 'Lack of Moral Fibre' – a fundamental flaw in character rather than a medical condition, and one to be regarded with appropriate censure and severity. One pilot described it as 'the most pernicious phrase' in all of the RAF's wartime vocabulary.[18] The Admiralty, for its part, continued to subscribe to the belief that all men suffering from battle exhaustion really needed was 'a special hardening course of treatment under strict naval discipline'; square-bashing would knock the shirkers back into line.[19]

Even within the RAMC, the treatment of battle trauma was often so eccentrically practised as to verge on the brutal. It was a science in its infancy, and opinions as to the proper clinical approach varied wildly. Some wartime research experiments became benchmarks in the postwar treatment of the mentally ill; Northfield Military Hospital near Birmingham proved foundational in the development of group-therapy techniques.[20]

But many psychiatrists had deeply invested in the Freudian school of psychoanalysis, and their 'defective' case studies were often described in a damning language of mental inadequacy. One soldier who had spent five months in heavy combat and had twice seen his tank blown apart had entered hospital in England complaining of lethargy, headaches and depression: he was written off as 'histrionic . . . self-centred and shallow' by his psychiatrist.[21]

Other doctors, looking for faster physical solutions, practised experimental lobotomies and narcotherapy with barbiturates and sodium pentathol.[22] Even Lieutenant-Colonel Thomas Main, psychiatric adviser to Montgomery's 21 Army Group in north-western Europe and a humane and sympathetic counsellor, had a 'compulsory mourning' programme for patients alleged to be suppressing feelings of grief. He would lock them in a small cell for three days in almost total darkness on a diet of bread and water.[23]

Whether or not any of these treatments worked, the army's ultimate concern was its own institutional efficiency rather than the long-term mental health of its conscripts. One of the main tasks assigned to the Directorate of Army Psychiatry was to weed out unstable men from the ranks before they could become a medical liability. Experience in the Western Desert of North Africa early in the war suggested that perhaps half of the army's psychiatric casualties should never have been called up in the first place, still less sent into action against the Afrika Korps.[24] The RAMC's psychiatrists set about identifying these misfits and either placing them in non-combatant roles far from the risks of battle, or else removing them from the army entirely. By 1944 almost half of all medical discharges were on psychiatric grounds.[25]

What happened to these men after their return to Civvy Street was not, however, a particular concern of the War Office, so long as they weren't a drain on the public purse. And by defining many psychological casualties as victims of pre-existing constitutional weaknesses unconnected to their military service, rather than the traumas of war, it was possible to deny thousands of pension claims. It has been estimated that only about 30,000 pensions were granted to British Second World War veterans for psychoneurotic problems, less than half those awarded after the Great War.[26] From the Treasury's point of view, it was a splendid outcome.

But for men permanently scarred by the events they had witnessed, there was no easy return to normality. Veterans like Bill Bates and Spike Milligan were silent victims of their own memories, besieged by inner demons that others could neither see nor understand. And there may have been tens of thousands of them released back on to the streets of Britain after the Second World War, undiagnosed and unassisted. Writing in the *Journal of Mental Science* in 1947, Thomas Main warned that as many as one-quarter of all 'healthy' demobilised men were having serious difficulties adjusting to peacetime life. 'They must be regarded as a sociological as well as a medical problem,' he wrote, 'an incubus on the mental health of the nation.' Few of them, 'in great but secret distress', were willing or able to seek psychiatric help for their problems:

Relatives will almost monotonously give the same story: *He was all right the first few days; he was so glad to get home. But he seems changed.*

*He used to be so cheerful. Now I don't know what to do with him.*
*Nothing I do seems right for him. He's a different man.*[27]

## Barbed-Wire Disease

'As I sit and write this, everyone has gone,' wrote Lieutenant George Chippington from his lonely Rangoon hospital bed in the autumn of 1945. 'This sense of being in a vacuum which has haunted me – if that is not too strong a word – ever since we first heard it was all over, has now intensified to the point of being unbearable':

> After so many years of the excitements and dangers of the campaign and the sufferings and privations . . . the sudden full stop to all purposeful activity, out of its very emptiness, has created an overpowering sense of isolation. I am now as it were a mere spectator doomed forever to stand off-stage while others act out the drama in which I no longer have a role.[28]

Chippington, an infantry officer with the Leicestershire Regiment, had been captured at the fall of Singapore in February 1942 and held in a succession of Japanese prison camps in Malaya and Thailand for the three and a half years that followed. The stories of Chippington and the other 37,583 Far East Prisoners of War (Fepows) who survived to return home would quickly become, within the English-speaking world, as emblematic of the horrors of the war as those of the Jewish victims of Hitler's 'Final Solution'. Systematically starved, beaten and worked to the brink of death by their captors, liberated Fepows in the summer of 1945 were scarcely recognisable as human beings. Betty Duignan, a WAAF stationed in Columbo, Ceylon, helped to receive liberated prisoners. 'One looked exactly like that man in the Belsen pictures who was sitting up in a pile of rags and who looked more like a skeleton than a man,' she wrote to her parents:

> Every bone in his body was showing through the skin – my finger and thumb would have circled the top of his arm easily – his neck

was sunk in a deep pit of bone and even his ears seemed to hang loose because all the flesh had receded. His eyes were right back in his head and they were surrounded by huge circles which made him look just like a giant panda . . . he was 24 and he lived near Barton Cross.[29]

Men had seen so little food during their imprisonment that upon release they would stand awe-struck outside bakeries, gazing at the tiers of fresh loaves.[30]

After years of this malnutrition and the ravages of tropical disease, few of the Fepows bore much resemblance to their prewar selves. A.K. Berrecloth, an RAF corporal who had been captured on Java in 1942, noted that he did not even recognise his own face when he first saw his reflection after liberation. 'It was grim looking, with jaw clenched and mouth turned downward at the corners. The lower half was covered by an irregular stubble of beard tending to redness . . . the eyes had whitish crow's feet each side due to wrinkling against the glare of the tropical sun. A morose and unhappy face, the face of a stranger!'[31] 'After the first shock of seeing your grey-haired, pot-bellied spindle shanked leprous Eurasian-looking husband . . . it'll take a lot of settling down to a normal life again,' wrote Colonel G.H. Shorland in an imaginary letter to his wife Betty in December 1944.[32]

If anyone had reason to celebrate the end of the war, it was these men. Yet Chippington admitted to oddly ambivalent feelings at his liberation. 'I suppose I should be happy,' he wrote:

> But I am not. In some strange, inexplicable way a feeling of apathy has crept over me – almost a sadness. I feel drained, empty – a shell, hollow inside as though suddenly in a vacuum. I have made no mention of this strangeness to others but, in some, I sense a similar attitude. Victory is ours. It is all over – surely a chance for rejoicing – yet oddly I am merely going through the motions.[33]

Berrecloth sensed he had 'no tremendous feelings of elation . . . no real excitement'.[34] Captain Ronald Horner, captured at Singapore, felt similarly confused. 'Somehow one can't help but feel anti-climax ... people [are] very irritable, having bottled up likes and dislikes for months. This extra strain finds them venting their spleen when previously they would have held themselves in.'[35]

This sense of anticlimax would soon be compounded by impatience at the delay in repatriation. The speed of the Japanese collapse in the summer of 1945 had caught the British authorities off balance. South East Asia Command (SEAC), which had been gearing up for an invasion of the Malayan Peninsula in September, suddenly found its military preparations superseded by a vast refugee crisis. Over 200,000 former prisoners, internees and corvée labourers were scattered from the Burmese frontier to the outermost islands of the Indonesian archipelago, thousands of miles to the east.[36] Like the Displaced Persons of liberated Europe, they needed urgent supplies of food, medicine, accommodation, and ultimately some way of getting back home.

The Recovery of Allied Prisoners of War and Internees (RAPWI) programme was tasked with taking control of former Japanese camps and preparing the surviving inmates for their return to their home countries. The first flights back to the UK left Singapore on 9 September 1945. But despite the high transport priority given to Fepows, their repatriation would be inevitably slowed down by the same shortage of aircraft and ships that was dogging the demobilisation process. 'An outside observer gets an impression of complete chaos,' wrote *The Times'* correspondent.[37] Horner felt that he and his comrades were getting 'a raw deal ... we're still living in the same conditions as we were under the Japs'. Resentment grew at the constant delays in embarkation and the lack of information given to Fepows. In the hospitals and ad hoc transit camps of Singapore, RAPWI became popularly known as 'Retain All Prisoners of War Indefinitely'.[38]

Whilst men in the Far East cooled their heels in frustration, for former prisoners of the Germans the return to Britain could be bewilderingly fast. During April and May 1945, the heavy bombers of the RAF and USAAF were hurriedly converted into troop transports to facilitate Operation EXODUS, the airlifting of the hundreds of thousands of Allied POWs who were being liberated in the final days of the war. By the end of May, 135,000 British ex-prisoners had been returned to the United Kingdom.[39]

The death rate amongst POWs in Europe – 5 per cent – was five times lower than in the Far East. But that is not to say that the men returning from Germany were in good condition. Food and medical care were always unevenly distributed between one laager or campo and another, and became considerably worse as Allied troops advanced on the territory of the Reich. By early 1945 tens of thousands of British Commonwealth and American POWs were being force-marched hundreds of miles westwards from their former prison camps in Silesia, Poland and East Prussia to escape the advancing Red Army; an unknown number succumbed to disease, exhaustion and starvation.

The physical state of many of the ex-POWs shocked the receiving staffs in Britain who were charged with debriefing them on their return. On 10 April 1945 the first batch of ninety-eight arrived at the Personnel Reception Centre at RAF Cosford in Staffordshire to be medically examined and interviewed. Three-quarters of the men were suffering from diarrhoea and were so ill that they could not raise themselves from their seats. They had been sent on a two-and-a-half-hour train journey from the airfield. There were no toilets on the train.[40] George Moreton, who had been shot down over Germany in September 1942 and held in a succession of Stalags until his liberation, was one of the luckier ones, being in reasonably good health. But he quickly noticed that his face had changed: 'haggard, lined and old with wrinkles where there had once been curves. My eyes were those of a captive on the run, expressing a suspicious fear as if being hunted.' At the RAF station on his return he felt like 'an animal on exhibit'; the sight of women unnerved him and the smell of rich food seemed nauseating and unsettling.[41]

Lieutenant H.C.F. Harwood of the East Kent Regiment, who had been captured along with many others of the British Expeditionary Force in France in May 1940, had been repatriated through Switzerland a few months before Moreton. He returned to London still wearing the battered and filthy battledress in which he had surrendered five years earlier. He could not get a connecting train home that first night, or find an empty hotel room. He discovered that his bag containing all the journals and sketches he had compiled while in the prison camp had been stolen. Harwood's legs shook: he began to suffer a panic attack. 'I have never felt like committing suicide in my life,' he recalled years later, 'but at that moment I can truthfully say that I came very near to it.'[42]

The schoolboy conviviality of postwar dramas set in the Stalags – *The Colditz Story* and *The Great Escape* – have helped to obscure just how dreary and destructive, mentally and physically, long-term captivity really was. Very few prisoners ever had the opportunity to attempt escape: most had little choice but to sit out the war as best they could until their uncertain day of release. And this captivity was often lengthy. The first British serviceman taken prisoner during the war, RAF Warrant Officer George Booth, whose Blenheim bomber crashed into the Kiel Canal on 4 September 1939, was exceptionally unlucky. But tens of thousands of other Britons had fallen into enemy hands during the military disasters of the first three years of war – the Dunkirk evacuation, the debacles in Greece and Crete, the surrender of Tobruk. By the spring of 1945 around 40,000 British POWs had spent more than five years in captivity. Despite attempts to arrange an exchange of these long-term detainees, a mixture of German intransigence and American indifference made such a scheme impossible.[43]

It had been expected for some years that even men liberated from Germany's and Italy's relatively humane prison camps would face a difficult psychological transition. Experience from the First World War had already demonstrated the problem of 'barbed-wire disease' in the happiest and most stable of prisoners. Most POWs had not suffered as much psychological trauma in battle as they did after their capture. What unsettled them was not a single dramatic event, but rather the steady attrition of their day-to-day captivity – their months and years of boredom, frustration and uncertainty, their almost total ignorance of what was going on in the outside world, and when or if they would ever get to see their homes and families again. Imprisonment chipped away slowly but relentlessly at the inmates' mental health.

Trevor Gibbens, a former POW himself, wrote about the phenomenon in a 1947 treatise on the psychology and psychopathology of prison-camp life. Barbed-wire disease was characterised in the typical captive by 'mild sadness . . . [an] unconscious preoccupation with his own small world . . . [a] bitter, cynical, disillusioned attitude to himself and others; suspicion, inability to find pleasure; apathy, fatigue, and loss of memory and concentration'. Concealed behind a false veneer of cheeriness, the liberated prisoner would often bring these neuroses back to civilian life with him undetected and untreated, their presence only manifesting itself in the weeks and months following repatriation when the initial excitement of homecoming had worn off.[44]

Early wartime experiences of prisoner release stood as a warning. Sergeant Ray Ellis escaped from a Ligurian campo in August 1943, and after a year of hiding amongst sympathetic Italian peasants, finally made his way southward to British lines. Walking through his Nottingham front door after his repatriation was, he remembered, 'the culmination of all the hopes and dreams' he had cherished for the previous five years. Yet within a few weeks he was an angry, disheartened man. 'I was in a highly emotional state, thoroughly miserable, and where I had been both friendly and sociable, I had now become a bitter and disillusioned loner,' he subsequently recalled:

It was to be many years before I was able to escape the clutches of those deep depressions which fell over me from time to time like an all-enveloping black cloak . . . I clearly remember that during those final days in Naples, visiting the opera and lazing about in the sunshine and on board the ship which brought me home, I had been completely happy and with not a trace of emotional upset. Now, in the space of a few weeks I was at odds with the world.

He remembered his father, thinking he was out of earshot, saying to a house guest, 'be very careful with Ray, he's as mad as a hatter'.[45]

In a study of forty other men who had escaped from Italian POW camps in 1943, thirty-six reported that within two or three days of their return home they had felt unhappy and restless. Many suffered from terrible nightmares; claustrophobia, panic attacks, and a fear even of close friends were common: 'They felt as if strangers were talking about them, laughing at them . . . a paranoid and aggressive pattern soon became obvious and caused an acute problem both to the ex-prisoner of war and his family.'[46]

It was disastrous homecomings such as these that prompted the War Office to establish Civil Resettlement Units (CRUs) for repatriated ex-POWs. Twenty CRUs were eventually set up across Great Britain, each capable of handling up to 450 former prisoners at a time. Typically, a man would stay at his CRU for about five weeks. The atmosphere was deliberately informal: the resident was 'treated like an individual . . . no parades, no reveille, no NCOs to chase him,' as one administrator put it.[47] The intention behind the CRUs was to provide a transitional bridge between prison and civilian life, to ease the former inmate out of his barbed-wire symptoms by a range of occupational and therapeutic distractions. Army psychiatrists were on hand to assist with emotional difficulties in the returnees, though with the stigma about mental illness still so strong the advertisements for the CRUs scrupulously avoided any mention of psychological counselling. Though the scheme was entirely voluntary, by April 1946 over 15,000 men had taken part; considering how blasé the Forces could be about the difficulties of readjustment, it stands out as a humane and imaginative initiative that must have done much good.[48]

Some men, though, deliberately ducked any attempt at psychological counselling, even though they knew that their experiences as prisoners had affected them badly. Major Corrie Halliday, captured by the Afrika Korps near Gazala, Libya, in May 1942, was conscious of the fact that he had become 'quite potty by ordinary standards' after years of captivity in Italy and Germany. But he was so afraid of being locked away as unstable that he feigned sickness to avoid a psychiatric examination after his release. He made his way to Lanark in central Scotland, trying to work out whether or not to kill himself: 'I thought *What's the point of it all? . . . I don't want to go on, there's no point, I've done my bit, I've had my time of life, there's nothing really left. . . .* I think if I hadn't had a family in Devonshire with a mother and father still alive and a sister who needed care I might well have done myself in.'[49]

Most cases of barbed-wire disease were expected to diminish after six months or a year of normal life. But not all horrors dissipated so easily. Ten minutes after his return to his home in Bolton, ex-Fepow Alan Dewhurst was already 'emotionally exhausted'. He 'was aware of a desperate feeling that I wanted to get out of the house, and at the same time was conscious that I couldn't do so'. As the weeks passed, his habits became more peculiar. He began collecting tin cans and hoarding them in his room. He became obsessed with cleanliness, constantly washing and rewashing his clothes. He drank to excess. He was on a permanent short fuse: he ended up at a police station after he assaulted a pedantic post-office clerk who was refusing to let him withdraw some of his back-pay. At the station desk Dewhurst showed his leave pass, identifying him as an ex-prisoner of war. The sergeant sighed and called out to the back room, 'we have another one here'. Apparently Fepows already had quite a reputation amongst the local constabulary. It took five years of this behaviour before Dewhurst calmed down.[50]

Jim Long did not have a lucky war. Posted to one of the British Expeditionary Force's field kitchen units in March 1940, he found himself swept up in the shambolic retreat to Dunkirk a few weeks later. That time he got away. The next time he was not so fortunate, arriving in Singapore ten days before its garrison surrendered en masse. He spent the next three and a half years as a slave labourer for the Japanese. The joy of Long's homecoming in the autumn of 1945 was short-lived. He was withdrawn, quiet, difficult to talk to. He found that he was too frightened to mix with strangers any longer, even to stand in a shopping queue. He resumed his old job at a butcher's shop, but could not summon up the courage to go to work in the morning. A sympathetic doctor prescribed a daily tot of Guinness and three valium tablets – the result of which was that he became addicted to valium. Slowly, agonisingly, he weaned himself off the pills and forced himself to be more sociable. But he had no psychological evaluation until 1980. Earlier counselling, he later said, 'would have made a 100% difference – I wouldn't have had all those years of misery and torment'. Even in old age his Fepow anxieties never entirely left him: 'I still fly off the handle . . . every so often I'll have a bad nightmare and for three or four days after that I won't want to talk to anyone.'[51]

Other ex-POWs had hair-trigger temperaments too. 'Many of us have a strange feeling that we are "different" . . . a difference which we sense is recognized by the "outsiders",' confided George Chippington in his diary in 1945.

> There is a wariness in their dealings with us as though beneath our courteous behaviour (in itself rather odd) they suspect a lurking monster, suckled on cruelty and suffering, impatiently waiting its opportunity to burst free from its bonds and wreak havoc and destruction . . . beneath all the kindnesses shown to us lies the wariness of the trainer in the circus ring even as he strokes and pats his placid tigers obediently obeying his commands.[52]

'For five years I've been under forced restraint, under enemy orders,' wrote one former prisoner to the *Manchester Guardian* just after his return from Germany: 'To disobey, to rebel was a duty – and often a necessity. Now I cannot suddenly assume voluntary restraint.'[53] Jack Russell, a former NCO in the Far East who had come home to his job as assistant manager in a grocer's shop, threatened to hit several customers who exasperated him.[54] When the NCOs at a Devon army camp tried to get returned Fepows to parade, they were warned by an officer not to provoke them: 'if you annoy them they'll kill you'. 'No-one bothered us after that,' recalled Alan Dixon: 'They obviously thought we might be dangerous.'[55]

Perhaps the POW experience was so alienating because it defied the national narrative of victory. For men like Jim Long and George Chippington, indeed for most former POWs, the Second World War ended on a sour note. Their experience was not one of glorious triumph over the enemy, but rather of personal defeat and a sense, however unwarranted, of shame. For the men swept up in the mass surrenders of the first three disastrous years of the war, the fighting came to a sudden and jarring halt. They were not fated to take part in the better years to come. Their role in the final defeat of the Axis was as passive bystanders. The injustice of this rankled.

Alan Dixon, who like Jim Long had been through the debacles of Dunkirk and Singapore, found himself seething with anger at the humiliations he had been forced to undergo on account of the blunders of other men. His regiment had had a disastrous war, yet those in command who had made such a mess of things were never punished. By the end of the fighting 'I had been pushed around and ordered about,' he wrote later, 'often by people who either ought not to have been in positions of authority over me, or in the case of the Japanese, had little interest in whether I lived or died. This feeling of resentment has never really left me.' He emigrated from England in 1954, still angry about the waste of six years of his youth.[56]

Through no fault of their own, some ex-prisoners of war were dogged by a sense of disgrace for the rest of their lives. Barbara Webb believed that it was the reason her father, who had been captured in North Africa, never joined the British Legion or any other veterans' organisation. One day, over twenty years after the war ended, he suddenly announced to his wife, completely out of the blue: 'I think we should have fought and not given ourselves up to those Italians without a fight.' 'Those years clearly preyed on his mind,' Barbara believed. 'I think he was always looking for some kind of peace that he never found. He was never at ease . . . he lived in a kind of half-life. In captivity, I think, he was so desperate to get back to ordinary life and imagined all his troubles would be over.' But the mental liberation he sought eluded him.[57]

## Getting Over It

Something has gone wrong inside my head.
The sappers have left mines and wires behind;
I hold long conversations with the dead.[58]

On the second to last day of 1945 the body of twenty eight year old Royal Engineers Major Arthur Moss was found in his car in the Derbyshire Peak District, dead by a bullet from his own revolver. Moss had been the first British officer to land in Norway in 1940 and had gone on to fight in Burma, but since his return home at the end of the war he had 'shown signs of strain'. The coroner's verdict was that the balance of his mind had become disturbed.[59] Earlier in December 1945 the Norwich coroner passed a verdict of 'suicide while of unsound mind' on the death of Private Alfred Salter, who had poisoned himself with disinfectant a few months after returning to East Anglia. Salter had spent three and a half years in captivity in the Far East. 'He could just not stand the change-over from being a prisoner all these years to coming back to normal life,' the court noted.[60] Almost the same day a twenty six year old Polish RAF pilot, Tadeusz Rybczynski, killed himself after gambling away his pay and his gold watch. His temperament in his last days was described as 'neurotic and morbid'.[61]

These were the most extreme responses to the stress of war. Many other demobilised men reported trouble sleeping, often for many decades after the war. Marjorie Hanstock recalled that after her husband John was demobbed from the Royal Navy he experienced 'shattering' nightmares in which he grabbed hold of her for grim life.[62] After half a century James Bellows, who had served with the Royal Hampshire Regiment, still couldn't put his arm around his wife at night because he tossed and turned so violently in his sleep.[63] Violent overreactions were not uncommon amongst other demobbed veterans either. 'I used to lose my temper a lot . . . I never used to be like that,' admitted Charles Tinson, a veteran of the African desert war.[64] John Gray, a driver with the British Liberation Army (BLA) in Germany, agreed: 'You seemed to be at your wits' end all the time, you got easily aggravated, bad tempered – all the things you weren't when you went in.'[65]

Some men were terrified by thunderstorms.[66] Royal Artillery NCO Harold Harper returned to Britain in 1946 and found himself scared to cross the road and unable to sit on the top deck of a bus.[67] Another former gunner, Ernie Hurry, was jumpy on his return to work; colleagues would scare him for a laugh.[68] Trauma could be revived in the most peculiar of ways. An officer who had been caught in a bomb blast in Dover collapsed whenever he heard 'God Save the King'.[69]

Responses to stress were never predictable, however. Ken Watson had some nasty memories of the fighting in northwestern Europe after D-Day. He had seen a comrade's head blown off by a *Panzerfaust* when his Sherman tank was attacked; he vividly recalled the sight of a wounded German prisoner, fully conscious, with two legs and an arm missing. But he never suffered any nightmares afterwards.[70] Arthur Cheetham, who had fought in the gruesome trench-warfare conditions of Anzio in 1944, felt that 'most people were perfectly normal and rational. I didn't know anyone who came out of action and didn't have a few drinks afterwards and be perfectly alright.'[71]

To this day many veterans remain unconvinced, indeed dismissive, of the benefits of therapy, a scepticism echoed in 1995 when Prince Philip, speaking of his career as a Royal Naval officer during the war, grumbled that 'we didn't have counsellors rushing around every time somebody let off a gun . . . you just got on with it'.[72] Theirs was a generation not given to visible displays of emotion. And of course, many men *did* 'get on with it' well enough. In many cases the transitional symptoms of resettlement – boredom, listlessness, irritability, anxiety, depression – passed away with time and the patience of loving families. But the reluctance of men to seek help who really needed it was understandable too. They had returned to a Britain in which mental trauma was still far from adequately understood, either by the general public or by the authorities, where the moral stigma that had been associated with 'shell shock' during the Great War still lived on to some degree. Many men must have hidden their torments, perhaps even from their wives or children, afraid of being called weak or mad.

Some help did exist for those who sought it. The Services' After-Care Scheme, organised by the National Association of Mental Health, was by 1946 looking after 10,000 cases in fifteen centres nationally. This formed a transitional bridge between military and civilian medicine.[73] But psychiatric treatment was patchy at best in postwar Britain. According to a 1946 survey conducted by the Ministry of Health, only 5 per cent of ex-soldiers discharged from the army on psychoneurotic grounds had received follow-up mental-health care since their return to civilian life, and almost all of those who did so lived near London.[74]

So it remains unknown how many demobbed men slipped through the cracks, unwilling to be identified as 'mad' or uninformed about how to seek help. One army psychiatrist estimated that about 35 per cent of the 12,000 battle-exhaustion casualties he had seen were suffering from chronic illnesses that were irreversible without professional treatment.[75] It is impossible to say how many men in similar conditions were released undiagnosed and untreated for years – or how long it would take for their buried injuries to appear. As late as the fiftieth anniversary of V-E Day, the Ex-Forces Mental Welfare Society was reporting that over a thousand veterans of the Second World War had approached them seeking counselling for the first time; many were finding themselves unexpectedly overwhelmed by TV images from half a century before which had provoked long-hidden memories.[76]

Henry Warnes, who sailed on forty-two Atlantic convoys as a fitter for the Fleet Air Arm, was sunk three times. 'At night time you're frightened to go to bed and sleep because of flashbacks,' he said in 1995: 'The thing to do to take your mind off it is to think of the girl you might have married . . . I'm heavily drugged. I take twenty-one tablets a day.' 'I still get battlefield nightmares and sleeplessness,' reported Gordon Trowsdale, who had fought at Nijmegen Bridge during the Operation Market Garden campaign in 1944. 'I get medication, the best they can do, but they can't perform miracles.'[77]

If anything, the problem is getting worse, not better. According to an extensive survey of hundreds of British Second World War veterans conducted in 2001, one in five is continuing to display war-related psychological distress. 'I used to be easy-going,' says one ex-Fepow today:

but when I came back I was withdrawn and used to cry at the least thing. It still comes back. I can still cry at anything that brings back memories. I don't think you can get rid of it.[78]

For such men, demobilisation can never truly be said to have ended – because the war has never ended.

# Epilogue

*The marks of the demobilised man have faded almost away.*
*He is no longer ex-service, he is just a man again.*
*Perhaps it is for the best.*[1]

Corporal Arthur Simmons REME
was demobilised, with a gratuity of
one hundred and twenty six pounds
shortly to be paid, a civilian identity card,
suit of clothes, underwear, overcoat
and a large sheaf of important papers.

At last, after four years, his young wife
was to be permanently his, his young son,
apple of his eye, fruit of an air-raid union,
eve of sailing, would enjoy the benefits
of personal paternal supervision
and the household come into impeccable order.

His old job of electrician would provide a larger wage
than ever in his history of eight and thirty years;

Gladys too had saved well. Henceforward
she would labour no more as a temporary booking clerk.
Her father had died six months back, fortunately
mother continued the tenancy in Willow Walk.[2]

The story of ex-Corporal Simmons appears in T.H. Jubb's poem 'Demobbed', published in a 1947 edition of *The Adelphi*. Arthur returns from the Second World War dreaming of cosy autumn evenings in a comfy chair, his son Bert tucked up in bed and Gladys curled up at his feet with hot cocoa and 'a brisk fire in the sitting-room grate'. But he is in for a few nasty surprises. First of all, there is a crash-course in the realities of 1947 austerity. A penny railway journey now costs threepence; newspapers are twice their prewar price, and half the size. At home the cupboard is almost bare: margarine, a few slices of wet and gristly bacon, and some links of pasty compound sausage are all that can be mustered up for a welcome home feast. Tobacco and beer are strangers to Willow Walk.

Arthur is shocked by his son's 'rubbishy and ruinous' shoes, and appalled when Gladys brings home black-market food – though with an empty belly he is not so appalled that he won't eat it. His wife informs him that they are £42 in debt: there is no possibility of her leaving her job any time soon. And the tools that he will need to become a self-employed electrician are prohibitively expensive. Arthur begins to feel 'very old and well browned off'. And there are few available shoulders to cry on in Civvy Street; Gladys is rushed and unsympathetic, and Arthur's friends are all still away in the Forces or off making munitions.

Eventually he falls in with Renee Evans, 'a showy bit' whom he takes on a clandestine date to the Odeon cinema – only to find his wife already there in the company of the assistant stationmaster. Disgusted with one another and with themselves, Arthur and Gladys conclude that it is postwar England that is the problem, and they agree to quit the country for good and sail to New Zealand on a friend's antique French crabber.

Arthur wasn't the only ex-serviceman to come to this conclusion. As demobilisation blues mounted in 1946 and 1947 – Civvy Street turning out not to be, as the veterans' newsletter of that name put it, an 'open and smooth highway', but rather a 'crowded and dirty lane, with terrific traffic congestion . . . delays, impatience, and exasperation'[3] – so a steady trail of applicants made their way to Australia House and Canada House to inquire about a fresh start in lands where ration books and rising damp were unknown. A free-passage scheme to the Antipodes for ex-servicemen was organised, with the first 200 families leaving in November 1946.[4] Indeed, the general gloominess of austerity was such that a year and a half later four out of ten Britons said that they would emigrate too if they were free to do so.[5] 'Disappointment is widespread,' as *Civvy-Street* lamented: 'everybody is giving vent to his thoughts on the deep depression which we have reached.'[6]

Emigration was one option: returning to the colours was another. Military life – with its comradeship, unselfishness, indeed civilisation – started to look all the more attractive by contrast with tired, cynical, postwar Britain.[7] Just a few months after the start of general demobilisation, a 'steady flow' of ex-servicemen were already reported to be showing up at recruitment offices asking about the possibility of rejoining the Forces.[8] RAF airman David Searle, who was demobbed in early 1947, was just one of the thousands of newly minted civilians with itchy feet, disenchanted with their dull new factory and office jobs. 'I stand by my engine-stand all day trying to decide what I should do,' he wrote to his wife Audrey. 'Oh, the conflict that goes on in my mind. I still have very strong service pulls and the recruiting office is only fifty yards from here.'[9] Former Durham Light Infantryman Tony Cameron was dismayed by his return to his job at Emner Colliery in Tyne and Wear: 'It was nowt like being in the Army . . . nowt like being in the bloody desert,' and by February 1947 he had decided to re-enlist.[10] One ex-soldier who had been compulsorily discharged for medical reasons pretended to be his deserter brother and surrendered to the authorities in Richmond, North Yorkshire; the prospect of two years' hard labour in the glasshouse paled beside the thought of having to remain a civilian.[11]

A few ex-servicemen even tried creating veterans' colonies, separate from the rest of the civilian community. In June 1946, at

Gumley Hall in Leicestershire, former Group Captain Leonard Cheshire VC unveiled the first of what he hoped would be a chain of self-sustaining farm communes of ex-service members and their families. Calling itself *Vade in Pacem* (VIP), the Gumley Hall colony was intended to be a pre-industrial commune of farmers, artisans and petty tradesmen as well as an experiment in practical morality, combining a quasi-Christian communitarian ethic with the encouragement of qualities and talents that had supposedly flourished in the Forces. The structure of the community was explicitly modelled on the services, with 'personnel' grouped into 'sections' and an HQ unit acting as a sort of general staff. VIP quickly expanded, acquiring a second colony at a Victorian estate in Hampshire. But by early 1947 it was being dogged by financial woes and ruinous quarrels between the members: Cheshire complained of 'too many parasites and unorganised individualists'. The project disintegrated shortly afterwards, though Cheshire was to turn the Hampshire property into his famous hospice for the disabled and dying.[12]

Without going so far as completely estranging themselves from civilians, other returning servicemen also wanted to perpetuate the distinctive culture of military life. Could the essence of wartime camaraderie be carried on somehow in Civvy Street? 'What better than to preserve some of the few good things that come out of war?' asked Rex Ransley in *Ex-Services Review*, one of the optimistic (and short-lived) attempts to create a veterans' community in print:

> The sense of comradeship, the spirit of community, the habits of hardship borne with a cheerful grin, sharing the burdens and dividing the last cigarette . . . are we fighters, when we have become ex-fighters, going to forget these things are precious possessions to be jealously guarded? Shall we drift singly away and be lost in the anonymity of our 'civvies'? Are we prepared to watch the things we've fought for hazarded and lost in a welter of narrow, selfish, conflicting interests, class struggle, political strife and national apathy?[13]

'Front-Line Generation', the brainchild of the eccentric Dutch-Italian writer and editor Peter Ratazzi, was another short-lived veterans' group which met in an Earl's Court basement room, trying to preserve and extend the wartime spirit of comradeship which had been born in danger and suffering. Described by a former member as 'a sort of Old Comrades' Club for the long-haired [intellectual] boys out of battledress', it flourished briefly in the months following demobilisation before fizzling out, like so many other ex-service clubs and collectives, sometime around 1947.[14]

Ex-service projects began to run out of steam in the late 1940s because those demobbed men who had not emigrated or re-enlisted were getting used to civilian ways again: despite their earlier complaints, perhaps even despite themselves, they were settling down. Len Newman spent several unhappy years on the railways, but in 1949 he became a clerk in a local government office, and there discovered the same kind of fraternal atmosphere he had once enjoyed as a fitter with the 8th Hussars.[15] Edward Grey was luckier; he found the camaraderie of the coal pit to be 'very much the same' as that of the army from the start, and enjoyed his job despite its gruelling physicality.[16]

The wanderlust and restlessness some men had experienced when coming immediately out of the Forces generally dissipated after a while. Dennis Middleton spent long periods of his demob leave in the Pennines in a remote hill cottage trying to decide what to do with his life, before he returned to his position at a bank. 'I can't say that it was a bad choice,' he reflected years later.[17] After five years of pseudo-military life as a uniformed bus conductor, John Frost decided to return to the umbrella and pinstripes of his old City job.[18] William Robinson arrived back in Britain 'bored and restless . . . I went on tramp, getting a lift here, a lift there, with lorry drivers . . . it was a release'. But eventually he found himself back at his old tailor shop in Essex.[19] Ex-servicemen eventually did settle back into civilian life and work, albeit with varying degrees of enthusiasm.

As *Punch* so memorably recorded in March 1946, wartime ambitions slowly evaporated with the passage of time:

During the barren progress of hostilities
I did not disguise from my comrades
The vast range of the agenda
Dammed up within me . . .

I declared I would start a nudist colony for air vice-marshals
With my gratuity
In a modest corner of Patagonia
We selected with a pin
One wet evening in a pub in Lincoln . . .

Alas! How ambition withers
And aspiration stalls in the rude blasts of peace!
I am become a loiterer for halibut
A hunter of sprats from slab to slab
A dumb waiter for chitterlings . . .

Ah woe!
I am tethered by the leaden chains of peace!
And toil's grim sister
(I refer to Lumbago)
Stalks me without pause
Now the war is over.[20]

The tribal loyalties of the Forces, so vital in wartime, began to decay too. Ex-POW John MacAuslan remembered meeting one of his former fellow captives working in a road-gang on Chancery Lane as he was walking towards the Law Society. 'We talked, and I was glad to see him and I think he was glad to see me,' he later recalled. 'But there was really nothing to say. It was all gone.'[21]

Old comradeships would continue to wither over the following decade, as jobs and wives and children replaced wartime bonds. The process was captured by Ray Galton and Alan Simpson in 'The Reunion Party', an episode in the long-running BBC TV sitcom *Hancock's Half-Hour*, first shown in March 1960. Tony

Hancock, the dour philosopher-king of 23 Railway Cuttings, organises a get-together with three of his wartime army pals from that undeservedly obscure unit, the 3rd East Cheam Light Horse. Hancock hasn't seen the boys – 'Smudger' Smith, 'Ginger' Johnson and 'Chalky' White – since their demob party fifteen years ago, but what does that matter? 'It was a wonderful feeling we had in those days,' he tells his sceptical housemate, Sid: 'A bunch of young chaps thrown together from all walks of life, but joined together with a sense of purpose, a mutual respect, and bound by a deep everlasting friendship that time will never erase.'

The boys, however, are not as Hancock remembers them. Smudger, formerly 'up to here in Chianti and women', has turned into teetotal vegetarian Clarence, with a shrewish spouse in tow and his old wartime dreams of being a lumberjack or crocodile hunter abandoned in favour of a bank clerk's stool ('sometimes at the end of the day we're five shillings short. It's quite thrilling!'). Ginger, once the life and soul of the party, is bald, myopic and forgetful. And Chalky's ribald stories have been retired now that he is a clergyman. Sid tries to conciliate the crestfallen Hancock: 'Fifteen years is a long time. People change. I bet they're thinking right now how much you've changed, and how pathetic you are.' It is a waste of time trying to re-enact faded glory days, he chides: 'you cannot bring back the past'.[22] Many of *Hancock's* viewers must have known exactly what Sid meant.

For as ex-servicemen were reabsorbed into their new lives in the decade that followed demobilisation, a quiet revolution in their attitudes took place. For many, the service experience had been one of contempt for the army or navy or air force as *institutions*, combined with intense personal loyalty toward their immediate mates. But as individual connections between men withered, so a more unformulated nostalgia for the Forces as a whole grew. Memories dulled and old grudges began to fade; men grew less attached to the particular, more sentimental about the general.

Already by 1947, three-quarters of ex-servicemen polled by the Central Office of Information said that, on the whole, they had enjoyed their time in the Forces.[23] *Punch* tutored demobbing soldiers about the melancholy they would experience some distant time in the future:

> Whenever you refer to your life in the Service, let your voice assume a mellow, almost nostalgic, note. This may at present be *difficult*. You may, indeed, detect, at such affectionate references to the Service, a look of alarmed surprise in the eyes of your friends.
>
> Do not despair, however. Nostalgia will come. In time . . .[24]

For some it took a *long* time. Although Stewart Irwin admitted that he learned a certain amount of resilience during his service with the King's Royal Rifle Corps, he also came out of the Forces 'very bitter and twisted – it took me fifteen years to get over it'.[25] Gordon Paterson thought that the one thing the Royal Navy taught him was 'never ever seek advice again'.[26]

By contrast, John Frost, a clerk with the 11th Armoured Division, had been 'a bit of a mother's boy' before the war, but life in the Forces had made him 'self-sufficient and disciplined'.[27] Ian Hammerton felt that he emerged from army life a much more confidant person with a much wider appreciation of life generally and of people.[28]

The mixed reflections of former Royal Engineers sergeant Geoffrey William Isaac on his time in the wartime Forces seems to have been widely shared. 'I was very glad to get out of the Army,' he made clear years later:

> Six years was a long time and a large slice out of my life. Before I was called up, I was just beginning to make a bit of money with the Prudential, the start of a good career perhaps. I never considered myself a real soldier. . . . I ask myself, what use was I to the British Army, and how did my small bit help the nation? All I can say is that I was but a little cog in a huge machine, and like many another, I aimed to do my best . . . it was amazing to me that I learned to accept the bawling and the boredom, the petty restrictions and the inefficiencies of being a soldier. *And yet my experience of being in the*

*Army was the greatest event in my life* [my emphasis] . . . the Army opened my eyes to many things about life and gave me a confidence that I lacked.[29]

By 1961 *The Times* could speak of the typical wartime ex-serviceman as a 'man of no regrets' – a sentiment difficult to imagine being accepted without demur fifteen years earlier.[30] What still remained of the squaddie, erk, or matelot in these men by the 1960s? Their serial numbers, 'bit deep into memory through countless repetition';[31] their demob suits, by now probably relegated to workshop or allotment wear; other sartorial flotsam from the quartermaster's store – light-blue RAF shirts, naval duffel coats, gas capes, badgeless berets, fading now and increasingly consigned to jumble sales; for many, membership in the local branch of the British Legion club, usually more for its cheap beer than its militaristic associations; and maybe regimental insignia and campaign decorations, preserved in the attic to show to the kids at Christmas, or perhaps affixed to blazers for march-pasts on Remembrance Sunday.

The anxious, testy, cynical boys of 1945 were now on the cusp of middle age: long married, their children approaching adulthood, their careers maturing, their lives on the whole sedentary and secure – though not, perhaps, without a share of private and secret regrets.

## Oh, It's Tommy This and Tommy That . . .

The British homecoming experience was as varied as the millions of people who lived through it. It was not necessarily a traumatic experience for every individual. Most men and women were glad to be coming home in 1945, more or less. Most of their families and friends were glad to see them back, a few pangs of apprehension notwithstanding. Most marriages survived, for better or worse. And most repatriates settled down – eventually. The demobbed returned to a poor and tired country, but one in which the basic political and social institutions had survived the severe test of six years of total war. Moreover, it was a *victorious* country, one that the great majority of ex-servicemen were proud to have fought for, however much they might have found the day-to-day experience of life in uniform vexing.

But even some of the most fortunate and ultimately well-adjusted of ex-servicemen later acknowledged that their return to civilian life in 1945 was difficult. Not every ex-soldier was scarred forever by the war, either physically or mentally, and it would be absurd to suggest otherwise. Yet to judge by contemporary evidence and subsequent testimony, the years immediately following the Second World War were a period filled with tension, anxiety and anger. Untold thousands of British families struggled with very real problems of reassimilating their menfolk after a profound, sometimes psychologically bewildering, transition from one world to another. That most ex-servicemen eventually overcame their homecoming problems, that demob ultimately proved to be a transitory and impermanent moment of disorientation, does not detract from its importance in the national story of the past.

And perhaps it was more than just a passing moment of domestic disruption. When one looks at the American experience of homecoming at the end of the Second World War, and the way in which the famous GI-Bill helped to propel a returning generation of US veterans into the middle classes, 1945 begins to seem like a lost, never-to-be-repeated opportunity to take the concentrated energy and ambition of four million men and use it to transform Britain's ossified mid-century social and economic order for the better. How very differently the second half of the twentieth century might have turned out had the lofty aspirations of many of the homecoming been tapped in a more inspired manner.

Still, if Britain did not always handle the return of its servicemen in the 1940s as deftly or imaginatively as it might have done, there were at least mitigating circumstances. The country was battered, near-bankrupt, and still reeling from an exhausting six-year war. Most of the population had been involved, overwhelming the limited resources of a tired and penurious people.

What's our excuse now? Britain in the twenty-first century is wealthy and peaceful; it has a tiny, all-volunteer army, navy and air force. Yet we still do a disgracefully inadequate job of demobilising our young men and women. The experiences of soldiers, sailors and airmen returning from tours of duty in Ulster, the Falklands, the Persian Gulf, Iraq and Afghanistan over the past thirty years have too often been unhappy ones, and the support network that they need to manage the transition back to civilian life has frequently been found wanting. One prisoner in ten in a British jail today is an ex-serviceman.[32] Amongst the homeless, it is one in four.[33] Young men who have served in uniform are three times more likely to commit suicide than their peers.[34] The country's highest-decorated soldier, Johnson Beharry, who was awarded the VC in 2005, has called the lack of mental health care provision for veterans 'a disgrace'.[35]

Reg Ellery's warning is as pertinent today, then, as it was sixty years ago: Demobilisation, he said:

> involves far more than a change of clothing – it is a task of the greatest magnitude . . . and one which calls for great skill and understanding from the men and women executives in all departments of national life.

> For, on the degree of success with which this problem is handled, much of the happiness of future generations will depend.[36]

# Notes

### Prologue

1. Timothy Corsellis, quoted in Howard Sergeant, 'Poetry and the Front Line Generation', *New Generation*, spring/summer 1946, 35.
2. Details from the National Archives, NA MEPO 3/2302.
3. *Daily Express*, 27 September 1945, 3.
4. Martin J. Wiener, *Men of Blood: Violence, Manliness and Criminal Justice in Victorian England*. Cambridge University Press, 2004, 289–92.
5. *News Chronicle*, 10 July 1945, 2.
6. Over half a million servicewomen were also demobilised from the British auxiliary forces at the end of the Second World War, and I would not like any reader to think just because they are largely absent from this book that I am unaware of their existence, or that I imagine their demob narratives are of no complexity or interest. On the contrary, although there was some overlap between the problems of resettlement that both men and women went through, the women's story was so different in key respects that I cannot do it proper justice within a book that concentrates so specifically on the experiences of men. There still needs to be a book written about the demob of the ATS, WRNS and WAAF.
7. Sheila Ferguson and Hilde Fitzgerald, *Studies in the Social Services*. HMSO, 1954, 3. This does not take into account the 40,000 British prisoners of war who were held in captivity for more than five years during the war.
8. George H. Gallup, ed., *The Gallup International Public Opinion Polls: Great Britain 1937–1975, Volume One: 1937–1964*. Random House, 1976, 62.
9. J.L. Hodson, *The Sea and the Land*. Gollancz, 1945, 216.
10. Anthony Burgess, *Little Wilson and Big God*. Penguin, 1988, 305.
11. Ibid., 85.
12. *News Chronicle*, 15 May 1946, 1.

13. Mass-Observation, *The Journey Home*. Advertising Service Guild, 1944, 102–3.
14. Reg Ellery, *Psychiatric Aspects of Modern Warfare*. Melbourne, 1945, 147–8.
15. Mass-Observation, *The Journey Home*, 102–3.
16. Quoted in *The Times*, 27 March 1944, 8.
17. Andrew Latcham, 'Journey's End: Ex-Servicemen and the State During and After the Great War'. Unpublished dissertation, University of Oxford, 1996.
18. Quoted in Bill Gammage, *The Broken Years*. Australian National University Press, 1974, 271.
19. Mass-Observation, *The Journey Home*, 43, 105; *Sunday Express*, 19 November 1944, 4.
20. C.E. Montague, *Disenchantment*. Brentano's, 1922, 111.
21. Anthony Burgess, *Little Wilson and Big God*, 272.
22. Quoted by Hodson, 10 January 1945, *The Sea and the Land*, 280.
23. Eric Dornan Smith, 'The League of Angry Men', *Daily Mirror*, 4 June 1945, 1.
24. Quoted by Hodson, 8 December 1943, *The Sea and the Land*, 140–1.
25. *People*, 14 January 1945, 2.
26. See *Daily Mail*, 5 July 1946, 2; Lt.-Col. J.H.A. Sparrow, *Report on Visit to 21st Army Group and Tour of Second Army 30th March–5th May 1945*, 14. NA WO/32/15772; T.A. Ratcliffe, 'The Pyschological Problems of the Returned Ex-Service Man', *Mental Health* (7: 1) 1947, 3.
27. Quoted in *The Times*, 17 November 1944, 8.
28. Mark Connelly, *We Can Take It! Britain and the Memory of the Second World War*. Pearson/Longman, 2004, 301.
29. There have been three popular accounts of demobilisation, largely anecdotal in style: Ben Wicks, *Welcome Home: True Stories of Soldiers Returning from World War II*. Bloomsbury, 1991; Tony Rennell and Barry Turner, *When Daddy Came Home: How Family Life Changed Forever in 1945*. Pimlico, 1996; Julie Summers, *Stranger in the House*. Simon & Schuster, 2008. Academic historians have given the topic short shrift. In 1994 the late David Englander was complaining that demobilisation at the end of the Second World War was still regarded as 'a non-problematic process hardly worthy of scholarly attention'. See David Englander, 'Soldiers and Social Reform in the First and Second World Wars', *Historical Research* 67: 164 (1994), 319. Exceptions include Rex Pope, 'British Demobilization after the Second World War', *Journal of Contemporary History* 30: 1 (1995); and Jeremy Crang, 'Welcome to Civvy Street: The Demobilisation of the British Armed Forces after the Second World War', *The Historian* 46 (1995).
30. Hodson, 13 February 1945, *The Sea and the Land*, 298.
31. *Spectator*, 22 February 1946, 190.
32. *The Army at Home, November 1945–January 1946*. NA WO 32/15772.
33. Nicholas Mosley, *Time At War*. Dalkey Archive Press, 2006, 171.
34. Quoted in John Ellis, *The Sharp End: The Fighting Man in World War Two*. Charles Scribner's, 1980, 326.
35. *Picture Post*, 21 April 1945, 7–9.
36. *Daily Herald*, 7 November 1945, 2.
37. *Daily Mirror*, 13 November 1944, 7.
38. *Woman*, 27 April 1946, 22.
39. Joanna Bourke, *The Second World War: A People's History*. Oxford University Press, 2001, 202.
40. *Daily Express*, 17 May 1945, 2.

41. *Daily Herald*, 25 May 1946, 2; *Daily Mirror*, 28 May 1945, 2.
42. David Kynaston, *Austerity Britain 1945–51*. Bloomsbury, 2007, 109.

### Chapter One: Now This Bloody War is Over

1. J.L. Hodson, *The Sea and the Land*. Gollancz, 1945, 365.
2. Details of the HMS *Northway* incident from NA ADM 116/6421.
3. Peter Daniel, 'The Mutiny on the *Javelin*', *Mariner's Mirror* 85: 4 (1999), 447.
4. Details of the HMS *Javelin* incident from NA ADM 116/6421. See also Henry Leach, *Enjoy no Makeshifts*. Leo Cooper, 1993.
5. Stephen Richards Graubard, 'Military Demobilisation in Great Britain following the First World War', *The Journal of Modern History* 19: 4 (1947); Andrew Rothstein, *The Soldiers' Strikes of 1919*. Macmillan, 1980.
6. *Daily Herald*, 10 August 1946, 2; *Manchester Guardian*, 26 February 1946, 4; *Manchester Guardian*, 13 June 1946, 4.
7. H.A. Wilson, *War Diary*, 7–8 May 1945. Imperial War Museum Department of Documents, IWM:D #80/5/1.
8. Martin Gilbert, *The Day the War Ended: May 8, 1945 – Victory in Europe*. Henry Holt, 1995, 268.
9. Sydney Beck, *War Diary*, 9 May 1945. IWM:D #03/28/1.
10. Harold Harrington. IWM Department of Sound Records, IWM:S #18484.
11. Beck, *War Diary*, 4 May 1945.
12. H.W.F. Charles, *World War II: Called Up!* IWM:D #02/19/1.
13. Christopher Seton-Watson, *Dunkirk–Alamein–Bologna: Letters and Diaries of an Artilleryman 1939–1945*. Buckland, 1993, 276.
14. Beck, *War Diary*, 2–5 May 1945.
15. J.H.A. Sparrow, *Report on Visit to 21 Army Group and Tour of Second Army*, May 1945, 6. NA WO 32/15772.
16. Eric Lord. IWM:S #19911.
17. Christopher Cross, letter, 4 May 1945. IWM:D #91/8/1.
18. George MacDonald Fraser, *Quartered Safe Out Here*. HarperCollins, 2000, 27–8.
19. A.M. Bell MacDonald, *War Diary*, 27 June 1944. IWM:D #Con Shelf.
20. Wilson, *War Diary*, 21 September 1944; George Teal. IWM:S #18698.
21. Martin Page, ed., *Kiss Me Goodnight Sergeant Major: The Songs and Ballads of World War II*. Panther, 1975, 182–6.
22. Sparrow, *Report on Visit to 21 Army Group*, 10.
23. Seton-Watson, *Dunkirk–Alamein–Bologna*, 277.
24. *Release and Resettlement: An Explanation of Your Position and Rights*. HMSO, 1945, 24–5.
25. Winston S. Churchill, *The Aftermath*. Charles Scribner's, 1929, 48.
26. Mass-Observation, *The Journey Home*. Advertising Service Guild, 1944, 84.
27. *The Times*, 23 October 1944, 5; Captain A.M. Bell MacDonald, *War Diaries 1939–1945*, 26 September 1944. IWM:D #Con Shelf; Wilson, *War Diary*, 24 September 1944.
28. Mass-Observation Topics Collection 27/3/E, September 1945.
29. Arthur S. Harris, 9 December 1945 and 8 February 1946. IWM:D #96/35/1.
30. *The Times*, 17 May 1945, 5.
31. *Manchester Guardian*, 13 December 1945, 4.
32. *Daily Mirror*, 3 September 1945, 2.

33. *Daily Herald*, 28 August 1945, 2.
34. R.B. McCallum and Alison Readman, *The British General Election of 1945*. Oxford University Press, 1947, 153.
35. *Let Us Face the Future: A Declaration of Labour Policy for the Consideration of the Nation*. Labour Party, 1945.
36. McCallum and Readman, *The British General Election*, 205–6.
37. Jeremy Crang, 'Politics on Parade: Army Education and the 1945 General Election', *History* 81: 262 (1996).
38. *The Times*, 24 August 1945, 5.
39. Corelli Barnett, *The Lost Victory*, Macmillan, 2–4.
40. Sparrow, *Report on Visit to 21 Army Group*, 2.
41. *Daily Mirror*, 3 September 1945, 2.
42. Quoted in *The Times*, 4 October 1945, 2.
43. Mass-Observation Topics Collection 27/3/E, September 1945.
44. *Daily Herald*, 21 December 1945, 2.
45. *New Statesman*, 9 September 1945, 1.
46. *Daily Mail*, 6 September 1945, 2.
47. Ibid.
48. John White, 7 October–10 October 1945, 23 May 1945. IWM:D #90/6/1.
49. Charles, *World War II*.
50. Mass-Observation, *The Journey Home*, 25.
51. *The Times*, 6 September 1945, 5.
52. *Manchester Guardian*, 3 October 1945, 4.
53. Rex Pope, 'The Planning and Implementation of British Demobilisation, 1941–1946'. Unpublished dissertation, Open University, 1986, 291.
54. I.C. Thimann, 'Vocational Training in the Services', *The Contemporary Review*, 170 (1946), 240.
55. *News Chronicle*, 23 October 1945, 2.
56. Charles Crichton. IWM:D #Con Shelf.
57. *Daily Express*, 8 August 1945, 3.
58. *Manchester Guardian*, 14 June 1946, 4. See also *News Chronicle*, 21 August 1946, 2.
59. For which see Chapter 4.
60. *Daily Mirror*, 26 October 1944, 2.
61. Letter to Mrs. Mary Jones, 22 August 1945. IWM:D #78/55/1.
62. See Jeremy Crang, 'The British Soldier on the Home Front: Army Morale Reports, 1940–1945', in Paul Addison and Angus Calder, eds., *Time To Kill: The Soldier's Experience of War in the West 1939–1945*. Pimlico, 1997.
63. Lt.-Col. J.H.A. Sparrow, *Tour of India and South East Asia Command, 28th June 1945–15th October 1945*. Imperial War Museum Department of Printed Books, IWM:PB #02(41).13 [South East Asia Command]/6.
64. E.W Browne, et al., *The Soldier and the Army: Opinions on Some Aspects of Army Life Expressed by Troops in SEAC*. South East Asia Command, 1946, 39.
65. Ibid., 40.
66. Roy McKelvie, *The War in Burma*. Methuen, 1948, 273; Les Ransom, *Where There's a Wheel*, 38. IWM:D #87/42/1.
67. Hannen Swaffer, *What Would Nelson Do?* Gollancz, 1946, 34–5.
68. Sparrow, *Tour of India and South East Asia Command*.
69. *Manchester Guardian*, 2 August 1945, 4.
70. *Manchester Guardian*, 1 September 1945, 4.

71. *Daily Mail*, 5 January 1946, 1.
72. *News of the World*, 14 October 1945, 1.
73. J.L. Hodson, 30 November 1945, and 10 January 1946, *The Way Things Are*. Gollancz, 1947, 75, 94.
74. *Westward Bound: Advice and Help for your Journey Home*. Homeward Bound Trooping Depot (Deolali), 1946, 40. IWM:PB #03(41).48/5.
75. Quoted in Pope, 'The Planning and Implementation of British Demobilisation', 256.
76. L.A. Gillam, *The Jesse Short Collection*. IWM:D #Misc 220 (3152).
77. *Manchester Guardian*, 12 December 1945, 4.
78. *Release and Resettlement*, 4.
79. *The Times*, 24 September 1945, 2.
80. David Duncan, *Mutiny in the RAF*. Socialist History Society, 1998; Richard Kisch, *The Days of the Good Soldiers*. Journeyman, 1985.
81. NA AIR 23/2899.
82. Bernard Shilling. *The Jesse Short Collection*, IWM:D #Misc 220 (3152).
83. Gerry Rubin, *Murder, Mutiny and the Military: British Court Martial Cases, 1940–1966*. Francis Boutle, 2005, 111–31.
84. *Manchester Guardian*, 2 January 1946, 4.
85. Wilson, postscript to *War Diary*.
86. NA ADM 1/18709.
87. *Daily Herald*, 12 November 1945, 3.
88. *Daily Mail*, 24 December 1945, 1.
89. *Daily Herald*, 24 November 1945, 1.
90. *Daily Mail*, 18 December 1946, 1.
91. D.N. Pritt, *Brasshats and Bureaucrats*. Lawrence and Wishart, 1966, 256–64.
92. Rubin, *Murder, Mutiny and the Military*, 132–94.
93. *The Times*, 11 October 1946, 5.
94. Central Statistical Office, *Fighting with Figures*, HMSO, 1995, 42.
95. Alan Bullock, *The Life and Times of Ernest Bevin, Volume II: Minister of Labour, 1940–1945*. Heinemann, 1967, 334, 365.
96. Quoted in *The Times*, 27 March 1944, 8.
97. *Daily Herald*, 10 August 1946, 2.
98. *The Times*, 5 September 1945, 5.
99. *Union Jack*, 16 July 1945, 3.
100. *Union Jack*, 6 August 1945, 1.
101. Letter to Mrs. Mary Jones, 22 August 1945. IWM:D #78/55/1.
102. W.A. Charlotte, 14 June 1945. IWM:D #93/19/1.

## Chapter Two: So, You're Back Then

1. Mass-Observation Topic Collection 27/3/E, September 1945.
2. H.A. Wilson, *War Diary*, Postscript. IWM:D #80/5/1.
3. Cecil Wareham, *A Portrait of our Family*, 129. IWM:D #96/31/1.
4. George Chippington, *Naked and Unashamed*, 647. IWM:D #PP/MCR/298.
5. W.M. Innes-Kerr, *Memoir*, 26. IWM:D #84/45/1.
6. Arthur Gilbert, *BBC People's War*. http://www.bbc.co.uk/ww2peopleswar/stories/07/a5011507.shtml. Accessed 20 January 2007.
7. Quoted in Tony Rennell and Barry Turner, *When Daddy Came Home: How Family Life Changed Forever in 1945*. Pimlico, 1996, 44–5.

8. Sheila Ferguson and Hilde Fitzgerald, *Studies in the Social Services*. HMSO, 1954, 3.

9. *Manchester Guardian*, 20 December 1945, 4. David Daniell (real first name Albert) later became a prolific children's author.

10. George Millar, *Horned Pigeon*. Heinemann, 1946, 423–4.

11. Anthony Burgess, *Any Old Iron*. Arrow, 1989, 162–3.

12. *Daily Mirror*, 7 November 1945, 2.

13. *Daily Mirror*, 2 July 1945, 7.

14. George Moreton, *The Barbed-Wire Medic*, 784. IWM:D #89/16/2(P).

15. Hugh Dewhurst, *A Japanese Interlude*, 51; *Memoir*, 3. IWM:D #02/32/1.

16. *Woman*, 29 September 1945, 7.

17. *Woman*, 13 October 1945, 8.

18. See, for example, *Daily Mail*, 18 March 1946, 2.

19. J. Danjoux, *Growing Up in the Second World War*. IWM:D #97/40/1.

20. *Woman*, 30 June 1945, 9; *Woman*, 8 August 1945, 15.

21. Jeffrey Weeks, *Sex, Politics and Society: The Regulation of Sexuality since 1800*. Longman, 1989 (2nd edn.), 237–8.

22. Hera Cook, *The Long Sexual Revolution: English Women, Sex, and Contraception 1800–1975*. Oxford University Press, 2004, 226–7.

23. Maurice Merritt, *Eighth Army Driver*. Midas Books, 1981, 177–8.

24. Harold Knowles. IWM:D #91/35/1.

25. A.M. Bell MacDonald, letter, 3 April 1945. IWM:D #Con Shelf.

26. *People*, 2 December 1945, 2.

27. Wareham, *A Portrait of our Family*, 130.

28. William Franklin, *Through Adversity to Attainment*, 112. IWM:D #04/17/1.

29. *John Bull*, 20 October 1945, 14.

30. *Daily Mail*, 4 July 1946, 2.

31. *Daily Mirror*, 13 November 1944, 7.

32. Dennis Rooke and Alan D'Egville, *Call Me Mister! A Guide to Civilian Life for the Newly Demobilised*. Heinemann, 1945, vi.

33. Eliot Slater and Moya Woodside, *Patterns of Marriage: A Study of Marriage Relationships in the Urban Working Classes*. Cassell, 1951, 215.

34. Jay Winter, 'The Demographic Consequences of the War', in Harold Smith, ed., *War and Social Change: British Society in the Second World War*. Manchester University Press, 1986, 152.

35. *Second World War Army Postal Services (1939–45)*. http://www.remuseum.org.uk/specialism/rem_spec_pcsww2.htm. Accessed 31 March 2007.

36. *Union Jack*, 18 October 1945, 3.

37. *Daily Mail*, 3 April 1946, 3.

38. J.L. Hodson, *The Home Front*, Gollancz, 1944, 299.

39. *Good Housekeeping*, June 1944, 104.

40. Alan Harris, unsent letter, 17 July 1944. IWM:D #96/35/1.

41. Slater and Woodside, *Patterns of Marriage*, 219.

42. Ibid., 223.

43. *Woman*, 9 June 1945, 22.

44. *Perfect Strangers* (1945), dir. Alexander Korda.

45. *Daily Mirror*, 13 November 1944, 7.

46. Philip Meninsky. IWM:S #12049.

47. *Daily Mail*, 25 July 1946, 2.

48. *Daily Mail*, 10 January 1946, 2.
49. *Woman*, 16 February 1946, 3; Slater and Woodside, *Patterns of Marriage*, 218.
50. *John Bull*, 13 July 1946; Lt. H.C.F. Harwood, *Oh Threats of Hell: The Diary of a Prisoner of War*, 296. IWM:D #84/33/1.
51. Dick Fiddament. IWM:S #17354.
52. See, for example, *News Chronicle*, 2 February 1945, 2; Douglas Hanson. IWM:S #4986.
53. Les Ransom, *Where There's a Wheel*, 38. IWM:D #87/42/1.
54. *Daily Mirror*, 3 September 1945, 7.
55. *Daily Herald*, 11 May 1946, 2.
56. *Woman*, 28 April 1945, 22.
57. *Modern Woman*, March 1946, 85.
58. Ferguson and Fitzgerald, *Studies in the Social Services*, 21–2. By 1944 the cost-of-living index was 30 per cent higher than it had been at the outbreak of war (Central Statistical Office, *Fighting With Figures*, HMSO, 1995, 237).
59. Ferguson and Fitzgerald, *Studies in the Social Services*, 6.
60. W.K. Hancock and Margaret Gowing, *British War Economy*. HMSO, 1949, 500.
61. For a lively memoir of the bourgeois woman's travails during this period, see Susan Cooper, 'Snoek Piquante', in Michael Sissons and Philip French, *Age of Austerity*. Hodder and Stoughton, 1963, 35–54. The 'domestic servant problem' is discussed in Elizabeth McCarty, 'Attitudes to Women and Domesticity in England, c. 1939–1955'. Unpublished dissertation, University of Oxford, 1994.
62. *Daily Mail*, 7 January 1946, 2.
63. Richard Titmuss, *Problems of Social Policy*. HMSO, 1950, 322.
64. *Daily Mail*, 16 March 1945, 3.
65. *Daily Mirror*, 28 July 1945, 3.
66. *News Chronicle*, 1 August 1946, 1.
67. *News Chronicle*, 14 June 1946, 3.
68. Anthony Weymouth, *Journal of the War Years*, vol. 2. Littlebury, 1948, 407.
69. Slater and Woodside, *Patterns of Marriage*, 216.
70. *Daily Mirror*, 2 July 1945, 7.
71. *Daily Mail*, 20 November 1945, 2.
72. *News Chronicle*, 12 February 1945, 2.
73. *Woman*, 24 March 1945, 22.
74. *News Chronicle*, 12 February 1945, 2.
75. Margaret Goldsmith, *Women and the Future*. Lindsay Drummond, 1946, 15.
76. *Modern Woman*, November 1945, 69.
77. *Modern Woman*, September 1945, 71.
78. *Daily Mail*, 31 May 1945, 2.
79. *Daily Herald*, 4 December 1945, 2.
80. *Daily Mirror*, 10 August 1944, 7.
81. Dr. H. Leonard Browne, *How We May Best Prepare Ourselves and Our Homes to Receive Those Returning from Captivity in the Far East*, 29 September 1945. IWM:PB #77/5.6(=41).
82. Jo Mary Stafford, *Light in the Dust: An Autobiography 1939–1960*. Trustline, 1990, 4.
83. Ibid., 20–1.
84. Ibid., 18.
85. Ibid., 4.

86. Titmuss, *Problems of Social Policy*, 434.
87. Ibid., 409.
88. There is a rich, albeit mostly anecdotal, literature of evacuation. See, for example, Bryan S. Johnson, *The Evacuees*. Gollancz, 1968; Ben Wicks, *No Time To Wave Goodbye*. Bloomsbury, 1988; Robert Holman, *The Evacuation: A Very British Revolution*. Lion, 1995; Martin L. Parsons, *I'll Take That One: Dispelling the Myths of Civilian Evacuation 1939–45*. Beckett & Karlson, 1998; Heather V. Nicholson, *Prisoners of War: True Stories of Evacuees*. Gordon, 2000.
89. Mrs. D. Pepper, *Child in the War*. IWM:D #96/26/1.
90. See, for example, *Housewife*, November 1944, 27–9.
91. *Good Housekeeping*, May 1946, 21.
92. Rennell and Turner, *When Daddy Came Home*, 76–7.
93. Mrs. J. Danjoux, *Growing Up in the Second World War*. IWM:D #97/40/1.
94. *New Statesman and Society*, 12 May 1995, 21.
95. Oliver Bland. IWM:S #19606.
96. *Civvy Street: The Magazine for all Ex-Service Men and Women*, October 1946, 4–5.
97. Ibid.
98. *Housewife*, July 1946, 76.
99. Rennell and Turner, *When Daddy Came Home*, 94.
100. Ibid., 95.
101. Ross McKibbin, *Classes and Cultures: England 1918–1951*. Oxford University Press, 1998, 172.
102. Quoted in Joanna Bourke, *Working-Class Cultures in Britain 1890–1960*. Routledge, 1994, 77.
103. Francis Lucas. IWM:S #28653.
104. Ibid., 93.
105. *The Times*, 16 June 1943, 5.
106. *Daily Mirror*, 25 October 1945, 7.
107. *Good Housekeeping*, January 1946, 42–3.
108. *Daily Mirror*, 25 August 1944, 3.
109. Central Statistical Office, *Annual Abstract of Statistics 1938–1950*. HMSO, 1952, 63.
110. Titmuss, *Problems of Social Policy*, 339–40.
111. Geoffrey Gorer, *Exploring English Character*. Cresset, 1955, 176.
112. Bourke, *Working-Class Cultures in Britain 1890–1960*, 90.
113. *Housewife*, December 1946, 81.
114. *Housewife*, July 1944, 74.
115. Alice Truman. IWM:S #12365.
116. *Woman*, 23 June 1945, 3. See also *Good Housekeeping*, November 1944, 105.
117. *Daily Mirror*, 9 April 1945, 7.
118. *Daily Herald*, 27 November 1945, 2.
119. 'Captain X' [William G.C. Shebbeare], *A Soldier Looks Ahead*. Labour Book Service, 1944, 167.
120. See Claire Lanhammer, 'The Meanings of Home in Postwar Britain', *Journal of Contemporary History* 40: 2 (2005).
121. Richard Hoggart, *The Uses of Literacy*. Chatto and Windus, 1957, 37.
122. Frederick Shaw, *The Homes and Homeless of Post-War Britain*. Barnes & Noble, 1985, 2.
123. B. Ifor Evans, *The Shop on the King's Road*, Hodder & Stoughton, 1946, 37.

124. Ferguson and Fitzgerald, *Studies in the Social Services*, 4.
125. George H. Gallup, ed., *The Gallup International Public Opinion Polls: Great Britain 1937–1975, Volume One: 1937–1964*. Random House, 1976, 119.
126. *EMPLOYMENT: General (Code 79[A]): Houses and Employment for Ex-Service Men – Effect on Morale. 1945–1949*. NA WO 32/11742.
127. *Enquiry into the Housing Conditions of People on Local Authority Housing Waiting Lists, for Ministry of Health*, July 1949. NA RG 23/535.
128. *John Bull*, 13 January 1945, 5.
129. J.L. Hodson, *The Way Things Are*. Gollancz, 1947, 205.
130. *Time*, 23 July 1945.
131. *News Chronicle*, 16 July 1945, 3.
132. *News Chronicle*, 21 July 1945, 1.
133. *News Chronicle*, 25 July 1945, 4.
134. *Enquiry into the Composition of Households, Dwellings and Amenities*, 1947. NA RG 23/526.
135. *Enquiry into the Housing Conditions of People on Local Authority Housing Waiting Lists*, Loc. cit.
136. Jack Clabburn. IWM:S #21721.
137. *Modern Woman*, April 1946, 64.
138. *News Chronicle*, 24 January 1945, 2.
139. *Daily Express*, 18 June 1945, 2.
140. *News Chronicle*, 2 February 1945, 2.
141. Lanhammer, 'The Meanings of Home in Postwar Britain', 343.
142. Mass-Observation, *An Inquiry into People's Homes*. John Murray, 1943, 171.
143. Arnold Whittick, *The Small House: Today and Tomorrow*. Crosby Lockwood & Son, 1947, 204.
144. J.L. Hodson, 7 January 1945, *The Sea and the Land*. Gollancz, 1945, 279. See also *Modern Woman*, April 1946, 64; *News Chronicle*, 20 August 1945, 2.
145. Barbara Kendall-Davies, *Memories of a Second World War Childhood*, 20. IWM:D #02/28/1.
146. *Daily Mirror*, 30 October 1944, 7.
147. *Woman*, 30 March 1946, 22.
148. *News Chronicle*, 7 February 1945, 2.
149. Quoted in Geoffrey Field, 'Perspectives on the Working-Class Family in Wartime Britain', *International Labor and Working-Class History* 38 (1990), 16.
150. O.R. McGregor, *Divorce in England*. Heinemann, 1957, 41–3. It is possible, however, that since no no-fault category of divorce yet existed, some of these claims may have been a legal contrivance.

## Chapter Three: My Faithless English Rose

1. *The Odyssey*, trans. Samuel Butler. Kessinger, 2006, 287.
2. These and all subsequent details of the Cairns' story can be found in the Metropolitan Police summary: NA MEPO 3/2719.
3. *News of the World*, 2 September 1945, 7.
4. *News of the World*, 9 December 1945, 9.
5. *Daily Herald*, 1 November 1945, 1.
6. *News of the World*, 9 December 1945, 3.
7. *Daily Express*, 15 May 1945, 3.

8. See, for example, *News of the World*, 2 December 1945, 3.

9. *John Bull*, 22 June 1946, 17.

10. Quoted in Geoffrey Field, 'Perspectives on the Working-Class Family in Wartime Britain', *International Labor and Working-Class History* 38 (1990), 16.

11. *Daily Mail*, 23 August 1945, 2; see also 8 January 1945, 2.

12. *Daily Herald*, 10 November 1945, 3.

13. Quoted in Sir Arthur S. McNalty, 'Influence of War on Family Life', in Sir James Marchant, ed., *Rebuilding Family Life in the Post-War World: An Enquiry with Recommendations*. Odhams, 1945, 133.

14. *Daily Express*, 14 March 1945, 3.

15. *Daily Mirror*, 31 January 1945, 2.

16. *News of the World*, 4 November 1945, 3.

17. *Daily Herald*, 25 May 1946, 3.

18. *News of the World*, 4 March 1945, 2.

19. *Daily Mail*, 15 March 1945, 3.

20. *Criminal Statistics for England and Wales 1939–1945*. Cmnd. 7227 (1947), 7.

21. Lawrence Stone, *Road to Divorce: England 1530–1987*. Oxford, 1990, 435.

22. *John Bull*, 22 June 1946, 17.

23. McNalty, 'Influence of War on Family Life', 133.

24. *Daily Mail*, 12 May 1946, 3.

25. *Daily Herald*, 11 July 1946. For a vivid picture of this creaking machinery see Julian Maclaran-Ross's short story 'Through the Usual Channels', in his *Selected Stories*. Dewi Lewis, 2004.

26. O.R. McGregor, *Divorce in England*. Heinemann, 1957, 36; Stone, *Road to Divorce*, 435.

27. McGregor, *Divorce in England*, 41–3.

28. Griselda Rowntree and Norman H. Carrier, 'The Resort to Divorce in England and Wales, 1858–1957', *Population Studies* 11: 3 (1958), 216.

29. Details in NA WO71/1139.

30. *Daily Herald*, 28 July 1945, 3.

31. *Union Jack* (Greece edition), 19 October 1945, 1.

32. Lt.-Col. J.H.A. Sparrow, *Report on Tour of Italy, Middle East and PAIC*, 3 November 1944, 13. NA WO 32/15772.

33. NA AIR 20/4583.

34. Lt.-Col. J.H.A. Sparrow, *Morale of the Army 1939–1945*. War Office, 1949, 8. NA WO 277/16.

35. Eliot Slater and Moya Woodside, *Patterns of Marriage: A Study of Marriage Relationships in the Urban Working Classes*. Cassell, 1951, 222.

36. Kenneth Howard, *Sex Problems of the Returning Soldier*. Sydney Pemberton, 1945, 47.

37. Alfred Torrie, 'The Return of Odysseus: The Problem of Marital Infidelity for the Repatriate', *British Medical Journal*, 11 August 1945, 192.

38. G.H. Shorland, *Diary*, 8 July 1945. IWM:D #95/17/1.

39. *Woman*, 12 January 1946, 22.

40. David Reynolds, *Rich Relations: The American Occupation of Britain 1942–1945*. Phoenix, 2001.

41. Martin Page, ed., *Kiss Me Goodnight, Sergeant Major: The Songs and Ballads of World War II*. Hart-Davis, MacGibbon, 1973, 121.

42. Ibid.

43. *Picture Post*, 26 May 1945.

44. *John Bull*, 8 September 1945, 11. See also *Daily Mirror*, 5 October 1945, 2. There were also fears about British women fraternising (or 'fratting') with Italian prisoners of war: see, for example, *People*, 29 July 1945, 3.

45. Jeremy Crang, *The British Army and the People's War 1939–1945*, Manchester University Press, 2000, 101–5.

46. Six in ten applications for compassionate home postings by men overseas were rejected, as were four in ten requests for early release (Sheila Ferguson and Hilde Fitzgerald, *Studies in the Social Services*, HMSO, 1954, 8–9).

47. Slater and Woodside, *Patterns of Marriage*, 222.

48. *The Times*, 2 April 1946, 5.

49. L.R. England, 'Little Kinsey: An Outline of Sex Attitudes in Britain', *The Public Opinion Quarterly*, 13: 4 (1949), 593. For an interesting, albeit polemical, discussion of Little Kinsey's methodology, see *Civitas Review* 3: 1 (2006).

50. Ferguson and Fitzgerald, *Studies in the Social Services*, 98.

51. *The Times*, 2 April 1946, 5.

52. Spousal wrongdoing was only confirmed in 50 out of 171 sample cases investigated by the Army Welfare Service's probation officers, though it was suspected in more. See Ferguson and Fitzgerald, *Studies in the Social Services*, 99.

53. Sparrow, *Report on Tour of Italy, Middle East, and PAIC*, 13.

54. Quoted in ibid., Appendix G.

55. *News Chronicle*, 30 July 1945, 2.

56. Field, 'Perspectives on the Working-Class Family *in Wartime Britain*', 17.

57. Page, ed., *Kiss Me Goodnight, Sergeant Major*, 122.

58. T.F. Main, 'Clinical Problems of Repatriates', *The Journal of Mental Science* XCIII (1947), 362.

59. *Daily Express*, 3 July 1945, 3.

60. *Daily Herald*, 16 February 1946, 3.

61. *Daily Express*, 27 September 1945, 3.

62. *Daily Express*, 15 November 1945, 1.

63. *Daily Herald*, 28 September 1945, 3.

64. Susan Gubar, ' "This Is My Rifle, This Is My Gun": World War II and the Blitz on Women', in Margaret M. Higgonet et al., eds, *Behind the Lines: Gender and the Two World Wars*. Yale University Press, 1987.

65. *Daily Mirror*, 12 January 1945, 2.

66. *The Times*, 11 April 1946, 5.

67. *John Bull*, 10 March 1945, 7.

68. Phoebe D. Bendit and Laurence J. Bendit, *Living Together Again*. Gramol, 1946, 77.

69. Howard, *Sex Problems of the Returning Soldier*, 56.

70. *Woman's Own*, 8 March 1946, 22.

71. *Woman's Own*, 5 May 1946, 22.

72. Ibid.

73. Geoffrey Gorer, *Exploring English Character*. Cresset, 1955, 148.

74. There were prewar precedents for this. In 1928 public opinion had swung to the defence of the acquitted Gloucestershire poisoner Beatrice Pace after it was revealed that her victim Harry had been a violent and abusive husband.

75. *News of the World*, 13 May 1945, 7.

76. *Daily Express*, 20 July 1945, 1.

77. *Daily Herald*, 21 November 1945, 2.

78. *News of the World*, 7 January 1945. The Army Welfare Department had been concerned about 'mischief-makers' for some time; see J.L. Hodson, 27 October 1943, *The Sea and the Land*. Gollancz, 1945, 127. For an account of a Local Army Welfare Officer's confrontation with a poison-pen writer, see Crang, *The British Army and the People's War*, 105.

79. See, for example, *Woman*, 28 April 1945, 22.

80. A point made by Sally Andrew, *Daily Herald*, 21 November 1945, 2.

81. J.B. Priestley, *Three Men in New Suits*. Heinemann, 1945, 154.

82. *People*, 22 July 1945, 2.

83. *People*, 4 November 1945, 3.

84. *People*, 18 March 1945, 8.

85. *Sunday Express*, 24 June 1945, 2. Similar concerns were also being expressed in the United States at the same time. See John Willoughby, 'The Sexual Behavior of American GIs During the Early Years of the Occupation of Germany', *The Journal of Military History* 62 (1998).

86. *People*, 4 November 1945, 3. Price, a successful novelist and broadcaster as well as a journalist, could perhaps be forgiven for taking a harsh line towards the defeated Axis: her husband was a recently released Fepow.

87. *People*, 18 November 1945, 3.

88. *News Chronicle*, 26 July 1945, 2.

89. *Sunday Express*, 8 April 1945, 3. For more on potential (and allegedly secret) marriages between British soldiers and German women see, for example, *People*, 21 January 1945 and 30 September 1945, 1; and *John Bull*, 22 June 1946.

90. See *People*, 5 August 1945, 3; 19 August 1945, 5; 7 October 1945, 3; 11 November 1945, 3. See also the *Daily Mirror*, 28 July 1945, 1; *News of the World*, 29 July 1945, 3.

91. *People*, 2 December 1945, 5.

92. *Soldier*, 29 September 1945, 23; see also the letter in the same edition, 2.

93. Geoffrey Field, 'Perspectives on the Working-Class Family *in Wartime Britain*', 16.

94. James Lucas, *The British Soldier*. Arms & Armour Press, 1989, 31–5.

95. Robert Lees, 'Venereal Diseases in the Armed Forces Overseas (1)', *British Journal of Venereal Diseases* 22 (1946), 154.

96. John Ellis, *The Sharp End: The Fighting Man in World War Two*. Charles Scribner's, 1980, 304.

97. Douglas Campbell, 'Venereal Disease in the Armed Forces Overseas (2)', *British Journal of Venereal Diseases* 22 (1946), 163.

98. The atmosphere of post-liberation Ostend is captured well in Alexander Baron, *The Human Kind*. Jonathan Cape, 1953, 130–45.

99. George MacDonald Fraser, *Quartered Safe Out Here*. HarperCollins, 2000, 182.

100. Paul Fussell, *Wartime: Understanding and Behaviour in the Second World War*. Oxford University Press, 1989, 37.

101. Mark Harrison, 'Sex and the Citizen Soldier: Health, Morals and Discipline in the British Army during the Second World War', in Roger Cooter, et al., eds, *Medicine and Modern Warfare*. Rodopi, 1999, 231.

102. Sparrow, *Report on Tour of Italy, Middle East and PAIC*, 13. See also T.A. Ratcliffe, 'Psychiatric and Allied Aspects of the Problem of Venereal Disease in the Army', *Journal of the Royal Army Medical Corps* 89 (1947), 127. Axis propagandists had spread (with evident success) the belief that prolonged treatment with the anti-malarial drug mepacrine induced impotence.

103. G. de M. Rudolf, 'Sex in the Fighting Services at an Isolated Station', *British Journal of Medical Psychology* 21: 2 (1948), 128.

104. *Statistical Report on Health of the Army 1943–1945* (1948), 265. NA WO 222/1566.

105. B. Seebohm Rowntree and G.R. Lavers, *English Life and Leisure: A Social Study*. Longmans, 1951, 213.

106. Philippa Levine, *Prostitution, Race and Politics: Policing Venereal Disease in the British Empire*. Routledge, 2003, 293, 264.

107. Roy Porter and Lesley A. Hall, *The Facts of Life: The Creation of Sexual Knowledge in Britain, 1650–1950*. Yale University Press, 1995, 242.

108. Harrison, 'Sex and the Citizen Soldier', 233.

109. For the rise of 'temperate masculinity' in Britain in the interwar years, see Alison Light, *Forever England: Femininity, Literature, and Conservatism Between the Wars*. Routledge, 1991.

110. Gorer, *Exploring English Character*, 151.

111. *John Bull*, 7 July 1945, 12–13.

112. *John Bull*, 23 November 1946, 19–20.

113. *Train of Events* (1949), dir. Sydney Cole et al.

114. Gorer, *Exploring English Character*, 147.

115. Ibid., 155.

116. Clive Emsley, *Hard Men: Violence in England Since 1750*. Hambledon and London, 2005, 77–93; Jon Lawrence, 'Forging a Peaceable Kingdom: War, Violence and the Fear of Brutalisation in Post-First World War Britain', *Journal of Modern History* 75: 3 (2003).

## Chapter Four: What the Hell Has Happened to this Country?

1. *Daily Express*, 15 November 1945, 2.

2. *Picture Post*, 2 February 1946, 4.

3. *Manchester Guardian*, 20 December 1945, 4.

4. Rev. W.G. Pollard, *Scrapbook*. IWM:D #93/9/1.

5. Maurice Merritt, *Eighth Army Driver*. Midas Books, 1981, 180.

6. *Civvy Street: The Magazine for all Ex-Service Men and Women*, June 1946.

7. Anthony Burgess, *Little Wilson and Big God*. Heinemann, 1988, 322.

8. Corporal D. Evans, *Memoir*, 247. IWM:D #92/37/1.

9. James Rochford, quoted in Paul Addison, *Now The War is Over*, Jonathan Cape, 1985, 24.

10. *John Bull*, 30 November 1946, 23.

11. L.C.F. Harwood, *Oh Threats of Hell: The Diary of a Prisoner of War*, 318. IWM:D #84/33/1.

12. *Horizon*, 10: 57 (September 1944), 152–3.

13. George Chippington, *Naked and Unashamed*, 653. IWD:D #PP/MCR/298.

14. *New Statesman and Nation*, 28 September 1946, 221.

15. Harwood, *Oh Threats of Hell*, 302.

16. Jean Crossley, *A Middle-Class War*, 56. IWM:D #04/13/1.

17. Mrs. E.J.F. Knowles, *Underage and Overseas*, 165. IWM:D #91/36/1.

18. S.C. Lawrence, 'Ad Astra', in *Civvy Street: The Magazine for all Ex-Service Men and Women*, June 1946.

19. J.L. Hodson, 10 April 1946, *The Way Things Are*. Gollancz, 1947, 123.

20. *Daily Herald*, 4 December 1945, 2.

21. *Picture Post*, 7 April 1945, 7.
22. *Punch*, 3 October 1945, 301.
23. Central Statistical Office, *Fighting With Figures: A Statistical Digest of the Second World War*, HMSO, 1995, 43.
24. John Ellis, *The Sharp End: The Fighting Man in World War Two*. Charles Scribner's, 1980, 162.
25. Ibid., 164.
26. Phil Davis, *Royal Air Force (RAF) Bomber Command 1939–1945*: http://www.elsham. pwp.blueyonder.co.uk/ raf_bc/.
27. J.M. Winter, *The Great War and the British People*. Harvard University Press, 1986, 73. Winter estimates that 6.1 million men served in the British armed forces at some point or other during the Great War. The Central Statistical Office's *Fighting With Figures* (38 and 41) gives the equivalent figure for 1939–1945 as roughly 5.5 million.
28. *Report on Civilian Attitudes to the Navy Compared with RAF and Army*, September 1941. Mass-Observation Topics Collection 29/1/A.
29. Army Questionnaire, June 1941. Mass-Observation Topics Collection 29/3/A.
30. Richard Titmuss, *Problems of Social Policy*, HMSO, 1950, 335–6.
31. Ibid., 324.
32. Anthony Weymouth, 28 February 1941, *Journal of the War Years*. Littlebury, 1948, vol. 1, 371.
33. *Report on Morale and Training in the Army*, June 1941. Mass-Observation Topics Collection 29/2/A at the University of Sussex, Adam Matthew Publications. Reel 143: FORCES (MEN), 1939–1956 (TC29), Box 2.
34. Weekly Home Intelligence Report, 11–18 June 1941. NA INF 1/292 WHIR.
35. 'Boomerang' [Alan Wood], *Bless 'Em All: An Analysis of the British Army, its Morale, Efficiency and Leadership*. Martin Secker & Warburg, 1942, 21.
36. Weekly Home Intelligence Report, 1–8 September 1942. NA INF 1/292 WHIR.
37. Ibid., 17–24 November 1942.
38. NA WO 32/15772.
39. Max Hastings, *Armageddon: The Battle for Germany, 1944–1945*. A.A. Knopf, 2005, 380.
40. *Summary of Total Strength of the RAF and WAAF, May 1, 1945*. NA AIR 20/1966.
41. George Millar, *Horned Pigeon*. Heinemann, 1946, 432.
42. J.L. Hodson, 21 September 1943, *The Sea and the Land*. Gollancz, 1945, 117.
43. Lt.-Col. J.H.A. Sparrow, *Tour of India and South East Asia Command*, 33. Chowringhee Road (now J.L. Nehru Road) ran through the commercial heart of Calcutta.
44. A point made by Sparrow in his confidential 1949 report to the War Office on *Morale of the Army 1939–1945*, 17. NA WO 277/16.
45. Lt.-Col. J.H.A. Sparrow, *Report on Tour of Italy, Middle East and PAIC*, 3 November 1944, 22. NA WO 32/15772.
46. Philip Furneaux Jordan, *Jordan's Tunis Diary*. Collins, 1943, 84.
47. Hodson, *The Sea and the Land*, 168.
48. Servicewomen were not included in the scheme. They received a cash payment (originally £12) and extra clothing coupons to construct a new civilian wardrobe. Many ex-auxiliaries complained that this settlement was 'farcical' given the paucity of goods in the shops. See, for example, *British Legion Journal*, December 1946, 274.
49. Arthur Charles Barker, *Nobby and Pincher in Civvy Street*. Rankin, 1950, 35–7.
50. George Cuthbertson, British Library National Sound Archive #F10884.

51. Eric Feakins, IWM:S #15607.
52. Tony Cameron, IWM:S #12918.
53. See, for example, Tom Hellawell, 'Some Folk Take Some Suiting', *Open Writing*. http://www.openwriting.com/archives/2004/01/some_folk_take.php. Accessed 8 September 2006.
54. *John Bull*, 17 March 1945, 2.
55. *Sunday Express*, 19 March 1944, 5.
56. *Union Jack*, 6 September 1945, 2.
57. *Daily Express*, 27 August 1945, 3; *Soldier*, 13 October 1945, 2.
58. *Union Jack*, 6 September 1945, 2.
59. James Herriot, *All Things Wise and Wonderful*. St. Martin's Press, 1998, 439.
60. Frank Luff. IWM:S #27267.
61. T.E.B. Howarth, *Prospect and Reality: Great Britain 1945–1955*. Collins, 1985, 45.
62. *Sunday Express*, 15 September 1945, 2.
63. *Daily Express*, 4 October 1945, 3; *News Chronicle*, 11 October 1945, 3.
64. Maureen Waller, *London 1945: Life in the Debris of War*. John Murray, 2004, 212. Note that a new suit for civilians cost twenty-six coupons.
65. *Soldier*, 13 April 1946, 2.
66. *Demobilisation Coupons: An Enquiry Made for the Board of Trade*, December 1945, 3. NA RG23/79.
67. *The Times*, 9 July 1945, 5.
68. Brian Poole, letter, 27 October 1946. IWM:D #Con Shelf.
69. *Punch*, 18 July 1945, 57.
70. Waller, *London 1945*, 163–4.
71. *Daily Herald*, 28 December 1945, 3.
72. Quoted in Kenneth Poolman, *The British Sailor*. Arms & Armour Press, 1989, 172.
73. *John Bull*, 8 December 1945, 14.
74. *Daily Express*, 2 February 1945, 2.
75. *John Bull*, 3 August 1946, 16.
76. *Punch*, 17 April 1946, 339.
77. *Daily Express*, 8 October 1945, 2.
78. *News Chronicle*, 26 September 1946, 2.
79. *Civvy Street: The Magazine for all Ex-Service Men and Women*, August 1946, 7.
80. *Daily Herald*, 1 October 1946, 2.
81. Victor Morrison, British Library National Sound Archive #F8629.
82. Brian Poole, letter, 12 September 1945. IWM:D #92/29/1.
83. B. Seebohm Rowntree and G.R Lavers, *English Life and Leisure: A Social Study*. Longmans, 1951, 7.
84. *Woman*, 17 November 1945, 3.
85. *Daily Mirror*, 6 November 1945, 2.
86. Arthur Harris, letter, 9 December 1945. IWM:D #96/35/1.
87. Ibid., letter, 12 January 1946.
88. Ibid., letter, 8 February 1946.
89. Lt.-Col. J.H.A. Sparrow, *Report on Visit to 21st Army Group and Tour of Second Army 30th March – 5th May 1945*, 1. NA WO 32/15772.
90. See, for example, *John Bull*, 31 March 1945, 14: 'I am in the British Liberation Army, and am worried about what people at home are saying and thinking about us. A pal of mine had leave in January and, while he was at home, friends kept showing clearly that they thought he was having a good time on the Continent.'

91. Victor Gollancz, *In Darkest Germany*. Henry Regnery, 1947, 198.
92. *Daily Mirror*, 18 July 1945, 4.
93. B.G. Horrocks, *30 Corps in Germany*, 1945, 52.
94. Ibid., 53.
95. *Manchester Guardian*, 14 June 1946, 4. See also *News Chronicle*, 21 August 1946, 2, which attributes the poor behaviour of British troops in Germany to the lack of entertainment.
96. Edward Kirby. IWM:S #16084.
97. Dennis Middleton. IWM:S #14986; Donald Sutherland, *Portrait of a Decade: London Life 1945–1955*. Harrap, 1988, 37.
98. Ian Harris. IWM:S #13389.
99. *Sunday Express*, 2 September 1945, 5. When the Board of Trade closed the loophole later that month, the purchasing power of the cigarette in the British Occupation Zone (BOZ) rose by 50 per cent in a matter of days. See *Daily Express*, 13 September 1945, 3.
100. *Daily Express*, 3 September 1945, 3.
101. *Sunday Express*, 12 August 1945, 4.
102. Letter to B. Charles, 12 December 1945, in Simon Garfield, ed., *Our Hidden Lives: The Everyday Diaries of a Forgotten Britain 1945–1948*. Ebury, 2004, 147. At this time British civilians received one egg a month.
103. *News Chronicle*, 3 May 1946, 1.
104. *News Chronicle*, 28 February 1946, 1.
105. George Forty, *British Army Handbook 1939–1945*. Sutton, 1998, 137–8; Jeremy Crang, 'The British Soldier on the Home Front: Army Morale Reports, 1940–1945', in Paul Addison and Angus Calder, eds, *Time To Kill: The Soldier's Experience of War in the West, 1939–1945*. Pimlico, 1997, 62.
106. See *John Bull*, 4 August 1945, 11.
107. *Punch*, 8 August 1945, 122.
108. *Daily Mirror*, 24 December 1945, 3.
109. *Woman*, 13 April 1946, 3.
110. Quoted in Lyn Smith, ed., *Young Voices: British Children Remember the Second World War*. Viking, 2007, 376–7.
111. *Daily Express*, 16 March 1945, 2.
112. *Daily Herald*, 7 May 1946, 1. See also *John Bull*, 15 September 1945, 11.
113. *News Chronicle*, 23 March 1945, 2.
114. *News of the World*, 11 November 1945, 4.
115. *Manchester Guardian*, 8 August 1945, 4.
116. *Manchester Guardian*, 11 August 1945, 4.
117. *Picture Post*, 9 June 1945, 3.
118. Harold Scull. IWM:S #14804.
119. Howard Baker, *Nanyo: The Story of a Family in Paradise and Hell*, 260. IWM:D #87/25/1.
120. *Manchester Guardian*, 2 October 1945, 4.
121. *John Bull*, 7 July 1945, 11.
122. J. Bartram, October 1945, Mass-Observation Topics Collection 27/3/E University of Sussex. Adam Matthew Publications. Reel 81: WORK: REGISTRATION & DEMOBILISATION, 1939–1946 (TC27), Box 3, Folder E.
123. *Union Jack*, 19 September 1945, 2.
124. *Union Jack*, 11 December 1945, 2.
125. *Manchester Guardian*, 20 December 1945, 4.

## Chapter Five: Clocking On

1. Len Newman. IWM:S #18705.
2. K.B. Huntbatch, *Diary*. IWM:D #01/39/1.
3. W.M. Innes-Ker, *POW Diary*. IWM:D #84/45/1.
4. *The Times*, 4 May 1946, 2.
5. *Soldier*, 31 March 1945, 2.
6. Bert Scrivens, IWM:S #29536.
7. Vic Emery. IWM:S #24731.
8. Fred Hazell. IWM:S #17229.
9. Ibid.
10. Bert Wolstenholme. IWM:S #27789.
11. Leslie Westcott. IWM:S #13946.
12. E.S. Conway, *Post-War Employment*. Jonathan Cape, 1943, 112.
13. Quoted in Simon Garfield, ed., *Our Hidden Lives: The Everyday Diaries of a Forgotten Britain 1945–1948*. Ebury, 2004, 51.
14. Rex Pope, 'The Planning and Implementation of British Demobilisation, 1941–1946'. Unpublished dissertation, Open University, 1986, 191–4.
15. *News Chronicle*, 28 May 1945, 2.
16. *Release and Resettlement: An Explanation of Your Position and Rights*. HMSO, 1945, 17–21.
17. George Taylor, 16 September 1946, Garfield, ed., *Our Hidden Lives*, 274–5.
18. *Daily Mirror*, 6 October 1944, 5.
19. Pope, 'The Planning and Implementation of British Demobilisation', 288.
20. *Union Jack*, 31 August 1945, 3.
21. Raymond Child. IWM:S #23138.
22. Cecil Wareham, *A Portrait of our Family*, 131. IWM:D #96/31/1.
23. Alan Hay. IWM:S #13079.
24. Walter Harris. IWM:S #20944. See also *John Bull*, 25 May 1946, 13–14.
25. Duncan McNie. IWM:S #19798.
26. Ron Ayers. IWM:S #21093.
27. *Daily Mail*, 10 June 1946, 1.
28. *John Bull*, 16 March 1946, 1.
29. *Daily Mail*, 30 August 1946, 3.
30. Ministry of Labour and National Service, *The Serviceman's Resettlement: Notes for the Guidance of all Concerned with Management*. HMSO, 1945, 10.
31. Reg Ellery, *Psychiatric Aspects of Modern Warfare*, Reed & Harris, 1945, 150.
32. M.M. Lewis, ed., *Teachers From the Forces: An Experimental Short Course of Training at Goldsmith's College University of London*. Harrap, 1946, 49.
33. *Union Jack*, 14 December 1945, 2.
34. *John Bull*, 13 October 1945, 9.
35. *Union Jack*, 13 August 1945, 3.
36. Ken Bean. IWM:S #27091.
37. A.M. Bell MacDonald, *War Diary*, 23 May 1944. IWM:D #Con Shelf.
38. Victor Bell. IWM:S #25936.
39. Joe Kidger. IWM:S #23200.
40. Harry Morrell. IWM:S #17824.
41. John Gray. IWM:S #20202.
42. Trevor Timperley. IWM:S #27493.

43. Robert Lees, 'Venereal Diseases in the Armed Forces Overseas (1)', *British Journal of Venereal Diseases* 22 (1946), 150.
44. J.L. Hodson, *The Way Things Are*. Gollancz, 1947, 92.
45. Figures in NA RAIL 1172/1968.
46. *Union Jack*, 13 August 1945, 3.
47. John Frost. IWM:S #22383.
48. George Bell. IWM:S #21137.
49. Corrie Halliday. IWM:S #15620.
50. *Army Tradesmen Statement at 30 November 1944*. NA WO 365/133; Lt.-Col. J.W. Gibb, *Training in the Army*, 319. NA WO 277/36.
51. *Comparative Statements of Establishment and Strength 1944–1945*. NA AIR 22/316. These figures do not include WAAF tradeswomen.
52. *Summary of Total Strength of the RAF and WAAF*. NA AIR 20/1966.
53. *Report on the Educational Preferences of a Sample of the Army*, September 1914. NA WO 32/9430.
54. J.B. Lindop, *AB RP3*. IWM:D #92/27/1.
55. *Daily Mirror*, 29 November 1945, 7.
56. *John Bull*, 6 October 1945, 14.
57. *John Bull*, 18 May 1946, 17.
58. Eric Horn, letter to Arthur Ebert, 28 October 1946. IWM:D #76/68/1.
59. *John Bull*, 6 January 1945, 12.
60. *Daily Mirror*, 21 August 1945, 5.
61. Pope, 'The Planning and Implementation of British Demobilisation', 288.
62. *Daily Mirror*, 20 September 1945, 7.
63. D. Evans, *Memoir*, 246. IWM:D #92/37/1.
64. Paul Addison, *Now The War Is Over: A Social History of Britain 1945–51*. Jonathan Cape, 1985, 144–56; Pope, 'The Planning and Implementation of British Demobilisation', 177–8, 306.
65. Addison, *Now The War Is Over*, 153.
66. Pope, 'The Planning and Implementation of British Demobilisation', 291.
67. *Manchester Guardian*, 24 May 1946, 4.
68. See, for example, *Manchester Guardian*, 27 August 1946, 4; *New Statesman and Nation*, 31 August 1946, 153.
69. *News Chronicle*, 17 December 1946, 5.
70. *News Chronicle*, 28 August 1945, 2.
71. Pope, 'The Planning and Implementation of British Demobilisation', 293.
72. *Daily Herald*, 7 February 1945, 2. For contemporary comparisons using the average income index, see http://www.measuringworth.com.
73. Hodson, 11 December 1945, *The Way Things Are*, 80.
74. *Location of Retail Business Orders Statistics, November 1945*. NA BT 64/180.
75. *Daily Mail*, 14 November 1945, 3.
76. *John Bull*, 18 August 1945, 13.
77. Ross McKibbin, *Classes and Cultures: England 1918–1951*. Oxford University Press, 1998, 47.
78. *Daily Mail*, 5 June 1945, 2.
79. *Daily Mail*, 14 January 1946, 2.
80. *News of the World*, 29 July 1945, 5.
81. *Daily Mail*, 5 June 1945, 2.
82. *Punch*, 14 November 1945, 410.

83. *News Chronicle*, 8 September 1945, 3. Evers continued to prosper in civilian life and in 1959 was made Lord Mayor of Dewsbury.
84. *Daily Herald*, 20 September 1945, 3. Nottingham City Transport's dilemma was resolved tragically when the plane bringing Wigginton home disappeared en route.
85. *Sunday Express*, 8 April 1945, 5.
86. *Sunday Express*, 5 August 1945, 7.
87. Martin Peter, 'Temporary Gentlemen in the Aftermath of the Great War: Rank, Status and the Ex-Officer Problem', *The Historical Journal* 37: 1 (1994).
88. Jeremy Crang, *The British Army and the People's War 1939–1945*. Manchester University Press, 2000, 21–44.
89. *News Chronicle*, 27 September 1946, 3.
90. *News Chronicle*, 4 January 1946, 3.
91. *Manchester Guardian*, 9 September 1946, 4.
92. *The Times*, 9 September 1946, 5.
93. *Spectator*, 11 January 1946, 38.
94. *The Times*, 14 September 1945, 5.
95. Arthur Vizard. IWM:S #16601.
96. Pope, 'The Planning and Implementation of British Demobilisation', 289.
97. *Spectator*, 11 January 1946, 38.
98. *The Times*, 18 May 1946, 5.
99. *The Times*, 26 August 1946, 7.
100. *News Chronicle*, 18 September 1946, 2.
101. *People*, 28 January 1945, 3.
102. *People*, 5 August 1945, 4.
103. *Manchester Guardian*, 5 January 1946, 4.
104. McKibbin, *Classes and Cultures*, 131.
105. *Daily Mail*, 31 December 1946, 2.
106. *John Bull*, 15 December 1945, 14.
107. *Picture Post*, 16 February 1946, 16.
108. *Manchester Guardian*, 4 September 1946, 4.
109. See, for example, *John Bull*, 27 October 1945, 12.
110. *Daily Mail*, 27 December 1945, 2.
111. *Woman*, 9 February 1946, 3.
112. *Writers of Tomorrow* 3 (1946).
113. *John Bull*, 12 May 1945, 10.
114. Ferdinand Zweig, *Labour, Life and Poverty*. Gollancz, 1948, 68.
115. Ibid., 165.
116. Ibid., 179–80.
117. Michael J. Bennett, *When Dreams Came True: The GI Bill and the Making of Modern America*. Brassey's, 1996, 242.
118. Suzanne Mettler, *Soldiers to Citizens: The GI Bill and the Making of the Greatest Generation*. Oxford University Press, 2005, 165.
119. Roy Lowe, *Education in the Post-War Years: A Social History*. Routledge, 1988, 62.
120. *Enquiry into the Frequency of Occupational Industrial and Geographical Change Amongst the Employed Population in England and Wales, for the Ministry of Labour*, 1949. NA RG 23/152A.
121. Ellery, *Psychiatric Aspects of Modern Warfare*, 146–7.

## Chapter Six: They Made Me a Fugitive

1. Dennis Rooke and Alan D'Egville, *Call Me Mister! A Guide to Civilian Life for the Newly Demobilised*. Heinemann, 1945, 51.
2. Morris Beckman, *The 43 Group*. Centerprise Publications, 1993, 19.
3. Ibid., 24.
4. Ibid., 53.
5. Ibid., 73.
6. Ibid., 203.
7. Ibid., 59.
8. Ibid., 198.
9. *They Made Me a Fugitive*, dir. Alberto Cavalcanti, 1947.
10. *The Flamingo Affair*, dir. Horace Shepherd, 1948.
11. *Spectator*, 4 July 1947, 13.
12. All figures that follow are for England and Wales.
13. *Annual Abstract of Statistics* 1938–1950, HMSO, 1952; B.R. Mitchell, *British Historical Statistics*, Cambridge University Press, 1988; Terence Morris, *Crime and Criminal Justice Since 1945*, Blackwell, 1989.
14. Leo Page, *The Young Lag*. Faber & Faber, 1950, p. 31.
15. *Daily Mail*, 9 November 1945, p. 1.
16. *John Bull*, 15 December 1945, p. 7.
17. Page, *The Young Lag*, p. 27.
18. *Soldier*, 24 November 1945, 11.
19. *Daily Mail*, 23 December 1946, 2.
20. *New Statesman and Nation*, 12 January 1946, 23.
21. *Civvy Street*, August 1946, 32.
22. *Soldier*, 11 May 1946, 11.
23. *New Statesman and Nation*, 3 November 1945, 293.
24. *New Statesman and Nation*, 28 September 1946, 227.
25. John Guest, *Broken Images: A Journal*. Longmans, 1949, 231.
26. *Manchester Guardian*, 29 January 1946, 4.
27. Cecil Wareham, *A Portrait of Our Family*, 129. IWM:D #96/31/1.
28. J.B. Lindop, IWD:D #92.27/1.
29. Charles Crichton. IWM:D #Con Shelf.
30. Philip Warner, 'Churchill, John Malcolm Thorpe Fleming (1906–1996)', *Oxford Dictionary of National Biography*, Oxford University Press, 2004; online edn., May 2006 (http://www.oxforddnb.com/view/article/62152, accessed 27 September 2008).
31. E.T. Williams, 'Carton de Wiart, Sir Adrian (1880–1963)', rev. G.D. Sheffield, *Oxford Dictionary of National Biography*, loc cit., (http://www.oxforddnb.com/view/article/32316, accessed 1 March 2009).
32. *New Statesman and Nation*, 27 October 1945, 277–8.
33. R.S. Ellery, *Psychiatric Aspects of Modern Warfare*. Reed & Harris, 1945, 146–7.
34. Ferdinand Zweig, *Labour, Life and Poverty*. Gollancz, 1948, 50.
35. B. Seebohm Rowntree and G.R. Lavers, *English Life and Leisure: A Social Study*. Longmans, 1951, 124.
36. *Daily Herald*, 3 January 1946, 2.
37. Raymond English, *The Pursuit of Purpose: An Essay in Social Morale*. Falcon Press, 1947, 123.

38. Perry V. Wagley, 'Some Criminalogic Implications of the Returning Soldier', *Journal of Criminal Law and Criminology*, 34 (1944), 314.
39. *Daily Mail*, 24 October 1946, 1.
40. *The Times*, 23 January 1948, 5.
41. *Daily Express*, 3 September 1945, 3.
42. *Army Officers and Men on Leave from BAOR Detected Smuggling*. NA CUST 49/3382.
43. *Spectator*, 18 April 1947, 419.
44. Donald Thomas, *An Underworld at War: Spivs, Deserters, Racketeers and Civilians in the Second World War*. John Murray, 2003, 361–6.
45. *The Army Overseas, Dec 1944–Feb 1945*. NA WO 32/15772.
46. *Soldier*, 27 October 1945, 2.
47. *Soldier*, 10 November 1945, 23.
48. *Spectator*, 12 September 1947, 327.
49. *Soldier*, 8 December 1945, 2.
50. Hermann Mannheim, *Social Aspects of Crime in England Between the Wars*. G. Allen & Unwin, 1940, 112–13.
51. *Soldier*, 5 January 1946, 23.
52. Anthony Burgess, *Little Wilson and Big God*. Penguin, 1988, 330.
53. Thomas, *An Underworld at War*, 183–95.
54. NA WO 71/1107.
55. *Daily Herald*, 31 July 1945, 3.
56. *Daily Mail*, 2 April 1946, 1.
57. *Daily Express*, 17 September 1945, 2.
58. *Daily Herald*, 14 June 1945, 3.
59. *Daily Herald*, 18 July 1945, 3.
60. Francis Selwyn, *Rotten to the Core? The Life and Death of Neville Heath*. Routledge, 1988, 23.
61. Ibid., 197.
62. Elizabeth Taylor, *A Wreath of Roses*. Alfred A. Knopf, 1949, 83–4.
63. *The Times*, 25 November 1941, 5.
64. *The Times*, 27 April 1942, 2.
65. *The Times*, 1 May 1942, 5.
66. See *The Times*, 14 May 1942, 8; Robert Ahrenfeldt, *Psychiatry in the British Army in the Second World War*. Routledge & Kegan Paul, 1958, 200n.
67. *Time and Tide*, 9 May 1942, 383.
68. Ahrenfeldt, *Psychiatry in the British Army*, 199–201.
69. J.L. Hodson, *The Sea and the Land*. Gollancz, 1945, p. 233.
70. *Good Housekeeping*, January 1945.
71. Lt.-Col. T.F. Main, 'Clinical Problems of Repatriates', *The Journal of Mental Science*, 93, 1947, 358.
72. Martin Dempsey, *Back in Civvy Street*. Samuel Walker, 1947, 19.
73. Nevil Shute, *The Chequer Board*. William Morrow, 1947, 323.
74. Ibid., 326.
75. Betty Miller, *On the Side of the Angels*. Hale, 1945, 133.
76. J.H.A. Sparrow, *Report on Visit to 21 Army Group and Tour of Second Army*, May 1945, 7. NA WO 32/15772.
77. *Daily Express*, 13 October 1944, 3.

78. *Daily Herald*, 15 December 1945, 1.
79. *Soldier*, 4 August 1945, 10–11.
80. Jim MacKenzie, 'Gimlet King'. http://www.collectingbooksandmagazines.com/gimlet. html. Accessed on 18 August 2005.
81. *Soldier*, 4 August 1945, 10–11.
82. *Soldier*, 8 December 1945, 5.
83. *Soldier*, June 1947, 18.
84. *Soldier*, 29 September 1945, 7.
85. *Daily Express*, 17 November 1945, 1; *Picture Post*, 4 August 1945, 17.
86. *Daily Herald*, 25 June 1946, 3.
87. *Daily Herald*, 26 June 1946, 2.
88. *Daily Herald*, 2 July 1946, 2.
89. *News Chronicle*, 29 June 1946, 3.
90. Robert Quixano Henriques, *The Journey Home*. Heinemann, 1944. Henriques (1905–1967) had an eccentric career. Born into one of the oldest Sephardic Jewish families in England, he was at various stages of his life a novelist, biographer, historian, broadcaster, soldier, big-game hunter and successful Cotswold farmer. He had served in the interwar Regular Army, and during the Second World War rose to the rank of colonel in the staff of Combined Operations HQ. After the war he became a passionate advocate for the state of Israel (though oddly he always denied that he was a Zionist), and at the time of his death he was preparing an elaborate history of the IDF (Israel Defence Forces).
91. Ibid., 206–8.
92. John D. Spencer, *Crime and the Services*. Routledge and Kegan Paul, 1954, 119.
93. Dale Archer and Rosemary Gartner, *Violence and Crime in Cross-National Perspective*. Yale University Press, 1984, 91.
94. *The Times*, 6 February 1946.
95. Arthur Harvey, *The Times*, 6 February 1946. A.V. Alexander, Minister of Defence, responded with a figure of 4.6 per cent for 1946.
96. See *The Times*, 15 and 17 December 1945, and 12 January 1946.
97. *The Times*, 23 September 1948, 6.
98. *Deserters from the Services Arrested for Criminal Offences: Annual Reports 1946–1953*. NA MEPO 2/7822.
99. Quoted in David French, ' "You Cannot Hate the Bastard Who Is Trying to Kill You": Combat and Ideology in the British Army in the War Against Germany, 1939–45', *Twentieth Century British History* 11: 1 (2000), 2.
100. Alex Comfort, *Authority and Delinquency in the Modern State: A Criminological Approach to the Problem of Power*. Routledge and Kegan Paul, 1950, 50–1, 56–7.
101. Quoted in the *New Statesman and Nation*, 12 January 1946, 23.
102. *The Times*, 23 May 1952, 7.
103. Joany Hichberger, 'Old Soldiers', in Raphael Samuel, ed., *Patriotism: The Making and Unmaking of British National Identity*. Routledge, 1989, vol. II, 51.
104. Philip Gibbs, *Realities of War*. Heinemann, 1920, 447.
105. Quoted in Hermann Mannheim, *Social Aspects of Crime in England Between the Wars*. G. Allen & Unwin, 1940, 10.
106. George MacDonald Fraser, *Quartered Safe Out Here: A Recollection of the War in Burma*. HarperCollins, 2000, 171.

## Chapter Seven: Something Has Gone Wrong Inside My Head

1. *Woman*, 24 March 1945, 22.
2. For HMS *Goodall*'s story see Vic Ould, *Last But Not Least: HMS Goodall, Torpedoed 29 April 1945*. Arcturus Press, 2004; NA ADM 199/1339.
3. J.L. Hodson, *The Way Things Are*. Gollancz, 1947, 5.
4. Francis McGovern. IWM:S #17825.
5. Robert Dare. IWM:S #18268.
6. Vernon Scannell, *The Tiger and the Rose*. Robson, 1983, 60.
7. Arthur Vizard. IWM:S #16601.
8. Richard Morris, *Cheshire: The Biography of Leonard Cheshire VC, OM*. Viking, 2002, 231–2.
9. Spike Milligan, *Milligan's War*. Michael Joseph, 1988, 182.
10. Humphrey Carpenter, *Spike Milligan: The Biography*. Hodder & Stoughton, 2003, 57–60.
11. Edgar Jones and Simon Wessely, 'Psychiatric Battle Casualties: An Intra- and Interwar Comparison', *British Journal of Psychiatry* 178 (2001), 243.
12. Wendy Holden, *Shell Shock*. Channel Four Books, 1998, 74. See also Robert Ahrenfeldt, *Psychiatry in the British Army in the Second World War*. Routledge and Kegan Paul, 1958; Ben Shephard, *A War of Nerves: Soldiers and Psychiatrists, 1914–1994*. Jonathan Cape, 2000.
13. Holden, *Shell Shock*, 71.
14. Harold Palmer, 'Military Psychiatric Casualties: Experience with 12,000 Cases', *The Lancet*, 13 October 1945, 456.
15. G.W.B. James, 'Psychiatric Lessons from Active Service', *The Lancet*, 22 December 1945, 802–3.
16. Hans Binneveld, *From Shell Shock to Combat Stress: A Comparative History of Military Psychiatry*. Amsterdam University Press, 1997, 156.
17. Quoted in Holden, *Shell Shock*, 94.
18. Mark K. Wells, *Courage and Air Warfare: The Allied Aircrew Experience in the Second World War*. Routledge, 1995, 194.
19. Holden, *Shell Shock*, 114.
20. T. Harrison and D. Clarke, 'The Northfield Experiments', *British Journal of Psychiatry* 160 (1992).
21. William Sargant, 'Chronic Battle Neurosis Treated with Leucotomy', *British Medical Journal*, 29 November 1947, 867.
22. Holden, *Shell Shock*, 88.
23. Ibid., 124.
24. Ben Shephard, ' "Pitiless Psychology": The Role of Prevention in British Military Psychiatry in the Second World War', *History of Psychiatry* 10: 4 (1999).
25. Ena Elsey, 'The Rehabilitation and Employment of Disabled Ex-Servicemen after the Two World Wars'. Unpublished dissertation, University of Teesside, 1994, 4.
26. Edgar Jones and Simon Wessely, 'War Pensions (1900–1945): Changing Models of Psychological Understanding', *British Journal of Psychology* 180 (2002), 377.
27. T.F. Main, 'Clinical Problems of Repatriates', *The Journal of Mental Science* 93 (1947), 355, 363.
28. George Chippington, *Naked and Unashamed*, 626. IWM:D #PP/MCR/298.
29. Betty Duignan, letter, 23 September 1945. IWM:D #PP/MCR/446.
30. *The Times*, 4 September 1945, 4.

31. A.K. Berrecloth, *Memoirs*, 270. IWM:D #PPR/MCR/297.

32. G.H. Shorland, *Diary*, November 16, 1944. IWM:D #95/17/1.

33. Chippington, *Naked and Unashamed*, 583.

34. A.K. Berrecloth, *Memoirs*, 264.

35. Ronald M. Horner, *Singapore Diary*, 175. IWM:D #Con Shelf.

36. *The Times*, 12 September 1945, 3.

37. *The Times*, 10 September 1945, 4.

38. Horner, *Singapore Diary*, 194–5.

39. Oliver Clutton-Brock, *Footprints on the Sands of Time: RAF Bomber Command Prisoners-of-War in Germany, 1939–1945*. Grub Street, 2003, 149.

40. Quoted in Ibid., 153.

41. George Moreton, *The Barbed-Wire Medic*, 780–3. IWM:D #89/16/2.

42. L.C.F. Harwood, *Oh Threats of Hell: The Diary of a Prisoner of War*, 312–16. IWM:D #84/33/1.

43. Arieh Kochavi, 'Why None of Britain's Long-Term POWs in Nazi Germany Were Repatriated During World War II', *Canadian Journal of History* 39 (2004).

44. Trevor Gibbens, 'The Psychology and Psychopathology of the Prisoner of War'. Unpublished dissertation, Cambridge University, 1947, 16–17.

45. Ray Ellis, *Once a Hussar*. IWM:D # PP/MCR/388.

46. Manfred Jeffrey and E.J.G. Bradford, 'Neurosis in Escaped Prisoners of War', *The British Journal of Medical Psychology* 20: 4 (1945–6), 428–9.

47. L. Bootle-Wilbraham, 'Civil Resettlement of Ex-Prisoners of War', *Journal of Mental Health* 6 (1946), 40.

48. A.T.M. Wilson, 'The Serviceman Comes Home', *Pilot Papers* 1: 2 (1946).

49. Corrie Halliday. IWM:S #15620.

50. Hugh Dewhurst, *Recounting the Experiences of Hugh Dewhurst, Royal Air Force 1937 to 1949*. IWM:D #02/32/1.

51. Jim Long. IWM:S #15350.

52. Chippington, *Naked and Unashamed*, 614. IWM:D #PP/MCR/298.

53. *Manchester Guardian*, 15 May 1945, 4.

54. Jack Russell. IWM:S #17606.

55. Alan Dixon, *Survival Course*, 32–3. IWM:D #91/35/1.

56. Ibid., 36.

57. Barbara Webb, personal correspondence, October 2004.

58. Vernon Scannell, 'Casualty – Mental Ward', *Soldering On: Poems of Military Life*. Robson Books, 1989, 69.

59. *Daily Mail*, 9 January 1946, 3.

60. *Daily Mail*, 4 December 1945, 3.

61. *Daily Herald*, 6 December 1945, 3.

62. Marjorie Hanstock. IWM:S #20711.

63. James Bellows. IWM:S #12913.

64. Charles Tinson. IWM:S #15255.

65. John Gray. IWM:S #20202.

66. Herbert Beddowes. IWM:S #20373.

67. Harold Harper. IWM:S #10923.

68. Ernie Hurry. IWM:S #14729.

69. Charles Tinson. IWM:S #15255.

70. Ken Watson. IWM:S #19096.

71. Arthur Cheetham. IWM:S #14779.

72. Quoted in *Daily Mail*, 15 August 1995, 5.

73. John Spencer, *Crime and the Services*. Routledge and Kegan Paul, 1954, 91.

74. Eric Guttman and Elsie Thomas, *A Report on the Re-adjustment in Civil Life of Soldiers Discharged from the Army on Account of Neurosis*. HMSO, 1946, 34.

75. Palmer, 'Military Psychiatric Casualties', 455.

76. *The Times*, 15 August 1995.

77. *New Statesman and Society*, 12 May 1995, 21–3.

78. Jonathan Moffat, and Audrey McCormick, *Moon over Malaya: A Tale of Argylls and Marines*. Tempus, 2002, 338.

## Epilogue

1. *The Times*, 12 November 1957, 9.

2. *The Adelphi* 4 (1947).

3. *Civvy-Street* (Incorporating 'Khaki and Blue'), Christmas 1946, 3.

4. *Daily Herald*, 12 September 1946, 3.

5. George H. Gallup, ed., *The Gallup International Public Opinion Polls: Great Britain 1937–1975, Volume One: 1937–1964*. Random House, 1976, 171.

6. *Civvy-Street*, Christmas 1946, 3.

7. *Manchester Guardian*, 8 April 1946, 4.

8. *Daily Mail*, 13 December 1945, 1.

9. Audrey and David Searle, 24 February 1947, *The What Else They Wrote About*. Pentland Press, 1994.

10. Tony Cameron. IWM:S #12918.

11. *Daily Mail*, 13 May 1946, 3.

12. Richard Morris, *Cheshire: The Biography of Leonard Cheshire VC, OM*. Viking, 2002, 223–48. The ex-service community described in Norah C. James's novel *There is Always Tomorrow* (Macdonald, 1946) may be based on VIP (and has a cautiously happier ending).

13. *Ex-Services Review* ('*A Forerunner – In Utility – of a National Magazine Planned for All Ex-Service Men and Women*') 1: 1 (Jan–Feb 1945), 4.

14. Derek Stanford, *Inside the Forties: Literary Memoirs, 1937–1957*. Sidgwick & Jackson, 1977, 121–6.

15. Len Newman. IWM:S #18705.

16. Edward Grey. IWM:S #16719.

17. Dennis Middleton. IWM:S #14986.

18. John Frost. IWM:S #22383.

19. William Robinson. IWM:S #17667.

20. *Punch*, 20 March 1946, 245.

21. John MacAuslan. IWM:S #8225.

22. 'The Reunion Party', *Hancock's Half-Hour*, no. 51. First broadcast 25 March 1960. Written by Ray Galton and Alan Simpson.

23. *Recruiting to the Territorial Army (and the Auxiliary Services)*, 1948. NA RG 23/529.

24. *Punch*, 23 October 1944.

25. Stewart Irwin. IWM:S #18210.

26. Gordon Paterson. IWM:S #22330.

27. John Frost. IWM:S #22383.

28. Ian Hammerton. IWM:S #8939.

29. Geoffrey William Isaac, *I Was a Sapper*, 62. IWM:D #06/41/1.

30. *The Times*, 28 September 1961, 13.
31. *The Times*, 12 February 1953, 9.
32. *Daily Mail*, 18 August 2007.
33. *Daily Telegraph*, 8 November 2002.
34. *Science Daily*, 6 March 2009 (http://www.sciencedaily.com).
35. *Independent*, 28 February 2009.
36. R.S. Ellery, *Psychiatric Aspects of Modern Warfare*. Reed & Harris, 1945, 146.

# Bibliography

## 1. Archival Materials

a. British Library National Sound Archive, Camden, London NW1 2DB
   Cuthbertson, George (F10884)
   Morrison, Victor (F8629)

b. Imperial War Museum Department of Documents, Southwark, London SE1 6HZ
   Baker, Howard (87/25/1)
   Beck, Sydney (03/28/1)
   Bell MacDonald, A.M. (Con Shelf)
   Berrecloth, A.K. (PPR/MCR/297)
   Charles, H.W.F. (02/19/1)
   Charlotte, W.A. (93/19/1)
   Chippington, George (PP/MCR/298)
   Crichton, Charles (Con Shelf)
   Cross, Christopher (91/8/1)
   Crossley, Jean (04/13/1)
   Danjoux, J. (97/40/1)
   Dewhurst, Hugh (02/32/1)
   Dixon, Alan (91/35/1)
   Duignan, Betty (PP/MCR/446)
   Ebert, Arthur (76/68/1)
   Ellis, Ray (PP/MCR/388)
   Evans, D. (92/37/1)
   Franklin, William (04/17/1)
   Gillam, L.A. (Misc 220 [3152])
   Harris, Alan (96/35/1)

Harris, Arthur S. (96/35/1)
Harwood, L.C.F. (84/33/1)
Horner, Ronald M. (Con Shelf)
Huntbatch, K.B. (01/39/1)
Innes-Ker, W.M. (84/45/1)
Isaac, Geoffrey William (06/41/1)
Jones, Mary (78/55/1)
Kendall-Davies, Barbara (02/28/1)
Knowles, E.J.F. (91/36/1)
Knowles, Harold (91/35/1)
Lindop, J.B. (92/27/1)
Moreton, George (89/16/2)
Pepper, D. (96/26/1)
Pollard, W.G. (93/9/1)
Poole, Brian (Con Shelf and 92/29/1)
Ransom, Les (87/42/1)
Shilling, Bernard (Misc 220 (3152))
Shorland, G.H. (95/17/1)
Wareham, Cecil (96/31/1)
White, John (90/6/1)
Wilson, H.A. (80/5/1)

c. Imperial War Museum Department of Printed Books, Southwark, London SE1 6HZ
   Browne, H. Leonard, *How We May Best Prepare Ourselves and Our Homes to Receive Those Returning from Captivity in the Far East*, 29 September 1945 (77/5.6[=41])
   Sparrow, J.H.A., *Tour of India and South East Asia Command, 28th June 1945–15th October 1945* (02[41].13 [South East Asia Command] /6)

d. Imperial War Museum Department of Sound Records, Southwark, London SE1 6HZ
   Ayers, Ron (21093)
   Bates, Bill (22327)
   Bean, Ken (27091)
   Beddowes, Herbert (20373)
   Bell, George (21137)
   Bell, Victor (25936)
   Bellows, James (12913)
   Bland, Oliver (19606)
   Cameron, Tony (12918)
   Cheetham, Arthur (14779)
   Child, Raymond (23138)
   Clabburn, Jack (21721)
   Dare, Robert (18268)
   Emery, Vic (24731)
   Feakins, Eric (15607)
   Fiddament, Dick (17354)
   Frost, John (22383)
   Gray, John (20202)
   Grey, Edward (16719)
   Halliday, Corrie (15620)

Hammerton, Ian (8939)
Hanson, Douglas (4986)
Hanstock, Marjorie (20711)
Harper, Harold (10923)
Harrington, Harold (18484)
Harris, Ian (13389)
Harris, Walter (20944)
Hay, Alan (13079)
Hazell, Fred (17229)
Hurry, Ernie (14729)
Irwin, Stewart (18210)
Kidger, Joe (23200)
Kirby, Edward (16084)
Long, Jim (15350)
Lord, Eric (19911)
Lucas, Francis (28653)
Luff, Frank 27267
MacAuslan, John (8225)
McGovern, Francis (17825)
McNie, Duncan (19798)
Meninsky, Philip (12049)
Middleton, Dennis (14986)
Morrell, Harry (17824)
Newman, Len (18705)
Paterson, Gordon (22330)
Robinson, William (17667)
Russell, Jack (17606)
Scrivens, Bert (29536)
Scull, Harold (14804)
Teal, George (18698)
Tinson, Charles (15255)
Timperley, Trevor (27493)
Truman, Alice (12365)
Vizard, Arthur (16601)
Watson, Ken (19096)
Westcott, Leslie (13946)
Wolstenholme, Bert (27789)


e. Mass-Observation Archive, University of Sussex, Brighton BN1 9QL
    Topic Collections 27/3, 29/1, 29/2, 29/3


f. National Archives, Kew, Richmond, Surrey TW9 4DU
    ADM 1/18709, 116/6421, 199/1339
    AIR 20/1966, 20/4583, 22/316, 23/2899
    BT 64/180
    CUST 49/3382
    INF 1/292
    MEPO 2/7822, 3/2302, 3/2719
    RAIL 1172/1968

RG 23/79, 23/152A, 23/526, 23/529, 23/535
WO 32/11742, 32/15772, 71/1107, 71/1139, 222/1566, 277/16, 277/36, 365/133

## 2. Personal Correspondence

Barbara Webb

## 3. National Newspapers

*Daily Express*
*Daily Herald*
*Daily Mail*
*Daily Mirror*
*Daily Telegraph*
*Independent*
*Manchester Guardian*
*News Chronicle*
*News of the World*
*People*
*Sunday Express*
*The Times*

## 4. Armed Forces and Ex-Service Newspapers

*British Legion Journal*
*Civvy-Street* (Incorporating 'Khaki and Blue')
*Civvy Street: The Magazine for all Ex-Service Men and Women*
*Ex-Services Review*
*Soldier*
*Union Jack*

## 5. Popular Magazines

*The Adelphi*
*Good Housekeeping*
*Horizon*
*Housewife*
*John Bull*
*Modern Woman*
*New Generation*
*New Statesman and Nation* (later *New Statesman and Society*)
*Picture Post*
*Punch*
*Spectator*
*Time* (United States)
*Time and Tide*
*Woman*

## 6. Government Publications and Official Histories

Browne, E.W., et al., *The Soldier and the Army: Opinions on Some Aspects of Army Life Expressed by Troops in SEAC*. Calcutta: South East Asia Command, 1946.

Central Statistical Office, *Annual Abstract of Statistics 1938–1950*. HMSO, 1952.

Central Statistical Office, *Fighting with Figures: A Statistical Digest of the Second World War*. HMSO, 1995.

*Criminal Statistics for England and Wales 1939–1945*. Cmnd. 7227 (1947).

Ferguson, Sheila, and Fitzgerald, Hilde, *Studies in the Social Services*. HMSO, 1954.

Guttman, Eric, and Thomas, Elsie, *A Report on the Re-adjustment in Civil Life of Soldiers Discharged from the Army on Account of Neurosis*. HMSO, 1946.

Hancock, W.K., and Gowing, Margaret, *British War Economy*. HMSO, 1949.

Horrocks, B. G., *30 Corps in Germany*. Germany (?), 30 Corps, 1945.

Ministry of Labour and National Service, *The Serviceman's Resettlement: Notes for the Guidance of all Concerned with Management*. HMSO, 1945.

*Release and Resettlement: An Explanation of Your Position and Rights*. HMSO, 1945.

Richard Titmuss, *Problems of Social Policy*. HMSO, 1950.


## 7. Books and Book Chapters

Addison, Paul, *Now The War is Over: A Social History of Britain, 1945–51*. London: Jonathan Cape, 1985.

Ahrenfeldt, Robert H., *Psychiatry in the British Army in the Second World War*. London: Routledge and Kegan Paul, 1958.

Archer, Dale, and Gartner, Rosemary, *Violence and Crime in Cross-National Perspective*. New Haven, CT: Yale University Press, 1984.

Barker, Arthur Charles, *Nobby and Pincher in Civvy Street*. London: Rankin, 1950.

Barnett, Corelli, *The Lost Victory: British Dreams, British Realities, 1945–1950*. London: Macmillan, 1995.

Baron, Alexander, *The Human Kind*. London: Jonathan Cape, 1953.

Beckman, Morris, *The 43 Group*. London: Centerprise Publications, 1993.

Bendit, Phoebe D., and Bendit Laurence J., *Living Together Again*. London: Gramol Publications, 1946.

Bennett, Michael J., *When Dreams Came True: The GI Bill and the Making of Modern America*. Washington, DC: Brassey's, 1996.

Binneveld, Hans, *From Shell Shock to Combat Stress: A Comparative History of Military Psychiatry*. Amsterdam: Amsterdam University Press, 1997.

'Boomerang' [Alan Wood], *Bless 'Em All: An Analysis of the British Army, its Morale, Efficiency and Leadership*. London: Martin Secker & Warburg, 1942.

Bourke, Joanna, *Working Class Cultures in Britain 1890–1960*. London: Routledge, 1994.

—— *The Second World War: A People's History*. Oxford: Oxford University Press, 2001.

Bullock, Alan, *The Life and Times of Ernest Bevin, Volume II: Minister of Labour, 1940–1945*. London: Heinemann, 1967.

Burgess, Anthony, *Little Wilson and Big God: Being the First Part of the Confessions of Anthony Burgess*. London: Heinemann, 1987.

—— *Any Old Iron*. London: Arrow, 1989.

'Captain X' [William G.C. Shebbeare], *A Soldier Looks Ahead*. London: Labour Book Service, 1944.

Carpenter, Humphrey, *Spike Milligan: The Biography*. London: Hodder & Stoughton, 2003.

Churchill, Winston S., *The Aftermath*. New York: Charles Scribner's, 1929.

Clutton-Brock, Oliver, *Footprints on the Sands of Time: RAF Bomber Command Prisoners-of-War in Germany, 1939–1945*. London: Grub Street, 2003.

Comfort, Alex, *Authority and Delinquency in the Modern State: A Criminological Approach to the Problem of Power*. London: Routledge and Kegan Paul, 1950.

Connelly, Mark, *We Can Take It! Britain and the Memory of the Second World War*. New York: Pearson/Longman, 2004.

Conway, E.S., *Post-War Employment*. London: Jonathan Cape, 1943.

Cook, Hera, *The Long Sexual Revolution: English Women, Sex, and Contraception 1800–1975*. Oxford: Oxford University Press, 2004.

Cooper, Susan, 'Snoek Piquante', in Sissons, Michael, and French, Philip, eds, *Age of Austerity*. London: Hodder & Stoughton, 1963.

Crang, Jeremy, 'The British Soldier on the Home Front: Army Morale Reports, 1940–1945', in Addison, Paul, and Calder, Angus, eds, *Time To Kill: The Soldier's Experience of War in the West 1939–1945*. London: Pimlico, 1997.

Crang, Jeremy, *The British Army and the People's War 1939–1945*. Manchester: Manchester University Press, 2000.

Dempsey, Martin, *Back in Civvy Street*. London: Samuel Walker, 1947.

Duncan, David, *Mutiny in the RAF*. London: Socialist History Society, 1998.

Ellery, Reginald Spencer, *Psychiatric Aspects of Modern Warfare*. Melbourne: Reed & Harris, 1945.

Ellis, John, *The Sharp End: The Fighting Man in World War Two*. New York: Charles Scribner's, 1980.

Emsley, Clive, *Hard Men: Violence in England Since 1750*. London: Hambledon and London, 2005.

English, Raymond, *The Pursuit of Purpose: An Essay in Social Morale*. London: Falcon Press, 1947.

Evans, B. Ifor, *The Shop on the King's Road*. London: Hodder & Stoughton, 1946.

Forty, George, *British Army Handbook 1939–1945*. Stroud: Sutton, 1998.

Fraser, George MacDonald, *Quartered Safe Out Here: A Recollection of the War in Burma*. London: HarperCollins, 2000.

Fussell, Paul, *Wartime: Understanding and Behaviour in the Second World War*. Oxford: Oxford University Press, 1989.

Gallup, George H., ed., *The Gallup International Public Opinion Polls: Great Britain 1937–1975, Volume One: 1937–1964*. New York: Random House, 1976.

Gammage, Bill, *The Broken Years: Australian Soldiers in the Great War*. Canberra: Australian National University Press, 1974.

Garfield, Simon, ed., *Our Hidden Lives: The Everyday Diaries of a Forgotten Britain 1945–1948*. London: Ebury, 2004.

Gibbs, Philip, *Realities of War*. London: Heinemann, 1920.

Gilbert, Martin, *The Day the War Ended: May 8, 1945 – Victory in Europe*. New York: Henry Holt, 1995.

Goldsmith, Margaret, *Women and the Future*. London: Lindsay Drummond, 1946.

Gollancz, Victor, *In Darkest Germany*. Hinsdale, ILL: Henry Regnery, 1947.

Gorer, Geoffrey, *Exploring English Character*. London: Cresset, 1955.

Gubar, Susan, ' "This Is My Rifle, This Is My Gun": World War II and the Blitz on Women', in Higgonet, Margaret M., et al., eds, *Behind the Lines: Gender and the Two World Wars*. New Haven, CT: Yale University Press, 1987.

Guest, John, *Broken Images: A Journal*. London: Longmans, 1949.

Harrison, Mark, 'Sex and the Citizen Soldier: Health, Morals and Discipline in the British Army during the Second World War', in Cooter, Roger, et al., eds, *Medicine and Modern Warfare*. Atlanta, GA: Rodopi, 1999.

Hastings, Max, *Armageddon: The Battle for Germany, 1944–1945*. New York: A.A. Knopf, 2005.

Henriques, Robert Quixano, *The Journey Home*. London: Heinemann, 1944.

Herriot, James, *All Things Wise and Wonderful*. London: St. Martin's Press, 1998.

Hichberger, Joany, 'Old Soldiers', in Raphael Samuel, ed., *Patriotism: The Making and Unmaking of British National Identity*. London: Routledge, 1989.

Hodson, James Lansdale, *The Home Front*. London: Gollancz, 1944.

—— *The Sea and the Land*. London: Gollancz, 1945.

—— *The Way Things Are*. London: Gollancz, 1947.

Hoggart, Richard. *The Uses of Literacy*. London: Chatto & Windus, 1957.

Holden, Wendy, *Shell Shock*. London: Channel Four Books, 1998.

Holman, Robert, *The Evacuation: A Very British Revolution*. Oxford: Lion, 1995.

Howard, Kenneth, *Sex Problems of the Returning Soldier*. Manchester: Sydney Pemberton, 1945.

Howarth, T.E.B., *Prospect and Reality: Great Britain 1945–1955*. London: Collins, 1985.

James, Norah C., *There is Always Tomorrow*. London: Macdonald, 1946.

Johnson, Bryan S., *The Evacuees*. London: Gollancz, 1968.

Jordan, Philip Furneaux, *Jordan's Tunis Diary*. London: Collins, 1943.

Kisch, Richard, *The Days of the Good Soldiers*. London: Journeyman, 1985.

Kitching, Edwin Howard, *Sex Problems of the Returning Soldier*. Manchester: Sydney Pemberton, 1945.

Kynaston, David, *Austerity Britain 1945–51*. London: Bloomsbury, 2007.

Leach, Henry, *Enjoy no Makeshifts*. London: Leo Cooper, 1993.

*Let Us Face the Future: A Declaration of Labour Policy for the Consideration of the Nation*. London: Labour Party, 1945.

Levine, Philippa, *Prostitution, Race and Politics: Policing Venereal Disease in the British Empire*. London: Routledge, 2003.

Lewis, M.M., ed., *Teachers From the Forces: An Experimental Short Course of Training at Goldsmith's College University of London*. London: Harrap, 1946.

Light, Alison, *Forever England: Femininity, Literature, and Conservatism Between the Wars*. London: Routledge, 1991.

Lowe, Roy, *Education in the Post-War Years: A Social History*. London: Routledge, 1988.

Lucas, James, *The British Soldier*. London: Arms & Armour Press, 1989.

Maclaran-Ross, Julian, *Selected Stories*. Stockport: Dewi Lewis, 2004.

Mannheim, Hermann, *Social Aspects of Crime in England Between the Wars*, London: G. Allen & Unwin, 1940.

Mass-Observation, *An Inquiry into People's Homes*. London: John Murray, 1943.

—— *The Journey Home*. Advertising Service Guild, 1944.

McCallum, R.B., and Readman, Alison, *The British General Election of 1945*. Oxford: Oxford University Press, 1947.

McGregor, O.R., *Divorce in England*. London: Heinemann, 1957.

McKelvie, Roy, *The War in Burma*. London: Methuen, 1948.

McKibbin, Ross, *Classes and Cultures: England 1918–1951*. Oxford: Oxford University Press, 1998.

McNalty, Sir Arthur S., 'Influence of War on Family Life', in Marchant, Sir James, ed., *Rebuilding Family Life in the Post-War World: An Enquiry with Recommendations*. London: Odhams, 1945.

Merritt, Maurice, *Eighth Army Driver*. Tunbridge Wells: Midas Books, 1981.

Mettler, Suzanne, *Soldiers to Citizens: The GI Bill and the Making of the Greatest Generation*. Oxford: Oxford University Press, 2005.

Millar, George, *Horned Pigeon*. London: Heinemann, 1946.

Miller, Betty, *On the Side of the Angels*. London: Hale, 1945.

Milligan, Spike, *Milligan's War*. London: Michael Joseph, 1988.

Mitchell, B.R., *British Historical Statistics*, Cambridge: Cambridge University Press, 1988.

Moffat, Jonathan, and McCormick, Audrey, *Moon over Malaya: A Tale of Argylls and Marines*. Stroud: Tempus, 2002.

Montague, C.E., *Disenchantment*. New York: Brentano's, 1922.

Morris, Richard, *Cheshire: The Biography of Leonard Cheshire VC, OM*. London: Viking, 2002.

Morris, Terence, *Crime and Criminal Justice Since 1945*, Oxford: Blackwell, 1989.

Mosley, Nicholas, *Time At War*. Rochester, NY: Dalkey Archive Press, 2006.

Nicholson, Heather V., *Prisoners of War: True Stories of Evacuees*. London: Gordon, 2000.

Ould, Vic, *Last But Not Least: HMS Goodall, Torpedoed 29 April 1945*. Hargate: Arcturus Press, 2004.

Page, Leo, *The Young Lag*. London: Faber & Faber, 1950.

Page, Martin, ed., *Kiss Me Goodnight Sergeant Major: The Songs and Ballads of World War II*. London: Hart-Davis, MacGibbon, 1973.

Parsons, Martin L., *I'll Take That One: Dispelling the Myths of Civilian Evacuation 1939–45*. Peterborough: Beckett & Karlson, 1998.

Poolman, Kenneth, *The British Sailor*. London: Arms & Armour Press, 1989.

Porter, Roy, and Hall, Lesley A., *The Facts of Life: The Creation of Sexual Knowledge in Britain, 1650–1950*. New Haven, CT: Yale University Press, 1995.

Priestley, J.B., *Three Men in New Suits*. London: Heinemann, 1945.

Pritt, D.N., *Brasshats and Bureaucrats*. London: Lawrence and Wishart, 1966.

Rennell, Tony, and Turner, Barry, *When Daddy Came Home: How Family Life Changed Forever in 1945*. London: Pimlico, 1996.

Reynolds, David, *Rich Relations: The American Occupation of Britain 1942–1945*. London: Phoenix, 2001.

Rooke, Dennis, and D'Egville, Alan, *Call Me Mister! A Guide to Civilian Life for the Newly Demobilised*. London: Heinemann, 1945.

Rothstein, Andrew, *The Soldiers' Strikes of 1919*. London: Macmillan, 1980.

Rowntree, B. Seebohm, and Lavers, G.R., *English Life and Leisure: A Social Study*. London: Longmans, 1951.

Rubin, Gerry, *Murder, Mutiny and the Military: British Court Martial Cases, 1940–1966*. London: Francis Boutle, 2005.

Scannell, Vernon, *The Tiger and the Rose*. London: Robson Books, 1983.

—— *Soldering On: Poems of Military Life*. London: Robson Books, 1989.

Searle, Audrey and Searle, David, *The What Else We Wrote About*. Edinburgh: Pentland Press, 1994.

Selwyn, Francis, *Rotten to the Core? The Life and Death of Neville Heath*. London: Routledge, 1988.

Seton-Watson, Christopher, *Dunkirk–Alamein–Bologna: Letters and Diaries of an Artilleryman 1939–1945*. London: Buckland, 1993.

Shaw, Frederick, *The Homes and Homeless of Post-War Britain*. Totowa, NJ: Barnes & Noble, 1985.

Shephard, Ben, *A War of Nerves: Soldiers and Psychiatrists, 1914–1994*. London: Jonathan Cape, 2000.

Shute, Nevil, *The Chequer Board*. New York: William Morrow, 1947.

Slater, Eliot, and Woodside, Moya, *Patterns of Marriage: A Study of Marriage Relationships in the Urban Working Classes*. London: Cassell, 1951.

Smith, Lyn, ed., *Young Voices: British Children Remember the Second World War*. London: Viking, 2007.

Spencer, John D., *Crime and the Services*. London: Routledge and Kegan Paul, 1954.

Stafford, Jo Mary, *Light in the Dust: An Autobiography 1939–1960*. Stourbridge: Trustline, 2002.

Stanford, Derek, *Inside the Forties: Literary Memoirs, 1937–1957*. London: Sidgwick & Jackson, 1977.

Stone, Lawrence, *Road to Divorce: England 1530–1987*. Oxford: Oxford University Press, 1990.

Summers, Julie, *Stranger in the House: Women's Stories of Men Returning from the Second World War*. London: Simon & Schuster, 2008.

Sutherland, Donald, *Portrait of a Decade: London Life 1945–1955*. London: Harrap, 1988.

Swaffer, Hannen, *What Would Nelson Do?* London: Gollancz, 1946.

Taylor, Elizabeth, *A Wreath of Roses*. New York: Alfred A. Knopf, 1949.

Thomas, Donald, *An Underworld at War: Spivs, Deserters, Racketeers and Civilians in the Second World War*. London: John Murray, 2003.

Waller, Maureen, *London 1945: Life in the Debris of War*. London: John Murray, 2004.

Warner, Philip, 'Churchill, John Malcolm Thorpe Fleming (1906–1996)', *Oxford Dictionary of National Biography*, Oxford: Oxford University Press, 2004.

Weeks, Jeffrey, *Sex, Politics and Society: The Regulation of Sexuality since 1800*. London: Longman, 1989.

Wells, Mark K., *Courage and Air Warfare: The Allied Aircrew Experience in the Second World War*. London: Routledge, 1995.

Weymouth, Anthony, *Journal of the War Years*. Worcester: Littlebury, 1948.

Whittick, Arnold, *The Small House: Today and Tomorrow*. London: Crosby Lockwood & Son, 1947.

Wicks, Ben, *No Time To Wave Goodbye*. London: Bloomsbury, 1988.

—— *Welcome Home: True Stories of Soldiers Returning from World War II*. London: Bloomsbury, 1991.

Wiener, Martin J., *Men of Blood: Violence, Manliness and Criminal Justice in Victorian England*. Cambridge: Cambridge University Press, 2004.

Williams, E. T., 'Carton de Wiart, Sir Adrian (1880–1963)', rev. G. D. Sheffield, *Oxford Dictionary of National Biography*, Oxford University Press, 2004.

Winter, Jay, 'The Demographic Consequences of the War', in Smith, Harold, ed., *War and Social Change: British Society in the Second World War*. Manchester: Manchester University Press, 1986.

Winter, Jay, *The Great War and the British People*. Cambridge, MA: Harvard University Press, 1986.

Zweig, Ferdinand, *Labour, Life and Poverty*. London: Gollancz, 1948.

## 8. Scholarly Journal Articles

Bootle-Wilbraham, L., 'Civil Resettlement of Ex-Prisoners of War', *Journal of Mental Health* (6), 1946.

Campbell, Douglas, 'Venereal Disease in the Armed Forces Overseas (2)', *British Journal of Venereal Diseases* (22), 1946.

Crang, Jeremy, 'Welcome to Civvy Street: The Demobilisation of the British Armed Forces after the Second World War', *Historian* (46), 1995.

Crang, Jeremy, 'Politics on Parade: Army Education and the 1945 General Election', *History* (81: 262), 1996.

Daniel, Peter, 'The Mutiny on the *Javelin*', *Mariner's Mirror* (85: 4), 1999.

Dennis, Norman, 'A Case Study of "Little Kinsey", BBC4, 5 October 2005', *Civitas Review* (3: 1), 2006.

England, L.R., 'Little Kinsey: An Outline of Sex Attitudes in Britain', *Public Opinion Quarterly* (13: 4), 1949.

Englander, David, 'Soldiers and Social Reform in the First and Second World Wars', *Historical Research* (67: 164), 1994.

Field, Geoffrey, 'Perspectives on the Working-Class Family in Wartime Britain', *International Labor and Working-Class History* (38), 1990.

French, David, ' "You Cannot Hate the Bastard Who Is Trying to Kill You": Combat and Ideology in the British Army in the War Against Germany, 1939–45', *Twentieth Century British History* (11: 1), 2000.

Graubard, Stephen Richards, 'Military Demobilisation in Great Britain following the First World War', *Journal of Modern History* (19: 4), 1947.

Harrison, T., and Clarke, D., 'The Northfield Experiments', *British Journal of Psychiatry* (160), 1992.

James, G.W.B., 'Psychiatric Lessons from Active Service', *The Lancet*, 22 December 1945.

Jeffrey, Manfred, and Bradford, E.J.G., 'Neurosis in Escaped Prisoners of War', *British Journal of Medical Psychology* (20:4), 1945–6.

Jones, Edgar, and Wessely, Simon, 'Psychiatric Battle Casualties: An Intra- and Interwar Comparison', *British Journal of Psychiatry* (178), 2001.

—— 'War Pensions (1900–1945): Changing Models of Psychological Understanding', *British Journal of Psychology* (180), 2002.

Kochavi, Arieh, 'Why None of Britain's Long-Term POWs in Nazi Germany Were Repatriated During World War II', *Canadian Journal of History* (39), 2004.

Lanhammer, Claire, 'The Meanings of Home in Postwar Britain', *Journal of Contemporary History* (40: 2), 2005.

Lawrence, Jon, 'Forging a Peaceable Kingdom: War, Violence and the Fear of Brutalisation in Post-First World War Britain', *Journal of Modern History* (75: 3), 2003.

Lees, Robert, 'Venereal Diseases in the Armed Forces Overseas (1)', *British Journal of Venereal Diseases* (22), 1946.

Main, T.F., 'Clinical Problems of Repatriates', *Journal of Mental Science* (93), 1947.

Palmer, Harold, 'Military Psychiatric Casualties: Experience with 12,000 Cases', *The Lancet*, 13 October 1945.

Peter, Martin, 'Temporary Gentlemen in the Aftermath of the Great War: Rank, Status and the Ex-Officer Problem', *Historical Journal* (37: 1), 1994.

Pope, Rex, 'British Demobilization after the Second World War', *Journal of Contemporary History* (30: 1), 1995.

Ratcliffe, T.A., 'Psychiatric and Allied Aspects of the Problem of Venereal Disease in the Army', *Journal of the Royal Army Medical Corps* (89), 1947.

—— 'The Psychological Problems of the Returned Ex-Service Man', *Mental Health* (7: 1), 1947.

Rowntree, Griselda, and Carrier, Norman H., 'The Resort to Divorce in England and Wales, 1858–1957', *Population Studies* (11: 3), 1958.

Rudolf, G. de M., 'Sex in the Fighting Services at an Isolated Station', *British Journal of Medical Psychology* (21: 2), 1948.

Sargant, William, 'Chronic Battle Neurosis Treated with Leucotomy', *British Medical Journal*, 29 November 1947.

Shephard, Ben, ' "Pitiless Psychology": The Role of Prevention in British Military Psychiatry in the Second World War', *History of Psychiatry* (10: 4), 1999.

Thimann, I.C., 'Vocational Training in the Services', *Contemporary Review* (170), 1946.

Torrie, Alfred, 'The Return of Odysseus: The Problem of Marital Infidelity for the Repatriate', *British Medical Journal*, 11 August 1945.

Wagley, Perry V., 'Some Criminalogic Implications of the Returning Soldier', *Journal of Criminal Law and Criminology* (34), 1944.

Willoughby, John, 'The Sexual Behavior of American GIs During the Early Years of the Occupation of Germany', *Journal of Military History* (62) 1998.

Wilson, A.T.M., 'The Serviceman Comes Home', *Pilot Papers* (1: 2), 1946.

### 9. Unpublished Dissertations

Elsey, Ena, 'The Rehabilitation and Employment of Disabled Ex-Servicemen after the Two World Wars'. University of Teesside, 1994.

Gibbens, Trevor, 'The Psychology and Psychopathology of the Prisoner of War'. Cambridge University, 1947.

Latcham, Andrew, 'Journey's End: Ex-Servicemen and the State During and After the Great War'. University of Oxford, 1996.

McCarty, Elizabeth, 'Attitudes to Women and Domesticity in England, c. 1939–1955'. University of Oxford, 1994.

Pope, Rex, 'The Planning and Implementation of British Demobilisation, 1941–1946'. Open University, 1986.

### 10. Motion Pictures

*Dancing with Crime* (1947), dir. John Paddy Carstairs.

*The Flamingo Affair* (1948), dir. Horace Shepherd.

*The Life and Death of Colonel Blimp* (1943), dir. Michael Powell and Emeric Pressburger.

*Perfect Strangers* (1945), dir. Alexander Korda.

*They Made Me a Fugitive* (1947), dir. Alberto Cavalcanti.

*Train of Events* (1949), dir. Sydney Cole et al.

## 11. Television Programmes

'The Reunion Party', *Hancock's Half-Hour* (1960), written by Ray Galton and Alan Simpson.

## 12. Websites

BBC *People's War* (http://www.bbc.co.uk/ww2peopleswar/).
*Gimlet King* (http://www.collectingbooksandmagazines.com/gimlet.html).
*Open Writing* (http://www.openwriting.com).
*RAF Bomber Command* (http://www.elsham.pwp.blueyonder.co.uk/raf_bc/).
*Royal Engineers Museum* (http://www.remuseum.org.uk).
*ScienceDaily*, 6 March 2009 (http://www.sciencedaily.com).

# Index